ISLAM, MODERNISM AND THE WEST

ISLAM, MODERNISM and the WEST

Cultural and Political Relations at the End of the Millennium

Edited by
GEMA MARTÍN MUÑOZ

I.B.Tauris *Publishers*
LONDON • NEW YORK
in association with
The Eleni Nakou Foundation

Published in 1999 by I.B.Tauris & Co. Ltd
Salem Road, London W2 4BU

In the United States of America and Canada distributed by
Palgrave Macmillan a division of St. Martin's Press
175 Fifth Avenue, New York NY 10010

A full CIP record for this book is available from the British Library

A full CIP record for this book is available from the Library of Congress

ISBN 1 86064-341-8

Digitally reprinted in 2004 by Bookchase

Typeset in Adobe Caslon by Hepton Books, Oxford
Printed and bound in Great Britain by Biddles Short Run Books, King's Lynn

Contents

Introduction

Part One   Relations Between Europe and the Muslim World: A Reinterpretation

Part Two   Islam and the West: Concepts of Civilization

Notes on the Contributors

Mohammed 'Abed al-Jabri: Born in Figuig (Uxda) in 1935. Professor of Philosophy and Arabic–Islamic Thought at Mohammed V University in Rabat, Morocco. Received Baghdad Prize for Arab Culture awarded by UNESCO in June 1988. His main books are: *Introduction à la critique de la raison arabe; Le discours arabe contemporain: étude analytique et critique;* and *La question de l'identité: l'Arabité, l'Islam et l'Occident.*

Fariba Adelkhah: Iranian social anthropologist. Researcher at the Centre National de la Recherche Scientifique (CNRS), Paris. Main works: *La révolution sous le voile. Femmes islamiques d'Iran;* and *Thermidor in Iran* (with F. Burgat and O. Roy).

Mohammed Arkoun: Born in Great Kabylia (Algeria). At present Professor Emeritus of History of Islamic Thought at the Sorbonne La Neuve/Paris III, and editor of the Arab studies journal *Arabica.* Member of the Ethics National Committee in France. Among his most outstanding works are *L'Humanisme arabe au IV/X siècle; L'Islam, religion et société* (with M. Borrmans); *Pour une critique de la raison islamique; La pensée arabe;* and *Ouvertures sur l'Islam.*

Maurice Borrmans: Father of the Missionaries of Africa (White Fathers). Born in Lille (France) in 1925. Has been a lecturer in Algeria, Tunisia, Bahrain and other Gulf countries. At present he is a professor at the Pontifical College of Arab and Islamic Studies and the Urbaniana in Rome. Editor of the journal *Islamochristiana.* Among his works are: *Tendances et courants de l'Islam arabe contemporaine I: Egypte et Afrique du Nord* (with G. C. Anawati); and *Islam e Cristianesimo: le vie del dialogo.*

Jocelyne Cesari: Born in 1962 in France. PhD in Political Science. Researcher in Political Science at CNRS–IREMAM. Professor at the Political Science Institute in Aix-en-Provence. Her field of research encompasses Islam in France and in Europe, transnational nets between Europe and the Maghreb. Publications: *Etre musulman en France*; *L'Islam en Europe*; *La vie quotidienne des musulman en France*.

John L. Esposito: Professor of Religion and International Affairs at the Georgetown University and Director of the Center for Muslim–Christian Understanding: History and International Affairs at the Edmund A. Walsh School of Foreign Service. He has served as president of the Middle East Studies of North America and American Council for the Study of Islamic Societies. He is editor of *The Oxford Encyclopedia of the Modern Islamic World* (4 vols). His publications include: *The Islamic Threat: Myth or Reality?*; *Islam and Politics*; *Islam and Democracy* (with J. O. Voll).

Abdou Filali-Ansari: Born in 1946 in Morocco. PhD in Philosophy. Professor of Philosophy at Rabat University (1970–73). Since 1985 Director of the King Abdul-Aziz Foundation for Islamic Studies and Human Science in Casablanca. He is editor of the journal *Prologues: revue maghrébine du livre* and he has published numerous articles on the contemporary Islamic thought and translated into French Ali Abderraziq's book *Islam and the Foundations of Political Powers*.

Bichara Khader: Palestinian professor at the Catholic University of Louvain and Director of the Centre d'Etudes et de Recherches sur le Monde Arabe Contemporain (CERMAC). Among his publications are: *Le Grand Maghreb et l'Europe, enjeux et perspectives*; and *L'Europe et le Monde Arabe, cousins, voisins*.

Gudrun Krämer: Holds the Chair of Islamic Studies at the Free University, Berlin. She was senior research fellow at the Stiftung Wissenschaft und Politik, Ebenhausen, (1982–94) and Professor of Islamic Studies at Bonn University. Additional activities: 1990–94 professional lecturer, School of Advanced International Studies (SAIS), The Johns Hopkins University in Bologna; 1995–96 visiting professor, Fondation Nationale d'Etudes Politiques, Paris. Publications: *Islam, sura und Demokratie. Studien zu Theorie und Praxis zeitgenössischer sunnitischer Muslime.*

Gema Martín Muñoz: Professor of Sociology of the Arab and Islamic World at the Autonoma University of Madrid and Director of North African and Middle Eastern Studies at the José Ortega y Gasset Foundation. She is in charge of the Arab Women Studies Section at the Institute of Women Studies at Autonoma University of Madrid. She was responsible for the Cultural Civil Forum of the Euromediterranean Conference (Barcelona, 1995). Among her publications are: *Política y Elecciones en el Egipto contemporáneo (1922–90); Mujeres, Democracia y desarrollo en el Magreb*; and *El Islam y el Mundo Arabe. Guía didáctica para profesores y formadores* (with Begoña Valle Simón and Mª. Ángeles López Plaza).

Ann Elizabeth Mayer: PhD in Modern Middle Eastern History from the University of Michigan and a JD from the University of Pennsylvania. An Associate Professor of Legal Studies at the Wharton School of the University of Pennsylvania, she has written extensively on Islamic law in contemporary legal systems with a particular focus on human rights issues. Her most outstanding book is *Islam and Human Rights: Tradition and Politics*.

Miguel Ángel Moratinos: Career diplomat. He was Director of the Spanish Institute for Cooperation with the Arab World and Director of the Africa and Middle East Section at the Spanish Minister of Foreign Affairs. At present, he is the representative of the European Union in the Middle East Peace Process. Co-author of *El Mediterráneo y Oriente Medio. Reflexiones en torno a dos escenarios de la política española (1989–95)*.

Jørgen S. Nielson: Director of the Centre for the Study of Islam and Christian–Muslims relations (CSIC), Selly Oak College, Birmingham, UK, and Hon. Professor at the University of Birmingham. At CSIC since 1978, he developed research on Muslims in Europe and has more recently been working on aspects of the relations between the Muslim world and the West. His publications include *Muslims in Western Europe*; and as editor *Religion and Citizenship in Europe and the Arab World* and *The Christian–Muslim Frontier*.

Tariq Ramadan: Professor of Philosophy and Islamic Civilization at the Friburg University (Switzerland). Director of the Foyer Culturel

Musulman de Genève. Author of *Les musulmans dans la laïcité; L'Islam. Le face à face des civilisations; L'Islam et les musulmans, grandeur et décadence*.

Mohammed Tozy: Professor of Political Science at Casablanca University, Morocco. His research focuses on the Islamist tendencies, in particular in Morocco. He has dedicated numerous articles to this subject, included in books such as *Polity and Society in Contemporary North Africa* (edited by I. W. Zartman and W. M. Habeeb) and *Intellectuels et Militants de l'Islam contemporain* (edited by G. Kepel and Y. Richards).

François Zabbal: Born in Beirut in 1948. PhD at the Sorbonne University and Doctorat d'Etat in Arts on *The Ulama, the Christian and the Soldier. Damascus and Lebanon in the Nineteenth Century*. He has taught philosophy for twelve years at the Lebanese University in Beirut (1972–84). Also taught sociology and political science at Paris III University (1987–89). At present responsible for the Unit of research and debate at the Institut du Monde Arabe (IMA), Paris. Editor-in-chief of the journal *Qantara*, and editor of *La Chaire* de l'IMA collection at Albin Mitchel publishers. Co-editor with Robert Bistolfi of the book *L'Islams d'Europe*.

Foreword

Europa was not a European, at least, not in the modern sense of the word. She was a Phoenician princess brought to Crete by Zeus who became enthralled by her beauty. This familiar Greek myth is not just a charming story. To some degree, it is a true illustration of what we collectively recognize as the origins of European culture. In the Middle Ages, however, 'Europe' was more or less synonymous with Christendom, indicating a sharp cultural divide between believer and non believer and finding its centre on the northern shores of the Mediterranean. Later, the Enlightenment and modernity secularized the concept, defining Europe in terms of territory, of economics and politics. In the process, the centre of Europe moved northwards.

Our mental map of Europe is still changing, a process that has accelerated over the last decade. The politics of Europe have become fluid to say the least. As a consequence, our idea of Europe changes. It goes below the political surface and turns towards questions of culture, of beliefs and identity. Not that any such contemplation means our return to the Middle Ages. Far from it; the issues of cultural identity in our post-modern world are far wider, more complex and dynamic than they were a thousand or fifteen hundred years ago. Frontiers are not easily drawn. Indeed, it is questionable to what extent they should be drawn.

Feelings like these and related matters prompted the Eleni Nakou Foundation to initiate our third symposium, this time on the theme of 'Europe and Islam', during which we hoped to highlight and reconsider some of the historical, cultural and political links between these two worlds. I am grateful to the Fundación José Ortega y Gasset for their prompt and enthusiastic acceptance of our proposal to hold a conference on this subject. I should also thank Professor Gema Martín Muñoz and her collaborators for their very efficient organization of the proceedings.

The Eleni Nakou Foundation symposium took place in Toledo on 11–14 April 1996. We were honoured by the presence of His Royal Highness the Príncipe de Asturias who not only presided over the opening of the conference, but also took part in some of the meetings. I was confirmed in my conviction that Toledo was the most appropriate venue to discuss the relationship between the world of Islam and present-day Europe. Spain, at intervals throughout its history, has happily contained both cultures. It is well placed, now and in the future, to serve as a bridge between them. I am in no doubt that we need such a bridge – and not just a bridge, but a real understanding that can create a sense of community combined with respect for differences.

The Eleni Nakou Foundation was established in 1990 with the aim of promoting cultural contact and understanding between the European peoples, particularly between those of northern and southern Europe. Every second year we initiate a symposium related to European culture. The first was held in Crete, in 1992, when a group of historians, sociologists, political scientists and journalists was invited to discuss the theme 'Images of Europe'. In 1994 a second symposium was convened at the Louisiana Museum of Modern Art near Copenhagen to debate the question 'What is European in European Modern Art?' I should stress that the aim of these symposia is not to follow a narrowly academic or arcanely specialist agenda. Of course, specialists are invited. But our invitation is to provoke searching discussions over a wide-ranging area. Nor are the books that we produce after the symposia presented as a record of the proceedings at these meetings. They mirror, of course, to a large extent what was discussed there, but they are edited as self-contained publications in their own right. I am delighted that this volume, based on the discussions in Toledo reflects these intentions.

Dr Erik Holm, Director, The Eleni Nakou Foundation

Preface

The studies assembled in this book had their origin in a seminar organized in Toledo by the José Ortega y Gasset Foundation on the initiative and under the auspices of the Eleni Nakou Foundation which entrusted me with its direction. The aim of the book is to bring together an outstanding group of scholars from various disciplines, and from a number of Western and Islamic regions, in order to debate the key questions posed today by these two worlds that are in constant interaction. Consequently, the main concern of the book is to deal with the most contemporary and up-to-date aspects of this relationship in an interdisciplinary framework.

A critical reassessment of history is one of the challenges that Muslims and Westerners are facing. On the one hand Islamic thought and its cultural heritage have not been for the most part acknowledged by the West. This is essentially a result of the idea that what belongs to Islam is inevitably alien and opposed to the West which in turn means that the Islamic world is denied its position in history. On the other hand, the extreme ideologization to which Islamic and European nations have been subjected has given rise to the use of history as an ideological weapon. This must be reconsidered because it is the result of the vision that each side has of itself, a vision that promotes exclusively its own respective values, thus conditioning the mental structures of both civilizations.

What is Islam? What is Westernization? These are questions that one should approach from a critical viewpoint, establishing the frontiers between the imaginary and the real aspects of the historical and cultural vision that has traditionally been employed to answer both questions.

Alongside this necessary intellectual exercise, the education of the new generation is a responsibility that must be assumed in order to consolidate this historical reinterpretation of relations between the West and Islam. This can only be made possible by a revision of the curriculum of Western and Islamic systems of education in order to reconstruct positive images of the 'Other'.

For these reasons, this book aims to provide a forum for the cultural and political debates taking place in the heart of the Islamic and Western worlds. However, we have tried not to follow the simplistic approach whereby the West falls into self accusation over its hegemonic and ethnocentric tendencies. As far as the Muslim counterpart is concerned, the attempt consisted in avoiding the common reproachfull attitude caused by its resentment over the colonial experience. This means making a controversial, but positive, interpretation of relationships between Islam and modernity (democracy, secularism, citizenship), considering Islamic specificity in dynamic terms in order to ask questions about its possible future in the fields of economics, politics, and society, and discussing Islamism and the nature of its relations with the West. In short, working towards integration and mutual concern, and against the theory of the 'clash of civilizations.'

Our puspose has been to promote an earnest and cool-headed analysis that can help to banish the prejudices and false images that have been reciprocally built up. Shared reflection and debate is the best way to dispel ideological stands which persist in upholding a restrictive view of the respective cultures: on the one side, the view of a monolithic, timeless and immutable Islam which absorbs fanaticism and archaism into the Islamic civilization. On the other side, the West percieved in terms of cultural and economic aggression which is used as an explanation for all of one's failures.

Islam is now also, as a consequence of immigration, part of Europe, and demands solutions and policies for the future. Islam is sociologically a community-based religion and the Muslims' way of experiencing identity and culture is largely conditioned by the relations they have with their environment. Thus a multicultural society is faced with a search for models by which this reality can be organized and accepted. Integration, communitization or new formulas? These are the elements which preside over the debate in which urban spaces play a predominant role.

The fifteen member states of the European Union must face the question of the integration of their foreign citizens and the existence of xenophobic attitudes affecting them. The stances of the European countries do not always coincide because each one of them has a different experience. To what extent do the European policies of security as well as its immigration and nationality policies contribute to an increased distrust and fear? What are the implications of the European Union's Mediterranean policy and what are its real objectives? The Muslim Mediterranean world is of real importance for Europe, in terms of its stability, its economic and social balance, and immigration movements. Therefore, Euro–Islamic relations in the framework of the European Union's Mediterranean policy are key elements of the current debate, even though they affect certain European countries more directly than others. Whatever the case may be, cooperation and partnership emerge as the pillars of a common future. But this cooperation must be envisaged as 'positive interdependence' to make it lasting. It is to this ideal that this book hopes to contribute.

Gema Martín Muñoz

Acknowledgements

We would like to express our special thanks to His Royal Highness the Principe de Asturias for His interest in the subject matter of the seminar. Although it is impossible to mention all those who took an active part in the debates during the seminar that gave rise to this book, the editor would like to give a special word of thanks to the following for their invaluable contributions: Nasr Abu Zayd, Sadiq Al-Azm, Niels Barfoed, Hamid Barrada, Brian Beedham, Halil Becktay, Sophie Bessis, Anna Bozzo, María Cordón, Bruno Etienne, Isabel Fierro, Salima Ghezali, Hassan Hanafi, Nadir Izzat Said, Ibrahim Karawan, Martin Kramer, Nagi Laszlo, Tuomo Melasuo, Caridad Ruiz de Almodóvar, Antoni Segura i Mas, Catherine Simon, David Waines, Elisabeth Zachariadou and William Zartman.

The editor would like also to express her gratitude to the Arabist Begoña Valle Simón for her contribution to the organization of the seminar, as well as to Ignacio Alvarez-Osorio, Isaias Barrenada, Luis Martin, M. Angeles López Plaza and Almudera Ruiz. We wish to thank Dr. Julia H. Juberias for her invaluable contribution to the editing of this book.

Introduction

1

Islam and the West, An Intentional Duality

GEMA MARTÍN MUÑOZ

The dichotomy Islam/the West has recently gathered impetus as a result of a dual perception arising from the post-Cold War division of the world into East and West. In its search for a new *opposite* since the late 1980s, the West has chosen to confront Islam, considering cultural issues as the trigger for conflict.

Why cultural or civilizational issues? It is clear that this is not unrelated to the transformations the global system has undergone since the end of the bipolar system. Such transformations have affected how the principle of security is interpreted, weakening the concept of the ideological–military threat of the past. The new situation, however, has unleashed attitudes that assert 'particularisms' and have lead to concomitant social developments at regional or local level. When the strategic value held by states in the previous order was changed, the domestic status quo of these states was challenged by the emergence, after years of repression, of socio-political, ethnic and cultural movements with the aid of the superpowers and their 'strategic assets'. These movements are today voicing their fears as they become engulfed in a process of globalization. Today's societies and nations are indeed dominated by the dialectic between universal integration and the assertion of difference in a framework of regimes whose survival depends more on their capacity to generate legitimacy and institutional efficiency than on support from abroad. Instead of understanding these ongoing changes within a socio-political or human context, they are being used by some to support arguments in favour of civilizational incompatibility.

The 'clash of civilizations' theory has recently been developed out of this misconception. This theory gives an interpretation of history based on confrontation and on an ethnocentric conception of coexistence amongst cultures, since it considers such coexistence to be dependent on the extent to which other civilizations on the planet are capable of 'Westernizing'. Furthermore, it ignores the conflicts which result from the disruption caused by the marginalization of established cultural codes in non-Western societies. A case in point would be the drastic civilizational clash caused by European colonization, the effects of which are still being felt today.

But why Islam? And why has the Islam/the West dichotomy been put forward so insistently over the last few years? Although a biased presentation of international events, such as the Gulf War, or regional events, such as those arising from the confrontation between Arab and Islamist regimes, has no doubt fostered the perception of a threat, the dichotomy established by many between Islam and the West is based primarily on the false perceptions which have been conveyed traditionally to the different peoples, as a result of a misinterpretation of history.

Far from explaining the differences between the sides by using the 'conflict of interests' principle and analysing cultural relations through the concept of intercivilizational interpenetration, as the Moroccan intellectual Mohammed Abed al-Jabri proposes in this book, the predominant historical interpretation of West–Islam relations has been focused on the ideological principle of antagonism (Byzantium against the Islamic Empire; the Christian kingdoms against al-Andalus; the Ottoman Turks against Europe, Arab or Islamic nationalism against the West).

The rivalry for political and economic hegemony between medieval Christendom and the Arab–Islamic Empire was interpreted as a confrontation between civilizations, which led Western consciousness to perceive Islam with hostility and mistrust and, as the Islamic expert Muhammad Arkoun points out, while Christianity and Judaism were integrated in the West into what is commonly known as the 'Judaeo–Christian civilization', Islam was peremptorily swept aside. The prejudices created by the Islamic–Christian confrontation in Spain, in the Crusades or the fight against the Turk, penetrated the Western collective subconscious so deeply that Hichem Djaït, in his book *Europe and Islam* (1990), expresses doubts that they may ever be eliminated.

Collective perceptions take as their reference accumulated experience, which has been misinterpreted in the case of Europe and Islam. Basically such misinterpretation stems from the methods and mistaken choice of instruments with which history has been interpreted. The methodology used by observers, analysts and some specialists in presenting or analysing issues referring to the Muslim world is characterized by two main misguided tendencies. Firstly, there is a persistent tendency to hold Western ideals up as the only benchmark and place them in opposition to those prevailing in Islam. This attitude has given rise to an approach to Islamic civilization from the viewpoint of how it differs from, and conflicts with, the West instead of considering it in its own right. Moreover, political and social developments in the Muslim world are accounted for quite simply as signs of extreme religiosity. To give an example, the Iranian Revolution was assimilated into the Western historical imagination as a fanatical expression of religious fervour, ignoring all the social, political and economic factors which gave rise to the revolutionary movement. For the same reasons, the Islamic phenomenon is reduced to an irrational religious regression and no thought at all is given to why it has emerged and spread throughout Muslim populations, or to what it means for those societies, or to the break from the traditional order which they produce in sociological terms. Terrorism and warfare, when they involve Muslims, tend to be explained as a consequence of Islam itself (and its alleged inherent inclination to *jihad*) and not as the result of specific political and socio-economic circumstances.

The problem stems from the fact that the history of Eastern peoples is usually explained according to Islamic determinism arising solely from the fact of 'being Muslim'. Collective and individual behaviour patterns among the peoples in Islamic countries are explained from the viewpoint of an abstract notion of Islam rather than being interpreted from a stance which takes into account geography and local history, social structure and human experience. All this leads to a view of the Muslim world as an immobile universe. As the Lebanese sociologist Halim Barakat points out, the 'static method' used in a large majority of studies conducted by orientalists on Arab and Islamic society has undoubtedly contributed to this view. As Barakat explains in his *Inquiry into Contemporary Arab Society*, any approach to reality must bear in mind that society 'is not a complete, constituted and finalized entity, but that it is in continual evolution transforming its identity, its conceptions, its culture and its institutions according to new circumstances and situations' and that it should not be treated as 'a star turning in its own firmament and on its own axis according to immutable internal laws, which is exactly how some orientalists have perceived, and still do perceive, Arab reality.'[1]

Europe was known to the Islamic world until the nineteenth century as 'Bilad al-Ifranj' (Country of the Franks, the medieval Arabic term to denote the Crusaders). This anachronism perpetuated the notion of the foreigner as enemy and the Islamic identity as the best protection for the 'I' against 'the other'. 'Pan-Islamism' was largely the nineteenth-century response to a far-reaching crisis of self-confidence caused by the sense of humiliation amongst the populations of the Ottoman Empire on suffering European invasion. Linking religion and nation, Jamal al-Din al-Afghani called for resistance against the West based on the unity of all Islamic states and the renewal of their societies.

At that time, when the Islamic and Arab world was trying openly and unashamedly to take advantage of the universal heritage of the Enlightenment and the French Revolution, it had to endure the traumatic experience of being subjected to protracted colonial rule by Europe acting in its own mercantile interests, despite the fact that Europe was itself the firmest advocate of this heritage. Consequently, the first attempts to adapt the Islamic political and social model to constitutional and representative principles were torpedoed by European powers in connivance with the most reactionary sectors of Islamic societies. Thus the process of 'digesting' the values of modernity and the cultural and political 'renaissance' under way in the Islamic world at the end of the nineteenth century came to a grinding halt. This is what happened to the Ottoman reforms (*tanzimat*) in 1880, to Jayr al-Din's draft for a parliamentary constitution in Tunisia in 1864 and to the proclamation of the Egyptian constitution in 1879.

Such ambivalence generated by Europe, together with the colonial ethnocentricity which justified such domination and disdain for the non-European world, leaving it bereft of its historical and cultural dignity, generated serious confusion and frustration within Muslim populations. From their viewpoint, a corpus of legislation accumulated over thirteen centuries was rejected in favour of a modernity which came with European domination, causing a substantial weakening of cultural self-assertion. The re-assertion of cultural identity is in fact one of the key issues for today's Islamist movements.[2]

Consequently, as well as the false perceptions of Islam in the European imagination, in the Islamic world there is a distorted image of an atheistic, materialistic, imperialist West which is demonized in its turn. Both impressions result from the ideological deadlock caused by the dialectic between European ethnocentricity and the culture of resentment this has created amongst the colonized peoples.

Modernity and Westernization

Moreover, the 'Islam/the West' antithesis tends to conjure up a series of cultural dichotomies which suggest an equivalent notion of opposition between tradition and modernity just as there is there is an inevitable association of modernization with Westernization given the origins of, and the centre from which modernization spread beyond the European world. Precisely because modernity has spread throughout the world and has been adopted by different forms of civilizations, it has acquired a content that evidently determines the West but also extends far beyond its limits and, therefore, Westernization cannot express the notion of modernization in its full scope. For example, the fact that much of the Muslim world is undergoing a process of Islamic re-assertion which, far from being strictly religious, is closely linked to the need to find its own political and cultural language, cannot be divorced from either the experience of colonialism or the failure of modernization and secularization processes set in motion by post-colonial elites during the 1960s and 1970s. In fact, Muslim re-assertion has revealed that so-called modern cultural values must be the fruit of internal dynamics within the societies adopting them to ensure the necessary conciliation with the local culture on one hand, and that they are not felt to be transmitted by categories perceived as culturally alien on the other.

Even though the elites in Muslim societies have become Westernized in varying degrees, this Westernization has only been partial. The imagination recreated in the name of religion, national struggle or counter-Orientalism, has deeply affected the collective subconscious and Western attitudes are only valued and adopted in a purely external way, there being no critical social thought which enables such

Muslim elites to grasp, accept and adapt Western society.[3]

Besides this, the capacity of secularized thought to instigate social mobilization in the Arab world has lost ground to Islamist movements since the 1970s, particularly during the 1980s. Today, Islam endows populations with an identity and 'ideological autonomy' with which to improve their resistance to the clash with the outside world, a role played by secularized Arab nationalism during the 1950s and 1960s.[4] What are the causes underlying the decline in the secularized tendency in the Arab and Islamic world?

Firstly, this decline goes hand in hand with the waning of both nationalism and Marxism, to which secularism has been linked since the 1950s. This has been caused by a series of political events (the 1967 defeat, the Syria–Iraq conflict, booming oil prices and the reinforcement of conservative regimes during the 1970s, the Iranian Revolution in 1979) and by political and socio-economic failures in the management of the state.

Secondly, this decline is largely due to the lack of steadfast popular support for the process of cultural modernization and secularization undertaken in Muslim countries which has never been legitimized either by the state or by society. The process is also limited mainly to the intelligentsia, the military and the middle classes, whether professionals or government employees. Consequently, the material benefits are perceived by major segments of the population as a privilege to which they have been denied access. The real problem, then, is that Arab and Muslim societies need to find a new kind of social contract because that derived from what may be termed the postcolonial era has reached crisis point.

When the new post-colonial states were being created, the different nationalist leaders tended, as in Europe, to strip religion of its role as the main organizer of society. The two main principles which were to replace religion were secularization and nationalism. The building of the nation became the new object of worship and the nation-state largely based its legitimacy on the building of the nation, its development and modernization.

The religious sphere and cultural references of identity widely used to achieve these two goals were full of 'amalgams' and contradictions, since they had adopted a form of secularism which had never been legitimized culturally by a state resorting to religion and the sacred only in the pursuit of political legitimization through Islam. The state was to sacralize an immutable Islamic order, linking cultural identity to the preservation of very conservative Muslim principles. The control over and supervision of such principles was entrusted to an 'official' religious establishment who, in exchange, provided regimes with an Islamic seal of approval, thus perpetuating their role as social intermediaries to interpret what is licit or illicit according to Islam. This led such states to fail in their aim of implanting secularization and to the accusation from independent Islamic sectors that they were transmitting the colonizer's values. In response to this delegitimization, states have leaned further towards official Islam which in turn has appropriated the most fundamentalist part of Islamist ideals in a vain attempt to eliminate their value as vehicles of dissent.

Meanwhile, the process of secularization and modernization was confined to a small urban social elite. This process came with the rapid socio-economic change taking place in these societies as a result of the transformations in habitat (rural exodus and accelerated urbanization) and the labour market (the switch from traditional occupations to employment in new industries or services), as well as widespread schooling (change in parent–child relations), women entering the salaried labour market (mainly in cities), emigration, global communications conveying different social models and so on. All these transformations brought about major changes for certain sectors of the population.

Besides these factors of limited change, a further element with far-reaching consequences should also be mentioned, namely the generational changes occurring in present-day Muslim societies. A large part of today's population has suffered the negative effects of such accelerated socio-economic changes. Rapidly increasing birth rates have given rise to a high proportion of young people in the population and a concentration of them in cities (the under fifteens in the Arab world are 44 per cent of the population in Algeria, 40 per cent in Egypt and Morocco, 41 per cent in Jordan, 60 per cent in Gaza, etc.). This burgeoning generation, born after independence, does not share the nationalist ideals of its elders. The failure of nationalism and communism, as well as the liberal experience which preceded them, all of Western making, leads these young people to seek a new model taken from their own Islamic cultural legacy. This new model also allows them to take an active part in public affairs which they were unable to do under the protective post-colonial state that prevented them from rising in the social scale and attaining political representation.

Thus, the social debate has ceased to be a debate on modernization as in the preceding decades, and has come to focus on identity, culture and faith. Whereas at one time the most pressing concern was to achieve modernization, now introducing morality into the political and socio-economic order has come to the fore as a result of the corruption and the marginalization that the state has generated. Law and order have been undermined and discredited by factors affecting the legitimacy of institutions and individuals: the arbitrary character of justice, corruption and 'black' economies. All this has engendered a conflict between the classes located within the system and the peripheral classes within a framework of the process of generational change. Such changes and such a rift exert considerable societal influence, since it is precisely with them that both the Islamists and their socio-political representatives are identified. Hence, however hard *official* Islamic circles defend the adoption of the *shari'a*, they are incapable of stemming the tide of the Islamist movement. Here, we should not overlook the fact that, under different circumstances, it was also within the context of a generational change – the break away from the land-owning and trading aristocracy in power which was identified with a bourgeois middle class – that Arab nationalism sprang up in 1952.

Today, the new generation is tending to break away from the established political and social order. Such a rift is seen within families and households where the principles of a patriarchal system conferring the authority of elders over the younger generations are being questioned. Among other reasons, this is occurring because the younger generations have had access to knowledge (i.e. literacy, schooling) which the members of the family in positions of authority lack. In the framework of the state, the generation rift is reflected in the political confrontation between the established power and the Islamist movement which stems particularly from the struggle for power between an elderly post-colonial elite and a new elite which can mobilize these large social strata effectively, as well as other sectors which have, after a long period of consideration, come to support the Islamist movement either through intellectual conviction or because of its political militancy.

The third major reason for the moribund state of secular forces in many Arab and Muslim countries is the polarization of the political field between the regimes in power and the Islamist opposition. This has often been accompanied by the neutralization of secular sectors and their co-option by the state which has reduced their capacity for social mobilization and diminished their credibility.

There has been an enormous increase in the regimes' ability to win over secularized elites who are reacting strongly against the Islamist movement. Some regimes have used the experience in Algeria as a persuasive argument over and over again since 1992. As a result, the stance taken by some of the secular opposition parties, left-wing intellectuals and secularized associations (which are usually identified exclusively with civil society) has come more into line with the regimes in power in an attempt to achieve 'consensus' against the Islamist movement. The Reagroupement pour la Culture et la Démocratie (RCD) and the Ittihadi in Algeria, the Mouvement de Démocrates Socialistes (MDS) in Tunisia and al-Tagammu' in Egypt clearly illustrate this situation as do some feminist movements which, leaving aside their fight against governments perpetuating sexual discrimination, have joined forces with them to convey the idea that 'Islamic fundamentalism' is the only real threat to Muslim women. Such tacit support, with its fragile balance, however, merely adds to the deadlock in democratic development and accentuates the possibilities of social conflict on two fronts, i.e. amongst the groups in the system itself and between these groups and the periphery.

The present-day secular currents in the Islamic, and mainly Arab, world stem from a common rejection of Islamist discourse although they are unable to unite in a single positive project. As one of the most prominent representatives of this trend, Fu'ad Zakariyya, acknowledges: 'The tendency includes nationalists, progressives, liberals and apolitical intellectuals, each with his own project for society. They are united only through their conviction that the kind of regime claimed by the Islamist movement would only make matters worse.'[5] In other words, secularism is becoming a front for rejection without any overall project or ideological unity.

Perhaps for this very reason, some Arab intellectuals such as Burhan Ghalioun or Mohammad Abed al-Jabri defend the view that secularism is a false issue and that democracy should be the overriding question given that secularism does not necessarily imply democracy (Ghalioun draws from the Soviet experience to support his argument) and that, as al-Jabri argues, the separation of the Church from the state resulting from secularism is impossible in Islam since there is no Church.[6]

The Islam that perceives the West

Since the end of the 1980s, as the Eastern enemy gradually crumbled, a hotchpotch of issues receiving widespread, badly presented and poorly explained media coverage (e.g. the Rushdie affair, the Gulf War, the issue of the veil in France or the out break of violence in Algeria) was to be the only Islamic reality depicted for Western public opinion. In view of the historical heritage of Islam as depicted in the West public opinion was inclined to assimilate whatever came from the varied Muslim world through a totalizing and essentialist conception of Islam and, therefore, an image of the East over-determined by its religious identity. The Muslim world is considered to be firmly entrenched in the Middle Ages[7] and Muslims are suspected of fundamentalist militancy in an international conspiracy against Western identity which is sweeping unchecked through Western societies. A case in point is the transformation of the way Arab or Turkish immigrants in Europe have been perceived socially over the last decade. They have gone from the status of worker, foreigner and person in transit to that of a Muslim believer transplanted into Europe. This has been interpreted merely as 'Muslim visibility', a sign of religious backwardness and a threat to secularism. This attitude prevents any true understanding of the phenomenon of the so-called 're-Islamization' of immigrants in its true social and cultural light, particularly in their relationships with their host countries. It also blinds us to the fact that it is perfectly feasible for immigrants to live and experience their Muslim faith in a modern way.

A further important point to be stressed is that, as a result of what could be termed the 'mirror effect', Western societies tend to identify and concede credibility only to actors in other societies who reflect their own image. Social movements based on our own Western model are the only ones we know and take into account, since their achievements are more easily grasped, whereas the same credibility is not accorded to other means of seeking individualization and breaking away from the established order. The issue of women provides a tailor-made example of this point.

Of all the negative ideas that have circulated about Islam in recent times, the condition of women has been the strongest. Only Western-inspired feminist movements in Muslim countries have been regarded as credible in Europe while little credibility is extended to other means of breaking away from the traditional order, such as those used by Islamist women. Our secular Western societies have been misinformed and become biased to such an extent that they cannot or will not understand that the problem of women in Islam is not a religious but a social issue – i.e. religion being used by a patriarchal society – and, therefore, Islamist militancy may actually allow women to develop a modern relationship with Islam and open up breaches in the existing patriarchal order, regardless of whether this complies with the ideology of Islamist males or not.

Political Islam may give rise to a semi-conflictual relationship with traditional structures, and, contrary to them, encourage individualized behaviour given that theoretically the individual is not subservient to the honour of the tribe but is solely responsible for his/her relationship with God. In this way, female Islamists are altering the traditional status of women through their religious commitment and militancy.

Armed with the weapons of their religious 'knowledge' and their task of proselytization, women are undoubtedly conquering an area of freedom and entering the social and political world. This religious and ideological evolution favours the emergence of women's individuality while opposition from the family is restrained since they are acting on behalf of Islam and within an area considered sacred, i.e. that of religion.[8]

Far from the superficial interpretation which associates the veiled woman with submission and the unveiled woman with liberation, the issue of dress conceals a diverse world full of signs and symbols which must be decoded. French society, instead of understanding this, merely demonized the issue in the well-known 'veil crisis'. There is a whole sociological language involved in the differences between the *hayk* and the *hijab* veils[9] or the *jillaba* of one kind or another, which marks out the difference between a country peasant and a city dweller, between girls who study and go out and those who are confined to the family home, between women who assert themselves and those who submit. Islamist women do not wear the traditional veil of their mothers, which for them symbolizes ignorance, superstition, seclusion – all that they have discarded thanks to their studies, to their education. The *hijab* allows them to signal their rift with elders, breaking down one of the basic hierarchies of the patriarchal system. Moreover, by appropriating and claiming the religious, women are in some way questioning a traditional order in which it is not the religious but patriarchal social norms that for them carry most weight, that is, religion acts as an ideology which obliges a woman to accept such patriarchal order (religious duties – prayer, pilgrimage – come second to their duties as wives and mothers). The violent reaction of Algerian Islamists against their female comrades during Ramadan in 1991, when the women had laid claim to the religious sphere by attending the mosque for their evening prayers after the *fitar* (post-fast meal), clearly revealed the extent of this rift and how deeply (Islamist and non-Islamist) men feared that women would cease to be above all 'the wives of believers'.[10]

During the democratization period between 1989–91, Algerian Islamist women joined forces with modernist feminist groups over certain issues such as support for paid work for women, the right to education, protection against domestic violence, etc. 'The interruption of the electoral process and the subsequent denial of pluralism in Algeria prevented two currents in this society destined to form a mutually enriching relationship from voicing and aligning their views.'[11]

Democracy and its alleged incompatibility with the culture of Islamic countries is a further issue which often conveys a distorted image of Islam in the West. 'Islam has not been hospitable to democracy', claimed Samuel Huntington in 1984.[12] In other words, on issues of democracy Islam has no sources from which to draw. If we transfer the meaning of 'submission', as understood in religious terms in Islam, to the political sphere, some would conclude that Islam, therefore, promotes despotic rule and passive acceptance amongst the faithful. The totalitarian nature of the faith implies that only a totalitarian state could put its dogmas into practice and that Islam would discourage the creation of groups that would oppose despotism. From this standpoint, we could draw the conclusion that in Muslim societies the state is stronger than society itself. Socio-political associations in the Muslim world, with their poor organization and lack of corporate identity, would be the exceptions and informal groups would be the rule, especially as such informal groups are instruments for cooperation and support for the powers that be and the elites, whose political links would stem from clientelism.[13] While political sociology was proposing the idea that a strong civil society was required for democratization to take place, arguments in this vein were used for quite some time to show that Islamic countries seem incapable of fulfilling such a requirement.

The Iranian Revolution, however, presented us with a picture of a weak state and a strong civil society (Iranian clerics and their supporters amongst the traditional bourgeoisie in the bazaar were a strong civil society capable not only of challenging, but also of overthrowing regimes), something gradually confirmed by the expansion of Islamism and its capacity for para-state social organization. Consequently, *ad hoc* interpretations emerged to suggest that a strong society versus an unstable state hampers the development of a true civil society and the advent of democracy. Analyses presented by Patricia Crone, Daniel Pipes or John Hall explain that Islamic civilization differed in its imperative to legitimize political authority. Pipes believes that all religions postulate ideals that human beings are unable to attain, but that only Islam includes detailed political ideals in its code. By setting ideals that are impossible to fulfil, Islam ensures that Muslims ultimately perceive any form of government as illegitimate.[14] The irony is rife, as Yahya Sadowski points out:

> When the consensus evolved and social scientists thought an acquiescent, undemanding society was essential for progress, the neo-Orientalists portrayed Islam as beaming with pushy, anarchic solidarities. Middle Eastern Muslims, it seems, were doomed to be eternally out of step with intellectual fashion.'[15]

All these theories, as well as others that stress there is no distinction between politics and religion – God and Caesar – the absence of the principle of freedom replaced by that of justice in Islam, the lack of a clear concept or definition of 'citizen' and the primacy of the community over the individual are all elements in their own right that would explain attempts to argue that Islam and democracy are alien.[16] These are deterministic models of analysis, based on an essentialist view of religion and they therefore consider it outside any historical, human, geographic or social context.

It is not that the tribe, the patriarchal system or religion in Muslim societies are unimportant. They undoubtedly are, but there is a problem with the methodology used to analyse these components. Determinism and the tendency to omit a contextual explanation of the component parts and to use them to account for missing components instead – in this instance democracy – distort the conclusions drawn from the hypotheses to which they give rise. The authoritarianism of the modern Arab nation-state is more closely related to factors such as the deficiencies in the decolonization process, outside interference, the artificial divisions of national borders, the process of legitimization of elites, the predominance of a protective state, the relations between social classes and urbanization or lack of economic development than it is to 'congenital defects' arising from Islam or the tribe. In any case, as Lisa Anderson points out:

> … we therefore find ourselves faced with a body of literature composed, not of closely reasoned or carefully researched arguments, but of self-fulfilling prophecies. There is virtually no effort to examine the actual causal connections between apparently correlated phenomena, such as attitudes, behaviour and institutions, nor is there any capacity for dynamic analysis in which change in one realm of human life could be predicted to precipitate change in another. Indeed, the implicit (and sometimes explicit) assumption that attitudes and beliefs born in the desert in the era of the Prophet are timeless, unchanging, and overwhelmingly powerful – in contrast to, say, the ideas and values of contemporaneous seventh-century Europe – is a reflection of an inability to think critically about change.[17]

Authenticity, cultural values and democracy

The Islamic Revolution in Iran, the assassination of Sadat and the emergence of Islamist movements firmly placed the 'Muslim dimension' on the agenda of political science studies:

> In a sense, the key role played by the religious in the mechanics of politics restored to the Arab world a specificity that the orthodox political scientist tended to deny in the name of the double universality of objects and disciplines. Gradually, the idea began to emerge that, after all, Arab countries, states, nations and political communities all had in them (thanks to their origins, history, experiences and organizational modes) the wherewithal to undertake a kind of independent development comparable to

other cultures, experiences, etc., but not reducible or assimilable to such cultures.[18]

The research community was divided over the analysis of Islam and a current emerged that fostered theories in favour of Islam's incompatibility with democracy, based on their interpretation of Islamist movements.[19]

Although Islamist movements have often used a language that negates Western democratic values, this negation should be understood in the light of two realities: firstly, the prejudices generated by the way in which 'democracy' has been experienced in these countries; secondly, the marginalization of the Islamic legacy in the debate on democracy and modernity. Whilst these debates have recognized the contribution of the Judaeo–Christian tradition they have denied the contribution of Islam in the field of political or social organization of the modern state. The arguments put forward by Mohammed al-Hachmi Hamdi clarify this point:

> Every objective observer would admit that the West is still very much involved in the day-to-day affairs of most Muslim countries, especially those in the Arab world. This involvement takes the sad form of an unholy alliance with corrupt, isolated elites who do not respect democracy in *any* form, Western or otherwise ... Here we see the true face of secularism in most of the Islamic world: a new form of submission to the same old colonial powers. These powers may have democratic polities, but it is democracy meant for Westerners only, and does not imply any moral duties toward other nations.[20]

While it is true that the adoption of the *shari'a*, the symbolic core of Islamist claims, involves retrieving Islamic legislation which has lagged behind social developments, it must be remembered that this has occurred because of the imposition/imitation of alien European values. It is equally true that this legal corpus will have to be updated when the utopian world of opposition becomes the crude reality of political responsibility and governance. Consequently, contrary to the generally held opinion, Islamist socio-political formulation is – although there are many radical and fundamentalist views – already underway and covers a wide range of interpretations, although it is not entirely devoid of internal differences. Prominent sectors of the Islamist movement react against the more authoritarian interpretations by trying to develop Islamic principles for participation and representation within a modern, pluralist framework and by standing up to resistance to this view from radical quarters.

A further important point we must also take into account is that, in sociological terms, Islamist militants advocate a modern experience of the faith which is in a semi-conflictual relationship with the traditional order. This will inevitably lead to the need to adapt to changes and the evolving political arena in which they occur.

The controversy over democracy stems from the fact that democracy is perceived as a system conceived through the experiences of the 'other', hence some sectors see the West as a model to be imitated while others reject it on the same grounds. This emphasizes the fact that today, in light of the experience of this century, the principle of cultural authenticity is a criterion of substantial credibility for a large part of the Muslim world. Therefore, how democratization, interpreted though such a legitimacy, is perceived and experienced must not be overlooked, since the great symbolic value it holds cannot be underestimated. The different theories on the development of Islamic principles such as *bay'a, al-ikhtiyar* or *shura* to form cultural bonds between the Islamic heritage and the building of democracy, as proposed by Tariq al-Bishri, Rashid al-Barawi, Fathi Osman, Rashid al-Ghannushi, Adil Husayn or Khaled Muhammad Khaled, set the symbolic goal of according Islam a central role in the creation of modernity.

Considerable thought should also be given to the possible consequences of allowing Islamist actors (recognized as agents for the re-Islamization claimed by Islamists) to take part in modern political procedures (elections, multi-party politics, representative government), as large sectors of this movement are urging. Could the Islamists play the role of agents for a more 'natural' introduction of modern political values, given that if such values were transmitted by the 'modernist' elites they would be rejected as factors of cultural assimilation? This is a key element in today's debate which affects not only the institutional political arena but also the issue of women's rights, the acceptance of modernity, etc. This should not be ignored or relegated in favour of an exclusively 'demonized' view of Islam, nor should we concentrate our attention solely on radical and violent minority sectors.

There are many analyses based on the idea that 'the tribe prevails over Islam' which consider that progress towards democratization must include the integration of cultural values from that social reality. For Mamoun Fandy 'instead of asking whether Islam and democracy are compatible, the question should be, are democracy and primordial "sentiments" like tribal allegiance compatible?'[21] This view is supported by the examples of Jordan and Yemen (within the processes of political liberalization culminating in the 1993 elections), that do not deny democracy but show that it is attainable only if tribal cultural values are accepted rather than through Islamist mobilization which is considered as an offshoot of the 'tribal issue'. This analysis obviously provides an advantage in that it does not preclude the possibility of democratizing the Islamic world because of its tribal structure although the conclusions drawn record a strategy rather than a reality. The advance of popular expressions of Islam (Sufism, brotherhoods etc.) as seen in Egypt and Algeria, or the social relations woven by tribal solidarity, as in Jordan, particularly reflect the search for a way in which to challenge the expansion of Islamism. The 'rise of the tribe' in Jordan's 1993 elections compared with results in 1989 is not so much due to the natural dynamics of predominant tribal allegiance as to the changes in electoral legislation which were designed to counteract Islamist success by increasing representation in the predominantly tribal regions of Jordan – traditionally faithful to the throne – at a time when Jordan was signing the peace treaty with Israel and thus needed consensus over this issue which was not forthcoming from the Islamists.[22]

In addition, election results often show that where Islamists are running for election they tend to win their votes through a clear straightforward political or ideological campaign rather than by the kind of tactics that are employed by other parties which often need to resort to traditional formulae to attract votes. Furthermore, Islamist success is greater the higher the degree of freedom and competition in the elections.[23]

This does not mean that predominating values in societies can be overlooked or that they may not form the basis for representation and participation systems to be set up to the satisfaction of the population, as Fandy or Rami G. Khoury suggest.[24] In the case of the Lebanon, for example, the institutionalization of communalism has allowed coexistence to be regulated. This country, belonged to a confessional group that historically preceded the setting up of the state; nor must we forget that the war was mainly the result of foreign interference from Palestine, Syria and the West which aggravated the imbalance of power between Christians and Muslims in a situation in which a negotiated solution could have been found. In Sudan, however, no such communal formula has been achieved and the country has been plunged into an endemic civil war.

As Khoury claims 'democracy is a process that can be used to translate cultural values into political structures, systems and goals. The Western debate about Arab democratization has largely failed to admit this. Instead, it has designated democracy as a criterion, measure and goal of Arab political culture, on the simplistic and presumptuous assumption that democracy should be a defining Arab value because it is the Western defining value.'[25]

Notes

1.   Barakat (1984, 29 ff.).

2.   François Burgat is not wrong when he says, 'However real its multiple 'stimulant' factors (economic, in particular) and however diversified its political expressions may be, Islamism today is putting down its deepest roots in the soil of the decolonization movement. After manifesting itself in the *political* field, then in the *economic* field, with the rhetoric of Islam as an opposition movement, the self-distancing from the former colonizing power is extended to the ideological, symbolic and more widely *cultural* fields, where the colonial clash was most traumatic ... primarily it is the reaction to the cultural effects of colonization which today is triggering the Islamist 'third stage' of the 'decolonization rocket' (1995, 77).

3.   Saaf (1995, 11–26).

4.   The first ideas on secularism arrived with the Napoleonic invasion of 1798, although Muhammad Ali's government would be the first to develop a secular trend in the Arab world which would continue throughout this century with reformists and thinkers such as Rifa'a Rafi'i al-Tahtawi, Shibli Shumayyil, Farah Antun, A. Lufti al-Sayyid, Taha Husayn, Sati' al-Husri, Michel Aflaq, Antun Sa'deh, etc. The development of a Marxist intellectual movement, together with the adoption of Arab socialism as the ideological basis by many regimes in the 1950s and 1960s, was to contribute to the rise in secularist trends in the region. See Hourani (1992), al-Husri (1944), al-Azmeh (1992), Arkoun (1981).

5.   Zakariyya (1986).

6.   Ghalioun (1991) and Abed al-Jabri (1990, 45–9). For a review of both thinkers see Ismail (1995, 93–112).

7.   'What would happen to the narcissism of European modernity if the

(Near or Middle) East were to emerge from its 'Middle Ages', from 'barbarity' or from an exoticism of 'the other' which we have always found necessary to establish the basis of our 'civilizing' identity? Japan, after all, is so far away that even if it defies Europe, the reflections do not burn us' (Corm 1989, 372).

8.   The surveys conducted by Belhassen (1979), Ferchiou (1989) and more recently by Bucaille (1994, 105–18) provide very interesting data on this point as do the works by Taarji (1991), Adelkhah (1991) and el-Bizri (1995).

9.   The *hayk* is the traditional veil, while the *hijab* is a modern veil which does not cover the face and is used by Islamist women. The *jillaba* is the long dress of traditional Arab culture.

10.   Hakiki-Talahite (1991, 123–42).

11.   Salima Ghezali, 'Una lucha contra todas la violencias', *El País*, 30 April 1995.

12.   (1984, 199).

13.   Bill & Springborg (1984).

14.   Pipes (1983).

15.   Sadowski (1993, 19).

16.   Lewis (1996, 52–63).

17.   Anderson (1995, 89).

18.   Vatin (1992, 19). When Islam is not the main component of the analysis in papers by political scientists, compared with studies by Arabists and experts on Islam, the tribe and Weber-type 'oriental despotism' as culturalist essence causing deadlock in the democratic process, are found in works by authors such as Pryce-Jones (1974) and Sharabi (1988).

19.   Islamism has actually become one of events in the Muslim world used by the mass media, public opinion and specialists to support their theories on the Islam/West antagonism, providing a good example of how collective conceptions become fantasized. The debate published in the American review *Middle East Policy*, 3 (1994): 1–21, is a good example of the different views circulating in Western academic and political circles on Islam and its socio-political role. The market has in fact been flooded with publications on this issue, some of which are excellent, others mediocre.

20.   Al-Hachmi Hamdi (1996, 84). Al-Hachmi Hamdi is the founder and editor-in-chief of the Arabic-language newspaper *al-Mustaqilla* and until 1992 he was a member of the Tunisian Islamic movement, al-Nahda.

21.   Fandy (1994, 50).

22.   In the 1989 elections, Islamists won almost 40 per cent of the seats. In 1993, they dropped to 23 per cent while seats won by tribal leaders rose considerably.

23.   See on Egypt Martín Muñoz (1992) and (1995, 142–74).

24.   Khoury (1995, 68–76).

25.   Ibid., p. 74.

Part One

Relations Between Europe and the Muslim World: A Reinterpretation

2

History as an Ideology of Legitimation: A Comparative Approach in Islamic and European Contexts

MOHAMMED ARKOUN

Our societies have become more opaque for themselves, uncertain of their present, their future and even, therefore, of their past. At the same time, the great unifying paradigms which acted as an all-embracing framework for the development of the social sciences have collapsed, as indeed has the functional model which, in general terms, they all shared. The project for a global history, (or total history), which guided the efforts of three generations of historians, has had to be set aside, at least provisionally.[1]

The topic of history as an ideology of legitimization concerns all societies and all cultures throughout every period in history, from the remotest times to the current day. From the very beginning, we should stress the anthropological and philosophical scope of our survey which focuses on only two fields, named Islamic and European contexts. I have chosen this name to stress even in the title of my paper that the terms Islam and Europe, or Islam and the West, which are so often juxtaposed even in the most respected scientific texts, constrain us within a series of difficulties which are curiously evaded, concealed or even ignored by a large number of distinguished experts in Islam (I am not referring to essayists, journalists, militants or ideologists at all levels and of all leanings). I have often given my opinion on the abusive use of the terms 'Islam', 'Islamic' and 'Muslim' compared with 'Europe', 'the West', 'European' and 'Western'. On the one hand, the name of a religion is used to refer to extremely varied societies, to very different cultures, and to the most profane spheres of existence

25

without bearing in mind different historical periods, or sociological, anthropological or institutional realities as in today's fundamentalist discourse or the reformist discourse of the past. On the other, we find that Europe and the West refer to a historical space, to societies and to mainly secular cultures which have been forged by modernity since the sixteenth and seventeenth centuries. On the subject of contexts, it is important to stress the methodological need to let societies and cultures speak for themselves. The same applies to different social groups within a given social context that is inadequately structured by centralizing state policies. In the case in hand, we will analyse the numerous historical differences that have deepened over the last 40 years between societies arbitrarily labelled Islamic and those linked to Europe or the West. In each case we will have to evaluate how Islam and modernity are present, how they intervene and what the irreversible actions and possibly transitory contributions of each are.

By the term 'Islamic context', I mean all the historical arenas marked to a greater or lesser degree by what I shall call the 'Koranic phenomenon' or 'Islamic phenomenon'. The European or Western context differs from it due to a basic defining characteristic of the West since the English, American and French Revolutions, namely the emergence of a constructed modernity, which was experienced and implemented as a continuous effort to ensure the independence of spheres, especially the religious, political, legislative, legal and judiciary spheres, which remained unseparated in all other civilizations.

This point is crucial to the study of our topic: history as an ideology of legitimization. The failure to separate these spheres is linked in effect to a stage of narrative reasoning where mythical knowledge still predominates over critical historical knowledge. This does not mean, however, that in a modern context historical writing is completely free of myth and ideology. History as the exhaustive and, above all, objective reconstruction of the past is a distant horizon towards which the most outstanding historians will always strive. J. Le Goff has just provided a further example of this constant search in his mammoth work dedicated to Saint Louis. This great historical character, for many years transfigured to the point of sanctification, gives us an idea of how much ground has been covered between the founding myths, hagiographic literature, the annals of the Middle Ages and the nationalistic history of events and today's history-problems and historical anthropology, sociology, and psychology.

We are still a long way off from such daring, enriching, de-mythologizing and de-ideologizing explorations of new territory in historical knowledge in the Islamic context. Even Western researchers working in Islam-related fields often fall short of the methodological progress and cognitive ambitions of their colleagues and fellow citizens studying Western topics. This is why the history of Islam as a school of thought, as a culture, as a system of trans-social and trans-historical beliefs and norms is still written, taught and used as an ideology of legitimization. This process began when the Prophet disappeared in 632 and there was a need to gather all the Koranic verses, to faithfully compile all the teachings of the charismatic leader and to write his biography (*sira*). This was to ensure that future generations would receive the true version of everything that had been perceived, understood and experienced as divine categories (*ankham*), and, therefore, intangible, supranatural and metahistorical categorizations of the whole reality of the world and the conditions under which human life was to be conducted. To advance in the comparative analysis of the cognitive status and ideological functions of history in both contexts described above, I shall consider the following points: religion and history; state, society and history; and I then continue with two examples, namely France and Algeria.

Religion and history

Under this general heading we may raise the same questions and use the same epistemological criteria for both the Islamic and the European and Western contexts. It is the religious phenomenon that affects more or less decisively the writing and the use made of history for ideological purposes, just as history imposes developments and even radical breaks which the orthodox masters refuse to acknowledge in all religions. While concentrating our critical attention on Islam, we often forget that, just like the Islamic world, the whole of Europe was subjected to divine categorizations of reality and existence which Christianity set down in canonical law and moral and political theology. We judge Islam and its works by the postulates and categorizations introduced by the reason of the Enlightenment and positivist science of the nineteenth century, forgetting that most of the intellectual works and cultural achievements of Islam belong to the medieval mental era (610–1400).

Monotheistic religions introduced two temporalities which have continually been interwoven, competing with each other and causing tensions in the field of education ever since the biblical and evangelical writings were taken up and enlarged upon in Arabic in the Koran, in the biographies of the prophets (*qisas al-anbiya*) and in the highly detailed lives of saints, imams, mahdis, mystical masters, and so on. The inextricable mutual interference of these two temporalities are to be found in religious literature as well as in historiographic works which have finally imposed a vague linear chronology in the mythically-structured writings raised to the status of historical information by exegetes and annalists. The works of al-Tabari (d. 923), an exegete and historian, give a perfect illustration of this mental attitude which in the Islamic context is revived by the fundamentalist view and discourse, albeit with a considerably impoverished memory, the loss of the sense of the exhaustive and of fidelity in the transmission of narrative units. The chronological time in the worldly history of mankind is set within the framework of, and draws its meaning from, the eschatological view of the History of Salvation. The historian H. I. Marrou, the Catholic philosopher J. Guitton, the Protestant P. Ricoeur and many Christian theologians since Saint Augustine, each in his own style and attitude to belief, have all shown the constant topicality of this problem, especially when faced with the progress and intellectual challenges of critical historical knowledge.

As long as political theology maintained its supremacy by conditioning political legitimacy both in Islam and in Christianity, the writing of history was constrained in its choice of subject matter, in the scope of its research, in the interpretation of documents, in the total submission to the system of beliefs, to the ethical–legal norms, to the divine categorizations explicated by theologians–jurists and applied, with the help of a secular arm, by specialized religious personnel who were administrators of the sacred and guardians of 'orthodoxy', that is, from the theological point of view, guardians of the promise or eternal Pact of Alliance (*ahd, mithaq*) which links the Creator with His creatures.

As we can see, the hierarchical relationship between theology and history reflects the relationship of dependency between the state (political power) and religion (the spiritual authority equals Thomas Aquinas' *potestas/auctoritas* and *sulta/hukm* in Islam). When, with

Spinoza, Thomas Hobbes, John Locke, and the philosophers of the Enlightenment, philosophy–politics gradually replaced spiritual legitimacy defined hitherto by theology–politics with a secular legitimacy, an intellectual, legal, institutional and political revolution (accompanied by the great scientific discoveries and the upsurge of capitalism) spread with varying degrees of violence throughout Europe and North America. What does this mean then for history as an ideology of legitimization?

The building of the nation-state favours the replacement of theology–politics by philosophy–politics since it monopolizes historiography for its own ends. We must remember that, in the three monotheistic religions, for centuries theology–politics upheld three grounds for legitimacy, namely: authority, Revelation and obedience. With the nation-state, drawing its legitimacy from universal suffrage, political power relegates Revelation to private beliefs and demands obedience to the law passed by the legislative powers. Historiography records all these changes as a necessary and universalizable progress of civilizations. For a long time historiography has particularly favoured official records setting down political and military events linked to the actions taken by the state; religion is confined to a specialist field and is mentioned in official history only when there is open confrontation with the state. In societies where the state has not yet achieved its independence from the predominant religion, however, history is constrained both by the official religion and by the state. And it is this situation that prevails in the Islamic context, especially when states created out of national liberation struggles bring religion under state control to be used as a tool of legitimization.

State, society and history

In the Islamic context, the state control of religion underscores the function of history as an ideology of legitimization: the state appeals to and utilizes the history of the official religion, declared to be the true religion just as in the Middle Ages, but there is no doctrinal pluralism, and none of the many theological–legal and philosophical schools known in Classical Islam (661–1258) are included. Classical Islam has long since been evinced from the collective memory and from intellectual circles. The Muslim public has decreasing access to historical works by Western researchers in the original language, not only because of the high cost of books but for a more serious reason, i.e. the monolingualism imposed by nationalist states and the spread of fundamentalist thought to a wide range of social classes. Instead of showing concern, the state takes advantage of this trend and brings more pressure to bear to direct history and historians towards the main task of constructing a *national* memory based on the model of nation-states forged in Europe since the eighteenth and nineteenth centuries. This aim could not be criticized during the years of the struggle for political freedom and later for economic growth and the reinstatement of a national identity. The states drew their legitimacy from their commitment to building effective national unity which was conceived as the first, necessary and undeniable step towards material and intellectual modernity. When we see how European nation-states today resist the high demands exacted for the construction of a transnational entity, it is easy to understand the impatience and determination of colonized peoples to accede as quickly as possible to the international dignity and national pride which had hitherto been denied to them or which they had never known.

A further essential dimension of history as an ideology of legitimization arises here. In the Islamic context, aspirations to nationhood and nationalist feeling did not emerge from the inner history of peoples who had been led down that road by leaders basing their political vocabulary, their strategies for fighting and their aims on European ideologies of the emancipation of 'man and citizen'. Instead, their basis comes from theoretical works of Sunnite and Shi'ite political theologies or from the political and administrative institutions of a caliphate or sultanate which have long since been forgotten or become obsolete in view of the auspicious models for liberal revolutions or scientific socialism offered by Europe. Nationalist Islamic leaders had neither any critical history of theology–politics and the real issues at stake in Islam, nor sufficient information on the (not always sufficiently critical) research by European historians into their own history and its philosophical and political consequences. The way was clear for ideological daydreaming, nationalistic romanticism, fervent assertions of national identity in clear opposition to the arrogant and imperialistic encroachment of nation-states led by a conquering bourgeoisie or a revolutionary proletariat.

Moreover, in many Islamic societies, historical research and educational institutions were practically non-existent until the 1950s and 1960s. Following independence, the number of universities has multiplied, but in many cases the teaching of history and social science still remains firmly under the ideological control of the states who use the demagogy of Arabization to mitigate the critical effects of disciplines such as sociology, anthropology, philosophy and linguistics. This has delayed the introduction of historical criticism, particularly in fields related to religious matters. This would account for the success of fundamentalist attitudes amongst students in exact sciences. They are sheltered from information and historical criticism of the state, society, religion, the anthropological structures of kinship, or political, social and historical imagination. The secularizing forces acting in economic, monetary and technological spheres only deepen the cultural and intellectual gulf between the rapid progress towards modernity in the material sense, especially in the rich oil-exporting societies, and the backwardness in the critical attitude to the search for meaning (the subject matter of the social sciences and philosophy). Learning institutions artificially maintain people's allegiance to the idea of their history as nationalist, backing this by religious apologetics and ensuring that at school, in social discourse and in the official harangues, stereotyped formulae and stock themes are recited either vehemently or routinely, according to the parties involved.

When the generations born in the 1950s, 1960s and 1970s appeared on the scene, they brought with them a new element in the working of history as an ideology of legitimization. Trained in the 'educational' system and the nationalist atmosphere of post-independence, millions of young people show a clear lack of historical memory: from remote history they may at best remember the names of some 'civilizing heroes' but are unable to place them in a geo–historical context and relate them to main areas of civilization or key moments in local history. As for the more recent contemporary period, it is clear that the 'historical leaders' and heroes of the liberation struggle have been forgotten or disqualified by both the religious and secular oppositions which tend to dominate today's political scene. The replacement of an essentially secular nationalist, though none the less mythological Model by an 'Islamic' Model for producing history as seen above, again stresses the gap between the critical history which historians are trying to develop into a positive science as the objective reconstruction of the past of a given society or identifiable social group on one hand, and manipulated history to feed and direct present-day political imagination on the other. This gap, which is readily perceived and extremely harmful in post-colonial societies is also present – although clearly to a lesser extent – in European and Western societies. Despite the presence of numerous and innovative historians, the scientific control exercised sometimes by the most qualified authors and institutions is unable to ensure that an accurate relationship, free from ideological bias, is maintained between each nation-society and its past. This applies to research, the education system and official discourse. In Europe too, there are serious gaps in the historical memory of nations. The state acts directly (education, official celebrations, political arguments, etc.) or imperceptibly through symbolic gestures (see below the example of the Bicentennial of the French Revolution) to use history in order to strengthen, readjust, reactivate or repersonalize certain ways in which the past is perceived and integrated into the present. In a democratic context where freedom to think, write and publish is guaranteed by the rule of law, differing points of view may be voiced, and all interpretations of highly controversial topics and moments in national history are permissible. However, there is still a tacit agreement between the state and the different representatives of civil society which leads to the elimination of, or to only partial controlled reference being made to, historical events which cast a shadow on national history. Examples include the history of colonization in France which comes into conflict with the great principles of the French Revolution, or the Nazi period in the history of Germany. The consensus stems from the need for a legitimizing, hence necessarily positive, overall image of the nation's history. In each case, the writing of history depends on the kind of relations permitted or forbidden between state and society, although, in all cases, the state retains the monopoly of control over all the symbolic capital accumulated during the course of history acknowledged as the heritage of the Nation. To give a more detailed review of these persistent obstacles to the writing and teaching of history, I have chosen the examples of France and Algeria, but not because they are special, but simply because I know them better than other equally interesting examples.

France and Algeria

It is a well-known fact that the Revolution of 1789–92 plays the role of a founding account (*récit de fondation*) for the secular republican tendency opposed to the Christian monarchical tendency of the French Nation. Emile Poulat has given an excellent description of this division in a work titled *Liberté, laïcité, la guerre des deux France et le principe de la modernité* (1987). War breaks out without exception every time attempts are made to alter the status of so-called free schools or secular, state schools. In 1989, President F. Mitterand and his socialist government wanted to give the celebrations for the bicentennial of the revolution a special mark of distinction. Numerous historical works appeared which again showed the controversial aspects of the revolution but did not quite manage to get beyond the ideological debate about the basis of any philosophical and political legitimacy as still conceived and defended by the two Frances. The closing ceremony of the celebrations took place on the 12 December 1989. In his wish to reconcile the two Frances, F. Mitterand chose Abbé Grégoire to be buried in the Panthéon. But Cardinal Lustiger refused to take part in the official ceremony since Abbé Grégoire had signed the civil constitution of the clergy under the revolution. So we can see here how the two readings of history as an ideology of legitimization come into conflict, two centuries after the event.

A further, significant episode marked the bicentennial celebrations. Edgar Faure, originally appointed as Chairman of the Organizing Committee, had the idea of setting up a commission of specialists and qualified representatives of the main religions with the remit of preparing a seminar to study the different ways in which the traditions of religious thought perceived the revolution and how the revolution perceived them. When he died shortly afterwards, the new chairman, Jean Noël Jeannenay, began his term of office by scrapping the commission which had already begun to work on the project.

The third example I should like to mention is even more important and revealing. I am referring to the book conceived and edited by Pierre Nora on *Les Lieux de mémoire* (1984–92). This work shows how, during the Third Republic, the French state selected a series of historical events to back its political project of uniting the French nation. These events were established as key landmarks in national memory and, with the consent of historians, researchers and teachers, were faithfully transmitted to the French people from primary school onwards. The independence of historical research from the state's ideological strategies has certainly improved since the end of the Cold War and the fall of communism. It cannot, however, be considered either total independence or indeed an irreversible achievement. In the quote at the beginning of this paper, J. Revel warned us of 'the great unifying paradigms ... of social science have collapsed'. In my lengthy critique of the work by C. I. Cahen, I show both why and how the 'orientalist' writing of history should urgently break away from past methods, and provide the revisions and new outlooks required for all historical writing in general.[2] The speed and quality of progress in this sense will depend as much on transcending the nation-state and moving towards transnational political concepts (such as the European Union which is emerging despite sacrosanct national egoisms) as on the ability of social sciences to rid themselves of functionalist descriptivism and local, short-term empirical aims.

Algeria differs from France in the scope of the heritage used to lay the foundations for historical memory, in the continued expansion of this heritage since Clovis[3] and its ideological utilization or exploitation by historiography. During the war of liberation (1954–62), ideological controversy raged amongst the French, including researchers and intellectuals, who maintained the historical thesis of a total absence of an Algerian nation on the one hand and nationalist militants on the other, backed by essayist–historians who in a mixture of fervour, indignation and ignorance argued that an Algerian nation had existed since Jugurtha and Massinissa, i.e. 'African resistance to Roman occupation' as proposed by Marcel Benabou in his doctoral thesis. Many factors converge here to encourage the manipulation of history for strictly ideological purposes: the pressure of colonial ideology throughout the Maghreb; the lagging behind of historical research on what E. F. Gautier aptly called 'les siècles obscurs du Maghreb'; the almost total lack of Arabic-speaking researchers and teachers; the prevalence of local orally transmitted memories, themselves no more than edifying tales or, at best, discontinuous and increasingly impoverished accounts with a mythical structure, which would automatically be disqualified by learned culture; the impossibility of access to historiography and archives in Latin, Arabic, Turkish, French, Spanish, Italian etc.; the growing importance of the reformist Islamic nationalist discourse (*salafiya*) hunting out the 'superstitions', 'deviations' and 'bad habits' of so-called popular or *marabut* Islam, and the intrusions of modernity considered contrary to orthodoxy as defined by self-proclaimed *ulama*.

Resorting to history as an ideology of legitimization comes up against a series of problems shared by all the Maghreb societies. Moreover, Algeria has had to face an added difficulty, the discontinuity of state organizations and the consequent dispersion and isolation of local memories until the National Liberation Front (FLN) state emerged. The same dispersion is to be found in Morocco and Tunisia although, especially in the case of Morocco, the state has enjoyed greater continuity since Islamization. The political will of the National Liberation Front (FLN) state created the illusion that this fundamental historical, sociological and anthropological factor could be overlooked by decreeing a national unity based on exclusively Arab and Islamic allegiance. These two pillars of identity take us back to the problems which have not received any critical examination within the still non-existent framework of a historical and anthropological thought free from ideological control. I have already addressed this vital question in several essays.[4] And I hope to make an in-depth study on the conditions of how thought is exercised in the Maghreb. Here I should merely like to point out that the different uses made of Islam since independence by states, intellectual elites, religious leaders and social agents in general have given rise to such hypertrophy of the ideological sphere that the first task for thinking in the Maghreb today is to render thinkable all the unthought and the unthinkable which has built up about the cognitive status and functions of the religious according to the example of Islam. For the Maghreb inhabitants and contemporary Muslims in general, Islam considered as a system of beliefs and non-beliefs, as a tradition of long-standing pluralist thinking before becoming monolithic, dogmatic and isolated from the intellectual sphere is an enormous unthought which the up and coming political forces wish to keep strictly within the category of the unthinkable (i.e. what cannot be thought for fear of committing blasphemy, or, in actual fact, for fear of weakening the ideology striving for power).

It is well known that Algeria still suffers more tragically than its neighbours from such stifling of all critical thinking. The single line of thought, imposed for thirty years by the adepts of 'scientific socialism', has been succeeded by 'the revealed Truth' of an Islam cut off even from its medieval thinkable. After the dramatic experience of two civil wars in only forty years, very few Algerians are willing to face the following question: who, in the past of this political and legal territory called Algeria, has handed me down the tools for thought, cultural values, ethics and historical founding works, that is to say a heritage that is the result of the slow reflection process of a people upon itself? A people which thinks of itself as Algerian by sharing this symbolic capital that enables each and anyone of us to carry out a great many vital tasks, such as: to put an end to the semantic disorder that paralyses the social discourse, to do away with the faulty representation of the self that burdens collective memory, and disrupts the social thinking of a people, to create the political, cultural and institutional conditions in order to have a critical view of the past, the present, the immediate or distant future, as well as of the present challenges on the world future?

The replies to this vital question, which is being addressed on several fronts, have so far come from the Koran, from the *shari'a*, from the great names in Arab cultures whatever their real geo–historical background and the era in which their works were produced. We are all aware of how the Iranians, the Iraqis, the Syrians, the Turks, the Tunisians, etc. dispute the 'ownership' of the great names of Ibn Sina (Avicenna), al-Farabi, al-Ghazali, Ibn Khaldun, amongst others. This reinforces the use of history as an ideology for the legitimization of everything that history itself as a scientific discipline of elucidation, demystification, dismantling of ideologies, and emancipation of social imagination, is supposed to delegitimize. Political experts, whose role should be to show up the weaknesses, manipulations, bad habits, arbitrariness and mental confusion generated by official discourse, religious discourse, educational discourse, media discourse and various everyday discourses, then appear on the scene. Instead of conducting the essential task of criticizing ideologies, many of these 'researchers' actually help spread semantic disorder by transcribing the various afore-mentioned discourses into European languages, describing them all as Islamist and offering them up with the scientific seal of approval of university degrees to Western journalists. These in turn assure that ideological works 'enriched', so to say, at each stage of transmission, are spread throughout the world.

With the obvious corrections appropriate for each case, everything that has been mentioned about Algeria may be applied to all countries which have been channelled to modernity through the colonial system, a process continued and aggravated in many contexts and situations by so-called nationalist state regimes. The enormous responsibility of the social sciences should also be stressed. Social science's methodology and choice of areas of study have barely looked either at the recurrent power games and dialectics of regimes or at the post-independence hangover from the past with the hegemony of the West on one hand and all satellite societies on the other. Historians particularly must continue to struggle relentlessly to mitigate the ravaging effects of all official historiographies placed at the service of the will for power.

Notes

1. Revel (1995).
2. See Arkoun (1996, 28–70).
3. Baptized in Rheims around 488, Clovis became the first barbarian Catholic king and the sole king of all of Gaul. This explains President Jacques Chirac's decision to include him in the founding heritage of the nation along with other great 'places of memory'.
4. See Arkoun (1984, 1993a, 1993b).

3

Europe and the Muslim World in International Relations

MIGUEL ÁNGEL MORATINOS

It should come as no surprise that the relationship between Islam and Europe from the standpoint of international relations should be discussed by a Spanish diplomat. It is hardly surprising either that my country, Spain, has, in one way or another, always included an Arab-Muslim dimension in its foreign policy. We shall not review here all the different stages of our international relations or even our own history, but, over and over again, year after year and century after century, we find many events closely linked to the Islamic world. To name but a few, there is the end of the Reconquest in the mythical year of 1492, perceived by some as the culmination of the unified homeland, while seen by others as the end of an era of splendor leading many of Granada's inhabitants to flee the Peninsula, just as 'Leo the African' had done before them, to settle on African shores. Or the battle of Lepanto and the all-pervasive opposition to the Turks in the Mediterranean. Or the so-called 'Question of Morocco' from the late nineteenth century to the present day, amongst others. All these examples are prominent landmarks in the history of Spain.

In view of this, it would not be mistaken to stress that what may be termed as 'the phenomenon of Islam' should be a familiar matter for Spain and the Spaniards. This familiarity should not mislead us, however, or blind us to the problems and tension that have troubled relations between Spain and the Arab-Muslim World throughout the ages.

Although this statement may seem obvious, there is no unanimity over the matter. One could even go so far as to say that since Spain acceded to political democracy, since joining the European Union, and from its vantage point of modernity, Spanish society seems to want to forget part of its own historical identity together with its outstanding political and economic commitments in the Muslim world. Spain seems to have taken a stance that is more in line with other European and Western partners and, hence, a more distant view of a world which, though close to it geographically and historically, seems to embarrass the West morally and intellectually.

We could also say that, from behind the protective shield of imported superficiality and false enjoyment of Westernization, we have lost sight of some of the defining components of our own identity. And this loss will not affect Spain alone, but the whole of Europe. We must acknowledge, however, that Europe is rediscovering its bonds with this region of the world. What is disconcerting is that, at least until very recently, the attitude towards this re-encounter has been intuitive and, above all, conflictive. The European approach to what could be termed 'Islam' is both largely unthinking and contradictory. Perhaps what is most serious and worrying is that this approach does not respond to any logical historical reason or serve to support and guarantee its many major interests in the region.

We are witnessing a permanent and gradual satanization or demonization of Islam which has overlooked the possible adverse effects such discourse and attitudes may have on the future of our own continent. There have been many turning points in this emerging European and Western attitude towards Islam. I have decided to pick out some of the more outstanding examples: questions of concepts, further instances referring to declarations and other examples of a political nature. First of all I shall deal with instances relating to the conceptual sphere and declarations, although the examples of a political nature preceded these events and, to a certain extent, pre-conditioned them.

Firstly, it was undoubtedly the article by the American political scientist Samuel Huntington on the inevitability of a clash between civilizations that caused the greatest negative impact, given its intellectual and doctrinal nature. Without a doubt, the article, published in the journal *Foreign Affairs* in the summer of 1993, paved the way for a series of attitudes opposing Islam. Still more dangerous, the article also created a harmful dialectic of support and rejection, which was sensationalist and lacked rigour, that is being used today as a 'boomerang' whenever this question is under serious discussion.

The Eaton professor, perhaps finding appeal in Malraux's maxim 'the twenty-first century will either be the century of religions or it will not be at all', used a series of semi-valid, semi-false arguments to construct a fully-fledged, academic laboratory theory which might well have had its own rationale and interest had it not dealt with one of the most sensitive and complex questions the contemporary world has to face which require a greater and more accurate understanding of the matter than the North American scholar has shown.

No one would deny how important the cultural and civilizational dimension is for present-day and future relations, not only between states, but also between nations and societies. However, while no sound analyst, either a philosopher, sociologist, historian or politician, could deny the major role played by the cultural, religious, human or civilizational factor in forming any kind of relationship, it is unacceptable that such relationships should be inevitably and intrinsically conflictive and expressed in terms of opposition and rejection, negation and confrontation.

The second turning point occurred as a result of the unfortunate statements made by Willy Claes, the former NATO secretary general. His justification of the NATO-Mediterranean Countries talks revealed a subconscious full of false fears and new threats. When he claimed that the priority aim of the talks was to fight against 'Islamic fundamentalism', he gave rise to legitimate and fierce criticism, not only from some of the Arab states involved, but also from NATO members themselves, particularly Spain. A new 'declared crusade' had been launched from the very hub of Western military power. No greater symbolism than this could have been expected. As a consequence, radical Islamic groups were provided with new weapons with which to stigmatize the West.

Besides these two factors involving concepts and statements, it was undoubtedly the impact of several political events in the area that led Europe to try and define a policy to deal with the Islamist phenomenon: the Gulf War, the Algerian crisis and the Sharm al-Shaykh summit held on 13 March 1996.

Without wishing to cast doubt on the legality and legitimacy of the actions undertaken by the international 'coalition' against the military occupation of one state by another, in this instance of Kuwait, we should not ignore the 'shock waves effect' that such action caused in the collective consciousness of the Arab-Muslim world. A strong and deep current of solidarity spread through a large majority of the population in the area. As the French political expert Bruno Etienne described it, the accumulated frustrations kindled the reappearance of the 'Andalusi' syndrome dating from the era of lost splendour, of past glories, when they saw how mythical Mesopotamia was being rased and destroyed.

The 'Desert Storm' operation was a military success in the short term, but left in its wake deep-seated social and psychological bitterness throughout the Arab world. Today we are experiencing the consequences which will have an effect in the mid and long term.

The Middle East Peace Conference in Madrid set the goal of proving that the West in general, and the United States in particular, were fully committed to ensuring that international legality and recognition of the legitimate rights of the Palestinians be duly applied, thus rejecting the accusations of 'dual morality'. Madrid was a positive sign and brought hope and confidence to Arab societies that greater and better mutual understanding was achievable. The deep wounds that the Gulf War opened in Arab collective consciousness and imagination must not, however, be underestimated.

A second event which shocked European public opinion, and also Western diplomatic circles, was the overwhelming victory of the Islamic Salvation Front (FIS) in the first round of the elections in Algeria in December 1991. This result and the 'kid-gloved military coup' that ensued almost immediately brought about a highly ambiguous reaction from Europe and USA. Although no country in the European Union approved the interruption of the elections and, consequently, the halting of the democratic process in Algeria, and even President F. Mitterand publicly spoke in favour of a rapid return to the democratic path, no-one actually managed to condemn the 'coup de force' by the military.

Thus started a long, contradictory process, with disorientation acting as the overriding factor. Few countries stuck to a line of coherence and perseverance. At the same time, Western military chiefs of staff began to conjure up a catastrophic scenario. New techniques were developed to study possible response scenarios. The crisis and contingency planning units found a new reason for their existence.

If we bear in mind particularly the fifty thousand Algerians who have lost their lives during this fratricidal and futile war, we could say that the only virtue the Algerian crisis has had is to raise a debate on the Islamic phenomenon and its impact on Europe. It should be clearly stated that this debate, however, has been manipulated and tainted with unacceptable appraisals and clumsy simplifications from the very beginning.

For example, an attempt was made to interpret the situation in terms of a struggle for influence between France and the United States. The Americans were accused of having 'opted' for the Islamists merely to displace French interests. Moreover, the democratic forces who wished to favour talks with the representatives of political Islamism were anathematized. Islam was relentlessly 'satanized' and it was all too easy to fall into the trap of only picking out the atrocities committed by one side, without having the courage to report the violence committed by other forces in Algeria.

Lately there have been some hopeful developments in the Algerian crisis, such as the high turnout recorded at the election of President Zerual, which prove that the vast majority of Algerians favour a peaceful, democratic solution to their problems. Hopefully this objective will be furthered by talks between the authorities and the different political forces, including the Islamist groups who reject violence.

Lastly, I should like to refer to the attacks claimed by an armed branch of the Palestinian Hamas group, known as the 'Izz al-Din al-Qasam', on the 25 February and 4 March 1996 and how the West responded firmly and immediately to this challenge from radical Islam. The convening of the so-called Sharm al-Shaykh peace-makers' summit deserves a few comments. The summit had a triple aim. First and foremost, the aim of safeguarding the peace process and supporting its two main instigators: Shimon Peres and Yasser Arafat. Both Israeli society and the Palestinian population had evidently lost their confidence in the peace process and a clear, firm message of support from the whole of the international community was needed. Secondly, the summit aimed to condemn any terrorist act to failure by setting up mechanisms for international cooperation. By achieving these first two aims, the third would automatically be assured, namely strengthening and guaranteeing stability in the region.

From the political and diplomatic viewpoints, these three aims were flawless. Certain preliminary points had, however, to be corrected. The original name of the conference itself overlooked the most outstanding political aspects and focused only on repressive instruments to fight terrorism, failing to bear in mind the political and economic reasons giving rise to terrorism. The first drafts of the final declaration were also guilty of this mistaken approach, as was the preparation of the working party for the follow-up to the conference. Finally a more balanced approach was achieved so that useful and efficient recommendations could be drawn up to reach the goals set out above.

Most countries consider, however, that the Sharm al-Shaykh initiative is destined to be short-lived and should under no circumstances replace the current structures of the peace process. It would be a serious mistake to discard the Madrid framework, both in its bilateral and multilateral aspects, as well as the various economic initiatives that have arisen over the past few years. The Peace Process initiated in Madrid is definitely going through one of its most critical periods. But we must bear in mind both the historical perspective and future challenges. It is difficult to set policies in the midst of internal and external pressures generated by tragic events. Sometimes diplomatic instruments are created as reactions to events, not as duly considered action. Perhaps the Barcelona Conference is the only process which reflects a thoughtful and negotiated strategy, with a due sense of history which goes beyond mere short-term considerations. But a compromise must be struck between design and implementation. This is our current task. The latest proposals such as Sharm al-Shaykh are more reactive than creative and seek immediate results. In any event, they must all take into account the possible consequences of a hasty response to solve today's problems without considering the possible long-term negative effects this may have for the future.

The great danger of Sharm al-Shaykh is that it may give a distorted image of a West willing to take action only when the security and interests of a given single country are at stake, while remaining passive and indifferent when the same situation involves an Arab-Islamic country. The impression that this was a new anti-Islam 'crusade' was corrected in this instance by most Western countries who took part in the meeting, especially by Spain. The speeches delivered by the King of Morocco and the King of Jordan stressed this key idea of discerning between a tolerant Islam and the attacks perpetrated by terrorist groups. Indeed their speeches strengthened the message Sharm al-Shaykh wanted to convey to the enemies of peace.

All these events forced Europe to define and specify its policy for the region. Since then, it could be said that Europe has undergone a catharsis as regards Islam which has prepared the ground for the first steps towards implementing a policy on the region.

Along these lines, Spanish diplomacy has attempted to start defining a series of recommendations in cooperation with its European partners who are more sensitive to the situation in this region. Many of these were included either directly or indirectly in the political declaration issued at the Barcelona Conference in November 1995. I feel that the following recommendations should be stressed.

Our respect for Islam, its religion and culture should be clearly stated, taking into account the sensitivity of Muslims themselves. We should avoid any confusion and clearly distinguish Islam from radical Islamism. We should show our respect for and interest in Islam, while we should denounce radical Islamism and reject the use of violence for purely political aims, under the banner of religion. Our firm rejection of any complacency on this matter should also be made clear.

We should also avoid giving the impression that we are involved in a global confrontation with the Muslim world by overstating the importance of the 'Islamist threat', and we should also avoid all official statements in public which deal with the Islamist phenomenon in terms of conflict or threat. Both Huntington's thesis and Willy Claes' statement fall into this category.

We should also show our understanding of the deeply rooted causes underlying the development of Islamist movements and stress our willingness to act on the root of these causes. In any event, we should adopt a specific case-by-case and country-by-country approach to the Islamist phenomenon which is multiple and diverse. Our approach cannot and should not be to reject Islam globally and indiscriminately. We should tailor our action according to the specific national features of Muslim states and their degree and pace of development.

This course of action was one of the main pillars of policy approved by the Barcelona Conference, with the aim of supporting Arab-Muslim regimes who accepted certain common principles to back them in their attempts to develop democratic institutions and a state governed by the rule of Law. Here we must definitely stress that the safeguard of political and religious pluralism is linked to the very existence of such a state.

Although the Barcelona declaration does not outline specific commitments, the spirit of the declaration reveals the willingness to encourage Muslim states not to exclude moderate Islamist movements from the political field and to foster the exchange of ideas. The Jordanian model should be taken as a positive reference point. Such support of dialogue and political integration of Islamist groups does not exclude the commitment to support Muslim states in their fight against any form of extremism or the setting up of joint cooperation initiatives against terrorism. Although consensus was extremely difficult to achieve on this article of the Declaration, as on others, today it stands as one of the greatest achievements of Barcelona. For the first time Syria and Lebanon, as well as Israel, accepted commitments in this field. But the European Union must be watchful and ensure that it reacts in the same way towards any event or incident that occurs in the area. Our understanding must reach Muslim populations who are victims of external aggression, terrorist action or the violation of human rights whether in Europe, the Middle East, Africa or Asia. In other words, we should reject any 'dual morality'.

Attempts were made at Barcelona to open up a process of dialogue and cooperation which will guarantee the change towards political and economic 'modernity' throughout the region, within a framework of security and parameters of dynamic stability. Hence the global approach of the initiative. Economic measures and instruments must go hand in hand with political and cultural initiatives. When we refer to so-called economic 'conditioning' or 'persuasion', it must be taken as an incentive for the implementation of structural economic reform required at all costs to improve the standard of living of these societies. At the same time, there should be no hesitation in rewarding those countries which can show clear improvements in respect for human rights or consolidation of the democratic state by offering them economic incentives. It seems essential that a policy of dialogue and cooperation should be favoured in relations between Islam and Europe, within organizations whose membership includes countries from the North and South of the Mediterranean. The different bodies and forums for debate created at the Barcelona Conference and the Mediterranean Forum should be ideal centres for consolidating such cooperation. The development of a pro-active cultural policy for Arab-Islamic countries should be a priority, and the outstanding historical contributions of the Arab and Islamic worlds to European culture should be publicized.

Lastly, the situation of Islam in Europe should be assessed, encouraging the emergence of a modern Islam among the Muslim communities living in Europe, seeking valid, representative and responsible interlocutors. The latest book by Gilles Kepel *A l'Ouest d'Allah* (1994) is highly significant. The crisis suffered by Arab-Muslim communities in France, Great Britain and the United States as a result of the lack of integration in a society they consider alien and their desperate attempts to create their own communities in clear opposition to the foreign model of civilization, is forcing European countries to take a closer look at this situation in its entirety.

The dilemma for citizens between either forming part of a Western state or being a member of an Islamic community, when both systems are governed by different conceptions and norms, has become acute. The Rushdie affair or the question of the 'veil' are recent examples that have opened up the necessary debate. The replies have not been entirely satisfactory. In some cases, the secular republican principles have been upheld, in others communities' rights have been reconciled. Perhaps a middle-of-the-road and innovative approach has been missing which is capable of generating a new plural, respectful reality which nonetheless remains firm on certain principles and universal values. A balance should be struck between respect for the individual and respect for the community. Perhaps Western societies should rethink their traditional outlooks. Instead of focusing on the exclusive desire to export their own cultural and civilization model, it is time for them to accept 'cultural imports' and to improve their understanding of an increasingly complex and interdependent world; it is time for them to combine their enthusiasm for 'teaching' with a humbler, wiser attitude of wanting to 'learn'.

This is the main message we can send out from Toledo today and all of us, politicians, diplomats, academics, scholars and journalists must work together and channel all our joint efforts into reaching the goal of making the Mediterranean an area of peace and stability where, as the great architect, Ricardo Bofill said: 'in this perverse cycle of progress and decadence, the singular, creative and inventive individual can take inspiration from this sea with its traditions and light, so that citizens, instead of becoming merely machines turning round on themselves meaninglessly like collective clocks, show a new control over time, or, in other words, the ultimate meaning of life: the art of living, living freely and in tolerance.'

4

The Euro–Mediterranean Partnership: A Singular Approach to a Plural Mediterranean

BICHARA KHADER

Because of its duality of being both North and South, the Mediterranean clearly depicts the complexity of the 'new world order' and constitutes the theatre of its contradictions, tensions and imbalances.[1] The Mediterranean as a whole embodies a series of decisive issues at stake for the future of Europe, in demography, economics, ecology, in the politico–military spheres and above all in socio-cultural issues. While it is true that the Mediterranean is both a link uniting all Mediterranean countries, a thoroughfare and a region of intense trade, it is nonetheless true, as stressed by M. Arkoun, that the Mediterranean has been, and still is, 'an area of insurmountable differences, deep-rooted identities, hereditary refusals, murderous wars and destructive passions.'[2] By way of an example, we need only recall the history of the great Mosque of Algiers turned first into a cathedral to later return to the status of a mosque, or the cathedral at Cordoba erected on the site of the prestigious Ummayad mosque; or, more recently, how Palestine has been converted into a Jewish state, besides many other present-day examples (Lebanon, former Yugoslavia, Cyprus, etc.) proving the 'implacable rivalry striving to appropriate symbolic wealth'.[3] We must always be aware of the dual character of the Mediterranean, namely as a point of contact and as an area of friction.

In purely economic terms, the balance sheet of European Community policy on the Mediterranean over the last 25 years is mixed. Private European investments have not prioritized the Mediterranean world. There are still high trade barriers. Financial cooperation has overall been limited. Furthermore, the global or revised policy

47

has remained fragmented, with differing bilateral arrangements such as free-trade agreements, customs unions or preferential agreements. The 25 years of cooperation have not provided any improvement in the 'mutual impression', have not checked resentment and have not fostered cultural exchange and mutual understanding. Mistrust has often won out over dialogue. The impression that the other party is an adversary with whom no real point of contact exists has even been reinforced at grass-roots level, in open contradiction with the official discourse claiming close proximity, cultural kinship, historical legacy and mutual interests.

And yet the two Mediterranean basins, i.e. the Western Basin (Maghreb) and the Eastern Basin (Mashreq and Turkey) together with their natural extensions (other non-Mediterranean Arab countries, in particular, the Gulf countries) remain, together with Eastern Europe, a recognized area of priority for European Union action. It is precisely in this Mediterranean area that the great imbalances of the 'three Ds' (development, demography, democracy), the challenges (in migration, ecology, scarcity of natural resources such as water) and major risks (destabilization of states, conflicts between neighbouring countries, territorial claims, the upsurge of national identities with the ensuing destruction of territorial solidarity, religious fundamentalism, widening of cultural differences and nationalist xenophobia, etc.) are concentrated.

In view of the build-up of these imbalances, challenges and risks, questions are being raised over European Union policy more than ever before. Over the past 20 years, the great disparities in birth rates and economies have widened, the claims of Mediterranean peoples for political participation, access to economic development and improved standards of living have been highlighted, while the states have shown basic flaws in their functioning (administrative chaos, inappropriate development strategies, the absence of political dialogue) and, lastly, the verticality of trade with the European Union has been confirmed to the detriment of regional cooperation and horizontal trade.

This is the backdrop against which the new policy called 'Euro–Mediterranean Partnership' must be understood.

From the Europe–Maghreb to the Euro–Mediterranean partnership

The project for a *Euro–Mediterranean Partnership* began to crystallize in the early 1990s. Since the fall of the Berlin Wall in 1989, Europe felt the need to set up a global strategic framework in the Mediterranean which entailed a wide range of proposals: The Conference on Security and Cooperation in the Mediterranean (CSCM), the 'Western Mediterranean' or '5 plus 5', the Mediterranean Forum and the interparliamentary CSCM.

All these proposals led to meetings being held, but at the end of the day they remained 'empty shells'. The proposals never acquired institutional status because of the Arab–Israeli conflict, the embargo on Libya, the Greco–Turkish dispute, the break up of former Yugoslavia or many instances of opposition from the British and Americans alike, as well as the indifferent attitude in Northern Europe to the fate of the Mediterranean.

The Madrid Conference (1991) between the Arabs and Israelis did, however, release some pressure and led European authorities to envisage support for the peace process, even extending it to cover the whole of the Mediterranean 'in order to ensure that areas of differing stability are not created.'[4]

This is the underlying reason behind the Communication of the Commission on the future relations between the Community and the Maghreb, dated 30 April 1992 (Sec/92/401) which emphasized the need to finalize financial protocols with the Maghreb states from 1996 onwards by signing a regional contract which would lead to a Euro–Maghreb partnership and the setting up of a free-trade area.

The European Council held in Lisbon (June, 1992) gave its backing to this project. Although the Council's Declaration of the 27 June 1992 was limited to the case of the Maghreb, describing it as a geographic region of 'common interest to the Union' in matters of foreign affairs and security policy and justifying bilateral political talks between the Union and the UMA, the declaration also contained several references to the Mediterranean basin as a whole, indicating that it should be possible to extend the project to the whole basin. The dispute between Libya and Europe and especially the Algerian crisis have somewhat diminished the determination of the Community. The Maghreb as such was overlooked and the Community merely proposed talks with Morocco and Tunisia to set up a free-trade area, postponing the aim of a customs union amongst the Maghreb countries to a later date.

Meanwhile, Arab–Israeli, and especially Israeli–Palestinian negotiations were going well. This spurred the Commission on to present two Communications. Firstly, the Communication dated 8 September 1993 on 'The future of relations and cooperation between the Community and the Middle East' (COM (93) 375) and secondly, 'Community support for the peace process in the Middle East', dated 29 September 1993. It was certainly not purely a matter of chance that the first Communication was issued after the announcement of the Oslo Agreement and the second followed the signing of the Washington Agreement on 13 September 1993. This highlights the importance that Europe attaches to stability in the Middle East as a major factor affecting security in the Mediterranean.

It is clear from both Communications that the EU wishes to see relations between Israel and its Arab neighbours on a sounder footing, consolidated by the setting up of a regional area of free trade along the lines of European integration.

The Communication dated 19 October 1994 from the Commission to the Council and Parliament entitled 'Reinforcement of the Community's Mediterranean policy: setting up a Euro–Mediterranean partnership' must be seen as one in a host of Communications issued on Euro–Maghreb partnership and the future of relations between Europe and the Mashreq. In this document, the Commission states that a Euro–Mediterranean area of political stability and security will never be created unless it goes hand in hand, on the socio-economic front, with the progressive creation of a Euro–Mediterranean free-trade area.

Although the broad lines of the Communication were ratified by the European Council held at Essen (9–10 December 1994), it was revised and re-issued as a set of proposals. A second draft was presented on 8 March 1995 with the aim of defining the main lines of the Euro–Mediterranean partnership, of setting priorities for financial and technical cooperation for the period 1995–99, and of outlining the instruments and manners of implementing a Euro–Mediterranean partnership.

The communication is based on the premise that peace, stability and prosperity in the Mediterranean region rank amongst Europe's top priorities, and that 'actions undertaken by the European

Community in the region should be directed towards the achievement of these priorities.' The three priorities for action adopted were 'support for economic transition, support for an improvement in socio-economic balance, and support for regional integration'.

For the Commission, these aims are to be achieved by means of two basic kinds of instrument, namely budget resources and loans against the EIB's own funds (European Investment Bank). According to the Communication dated 19 October 1994, the Commission had allocated an indicative figure of 5,500 million ECUs in budget funds and a further 5,500 million from EIB funds for the 1995–99 period, that is, a total of 11 thousand million ECUs, to be shared out amongst all those countries included from 1997 onwards in the MEDA programme. In Cannes (June 1995), however, the Council cut the figure for community budget funds to 4,685 million ECUs.

That, then, was the main thrust of the project for Euro–Mediterranean partnership discussed and decided upon at the Euro–Mediterranean Conference in Barcelona (27–28 November 1995).

The final document adopted by participants at the Conference really amounts to a watered down version of the 19 October 1994 Communication, as the objections and susceptibilities encountered during the preparatory meetings had to be taken into account.

Although the Barcelona Conference, which had been carefully prepared by the Spanish Presidency, was a great media event, it was unable to allay fears or silence criticism. Indeed, besides those who felt the name 'Euro–Mediterranean' was inappropriate as it lumped together the names of a continent and a sea, there were others who thought that the Euro–Mediterranean concept weakened Euro–Arab relations and doomed the idea of re-starting the Euro–Arab dialogue.[6]

The Arab League, moreover, felt it had been unfairly treated since the non–Mediterranean members of the League had not been invited to attend the Conference, while *all* members of the European Union took part, including member states which are further from the Mediterranean than Saudi Arabia or Qatar.

Added to all this was the reluctance of particular countries, especially of the United States which was concerned to maintain exclusive control over the Arab–Israeli process, claiming that bilateral negotiations were the 'only recognized and approved framework for Arab–Israeli contact', and that the Barcelona Conference was not intended to replace any other action or initiative undertaken to promote peace, stability and development in the region.

The Euro–Mediterranean partnership: the promises

From the European Union standpoint, improving the economic situation of the Mediterranean aims first and foremost to meet a 'need for security'. Such improvement would relieve the pressure of immigration, the growth in population and the rise of extremist political movements and would dispel the threat of internal conflicts spreading beyond national borders.

But there is not only the security argument to bear in mind. There is also a real economic and political interest for the European Union to encourage the creation of a vast area of prosperity in the Mediterranean. The reasons for this are numerous.

The Mediterranean (including the Arab hinterland) is rich in natural resources needed in Europe. The area enjoys an exceptionally privileged geographic situation at the intersection of three continents. The Mediterranean also possesses capital, currently drained away from the area but which could be easily mobilized, besides the considerable pool of well-trained managers and 'cheap' labour.

The Mediterranean is a considerable potential market capable of substantially boosting European exports in the event of a return to growth and emergence of solvent demand. Henry Regnault[7] has shown that $10,000 in the GAP of Third Mediterranean Countries (TIC) generate around $1,300 in Community exports. G. Kebabdjian deduced from this fact that a further percentage point of growth in TMCs would increase European exports by nearly $400 million, no mean figure in terms of potential markets.[8]

This author concluded that 'in the longer or shorter term, the Mediterranean will be the only geographical area of expansion for Europe.' It is true that the Mediterranean faces competition from East European countries (PECOS) which became a priority area of regional expansion for the European Community after 1989. But this competition is not destined to last indefinitely, since sooner or later, these countries will join the EU.

The Mediterranean has the advantage of geographic proximity. It is true that this advantage has not been exploited sufficiently to date, and that European relocation efforts have tended to reject the nearest countries. Everything seems to point to a progressive 'regionalized relocation', that is, a tendency to set up regional networks for production and supplies. Geography is taking its revenge on technical progress which enabled distant relocations to go ahead (to Asia, for example) in view of lower transport costs. But the advantage afforded by proximity alone can only be fully exploited by TMCs if they can improve their infrastructure, their communications and transport systems and invest in training their work force and modernizing their institutions.

The Mediterranean has the advantage of cultural proximity. Despite certain xenophobic discourses, there is an enormous cultural kinship throughout the Mediterranean. Obviously Arabs, Orientals and Muslims are different from Europeans, but it is the closest, most intimate, of differences. There is clearly more socio-cultural affinity between the Spanish and the Moroccans than between the Spanish and the Chinese.

In socio-cultural terms, the Mediterranean provides an added advantage, in view of the general trend in the world economy towards the services sector (tertiarization) and of the important role cultural affinity plays in the development of this sector.

Overall, Europe has a real economic interest in the development of the Mediterranean. Besides its abundant natural resources, the Mediterranean offers real potential for exports, provides an area of economic expansion for the European Union and offers geographic and cultural proximity.

Partnership and free trade in the Mediterranean: the shadow areas

In theory, the creation of a free trade area aims to facilitate the circulation of goods and capital, to extend markets and promote a competitive supply, stimulated by improvements in productivity and quality. This naturally takes for granted that there are no hindrances to the opening up of markets, that TMCs are in a position to cover the costs of dismantling trade barriers and the accompanying adjustments in order to take full benefit from the regional economic liberalization. It is by no means certain, however, that all these prerequisites can be met within a reasonable time span. Here lies the main shadow area of the proposed project: the losses are immediate, while the gain is deferred and conditional.

First of all, the dissymmetry existing in the demand for commercial liberalization should be stressed. Mediterranean countries are being asked to open up and liberalize their economies, although the EU is not prepared to do the same in such a vital market as agriculture.[9] In theory, the macro-economic benefits of creating a partnership leading to a free trade area (FTA) are all the more important, the more a country is open to foreign trade. Unfortunately, those Mediterranean countries which are indeed open, are often also those which either specialize in hydrocarbons, often sold as crude oil, or in textiles with well-known and standardized technology. For the moment there is no major, competitive supply available in any other sector (mechanical and electrical engineering, electronics or agri–business).

This does not render the project of a partnership null and void, however. But for the project to be acceptable, it must go hand in hand with compensation measures against the effects of polarization (the EU has already invested vast sums to bring certain European countries up to par). It must also favour foreign capital investment, help states increase their attractiveness to investors by means of an accompanying policy to promote training of the work-force and the setting up of an institutional, administrative, communications and transport infrastructure. Such a policy should also make provision for certain mechanisms enabling TMCs to promote sectors of potential future growth in a flexible framework and encourage horizontal (regional) integration, without which a free trade area would be meaningless.

It should also be stressed that the project for a Euro–Mediterranean partnership does not get away from the logic of assistance to move towards real aid in setting up more consolidated, more diversified and competitive productive systems in the south of the Mediterranean, capable of responding to the demands for accumulation of wealth and the need to provide employment. Finally, the question of foreign debt should be highlighted. From the preceding information, it is clear that all Mediterranean, especially Arab, countries, are toiling under the strain of an unbearable debt, both in terms of overall amounts (outstanding debt) as in the ratios between debt/exports, debt/GDP, interest on debt/exports and interest on debt/GDP. For the Arab countries as a whole, the amounts paid as interest on their debt came to a total of 16.2 thousand million in 1992.[10] The real figure is quite likely to be substantially higher if we consider that the central Maghreb countries alone paid out almost 8 thousand million in 1992 and that their debt was just over one third of the total Arab debt (56 thousand million, compared with 152.9 thousand million).[11]

Apart from the figures alone, what is even more alarming is that the debt has fostered corruption, has encouraged the 'flight of capital', engendered a 'new social class' with its economic foundations based on capital linked to international cooperation and on export receipts for raw materials. In sum, the 'aid' system and foreign debt have contaminated the political class to such an extent that, with help from abroad, it can survive without any 'grass roots' support.

This situation is not tolerable and cannot last. The Euro–Mediterranean partnership would fail to fulfil its aim if it merely allocates 10,200 million ECUs (own resources and loans from the EIB) for 12 Third Mediterranean Countries (excluding Libya) over a five-year period. This sum, apart from being insufficient to warrant the name of a true 'financial Marshall Plan', would only have a very limited impact if not accompanied by a generous and daring policy on foreign debt. All in all it is not a question of giving more, but of taking less. This can be achieved by reducing, or indeed halting the impoverishing drain on resources, by rebalancing the terms of trade to ensure greater fairness and by setting up some control over speculative fluctuations in currencies.

The European Union, as the major creditor with over 50 per cent of the total debt owed by TMCs, cannot turn a blind eye to a demand that has repeatedly been voiced. One can easily understand the difficulties involved in this task. But without a bold policy on this matter, there is a grave risk of confirming the Mediterranean as the periphery and of seriously jeopardizing the success of the proposed partnership, given that the new funds would be devoted to paying the interest on foreign debt, while the expected foreign investments would still be hampered by the lack of adequate facilities caused by the scale of the debt and prospects of insolvency.

Adjustment and Euro–Mediterranean partnership

The problems and difficulties of the Structural Adjustment Programmes (SAP) should not lead us to reject the reforms, and hence the project of a Euro–Mediterranean partnership inspired by them, out of hand. A return to macro-economic stability, together with a 'safety net', is required now more than ever. However, the macro-economic reforms would be largely ineffective if they did not go hand in hand with a strengthening of scientific, technological and managerial skills and an improvement in institutional structures. Devaluation and deregulation will not guarantee sustainable economic development if institutional structures cannot inspire confidence in potential investors. Joan Prats Catalá has clearly shown this to be the case in Latin America.[12]

The success of the reforms thus depends both on appropriate demand (opening up of markets) and a competitive supply (competitive in quality and quantity), as well as on a coherent institutional framework, mechanisms for incentives and scientific research in tune with the reality of the country and competent managers. In other words, efficient institutions, motivating structures, experienced managers and, particularly, a reformed state.

'The imperative does not lie in the limitation of the State's role, but in State reform to convert it into the instrument ... of structural transformation and the building of comparative dynamic advantages in industrial activities subject to dynamic external factors.'[13] Needs to introduce this quote

However important privatization may be, as the Commission insists, it is not a panacea in itself. There are several reasons for this, as follows: There would be no gain in efficiency by replacing a state monopoly with a private monopoly. Empirical evidence shows that competence plays a more active role than ownership in attaining efficiency. Public corruption may be stimulated by private companies seeking to win contracts. It is by no means proven that privatization eliminates all the rigidity linked to trade barriers and differing economic management strategies. The local bourgeoisie often lacks business spirit and prefers to opt for quick profit, easy gains and speculation rather than productive undertakings.

To conclude on this point, if a Euro–Mediterranean free trade area is definitely an unquestionably worthwhile goal, then a lengthy period of adaptation will be needed to reform institutions, to modernize structures and to prepare the population. It is true that the project for Euro–Mediterranean partnership has provided for a transition period, and this time must be used to full advantage. But the measure may turn out to be relatively ineffective unless efforts are made simultaneously to reduce the development gap between the different partners by promoting scientific and technological innovation, i.e. the only means of promoting a competitive supply.

The cultural dimension of the Euro–Mediterranean partnership

Within overall relations between Europe and the Arab–Muslim world, Euro–Mediterranean cultural ties constitute a 'shattered relationship'. The shared destiny of Euro–Mediterranean countries has suffered many cultural rifts down the centuries. The first of these rifts was brought about by the Crusades (1099–1289). The ninth centenary of the Crusades was celebrated precisely on the day the Barcelona Conference was opened.[14] Later there was the seizing of Constantinople (1452), and then, particularly, the fall of Granada (1492) which put an end to centuries of trade and interaction between East and West, marking the beginning of a concealment and rejection of the Arab legacy, which had been decisive in the evolution of the Mediterranean region',[15] opening up the way for the expulsion of the Muslims from Spain in 1492 and 1609 and then the Spanish Inquisition.

The second rift was caused by colonization which brought tragic opposition and irreparable splits. The third rift came about with the creation of the state of Israel and the unshakable backing given to it, despite the glaring injustice to an Arab people, namely the (mostly Muslim) Palestinians. The fourth rift came with the 'tripartite aggression' (1956) against Nasser's Egypt in the form of the Suez expedition, the Algerian war (1956–1961) and the Six Day War in 1967 in which the overwhelming majority of Europeans took the side of 'little David' threatened by the 'Arab Goliath'.

The most recent rift came with the two Gulf Wars (the Iran–Iraq war, and the war against Iraq). The tangible result, in the eyes of Arab and Muslim opinion, was the weakening of two states with considerable past and present influence in the regional arena. The fact that both these states provided grounds for their weakening (Iran) and devastation (Iraq) does not mitigate the devastating effect of the two crises on the mutual perception of East and West.

We must bear in mind all of these above-mentioned rifts, which were not produced by Islam (cf. 'The Clash of Civilizations' by Samuel Huntington, 1993), but by actions often taken by Westerners and

Europeans on Islamic land in attempts to heal the cultural relationship between Europe and the south–eastern Mediterranean, and set it upon a new footing.

To do so, we should take a closer look at four main ideas: the confrontational approach, as prophesied by Samuel Huntington and certain members of NATO for want of 'new enemies', could turn out to be a 'self-fulfilling prophecy' unless care is taken. By continually seeing the Other (the Arab, the Muslim) as an enemy, he may end up by behaving like one.

Islamism is the product of a given space and time. You do not need to search in the Koranic texts to understand Islamism. Instead, you need to analyse and interpret the social, political and economic realities in which it has developed. The explanation lies not in theology, but in the human sciences.

This also accounts for the diversity of Islamist groups, the marked differences in their relations with states and the different approaches adopted by states (an inclusion strategy, such as in Jordan, selective co-opting as in Egypt or exclusion as in the case of Tunisia). Whatever concept Europe holds of Islamist movements, they do not represent a pathological phenomenon and should not be treated 'surgically'. Quite the opposite, Europe should encourage dialogue between governments and moderate groups amongst Islamists so as to ensure their integration in, rather than exclusion from, the political arena.

Conflicts between the North and the South of the Mediterranean have more to do with interests than with values. However, the fact that interests are the real issue is disguised by a strong emphasis on values. The conflict of values should not be underestimated. A real conflict indeed exists. But this should not be used to conceal the real issues at stake: in politics (democracy), in society (development for all), in geopolitics (security for all), and in culture (access to accepted and controlled modernity).

Having said this, the crusade to defend values should not stop where interests begin. Such ambivalence is contrary to the interests of all concerned. There can be no successful partnership in the Mediterranean without a strategy of jointly belonging to one and the same Mediterranean space,[16] based on solidarity in the Mediterranean rather than on solitary Mediterranean states.[17] This involves providing an innovative solution for the problem of Cyprus (a federal or confederate solution), an honourable outcome to the problems of the Western Sahara, Gibraltar and the Spanish possessions in Ceuta and Melilla, and especially solving the conflicts in former Yugoslavia and the Middle East.

All these ideas point to the urgent need for a pedagogy for cultural exchange. Andalusia's past history provides us with a successful illustration. It would also be fitting for the EU to set up a 'MED Culture' programme along the same lines as other programmes (MED-Campus, MED-Urbs, MED-Invest, MED-Media, MED-Techno, MED-immigration, MED-associations). Only such a programme could guarantee that the Mediterranean once again becomes a linking bridge rather than an ever-deepening gulf.

More and more, the search for stability and democracy should be seen as a solution to the internal dramas affecting populations in the southern and eastern Mediterranean basin rather than an instrument to simply ensure the preservation of European and Western interests.

Moreover, while democracy in the West is based on the principle of 'one man, one vote' and on individual liberties, it is not yet possible to repeat this model within the complex social and human reality of the Arab Muslim world where the collective rights of communities, of ethnic and linguistic groups must be preserved. 'Representative' democracy alone is not the cure for all evils. We must not forget that Islamist contestation in Mediterranean countries is more the product of social inequality and the economic inefficiency of states and their incapacity to redistribute wealth than of their authoritarian nature. Democracy must, therefore be accompanied by a fairer distribution of wealth which, in turn, requires an adequate institutional framework able to define the 'rules of the game'.

This revised cultural approach should be backed both at school and university levels by an educational policy more open to difference. In this sense, Europe should encourage and support initiatives which aim to revise teaching materials to avoid perpetuating a stereotyped, even racist, view of other peoples, to promote the study of Mediterranean languages, the translation of basic texts, school and student exchange programmes, the twinning of schools and towns, the introduction of courses on the Mediterranean in university curricula, the funding of EU professorships on 'the Mediterranean', setting up scientific networks, or more specific actions (cartoons giving a more positive view of Mediterranean partners, comic strips for adults, etc.).

We must welcome the creation of the Euro–Arab University in Granada along these same lines, since the curriculum has a common-core syllabus of general culture on Europe, the Mediterranean and the Arab World. This is what I have termed the EMMA programme (Europe–Méditerranée–Monde–Arabe).

But learning must be a two-way process. Centres for European studies should also be set up at the main Mediterranean universities. Television broadcasts should afford a greater insight into European reality. Joint co-productions of films could be encouraged.

Cultural activities should target all kinds of public. Decentralized cooperation programmes should be continued, complemented with new programmes (MED-Culture, MED-Regions) with improvements in management and running by leaving the choice of topics and the organization of training up to the countries of the South. Initiatives by NGOs in education and decentralized cooperation should be duly recognized and supported.

To help the Euro–Mediterranean partnership flourish through creative thought and proposals, the EU should set up a small working group of top experts on the Mediterranean, centred around a renowned scientific personality who would be entrusted with the task of drawing up notes and appraisals of any actions undertaken and policy proposals. The group would also centralize documentation on the Mediterranean and ensure access for students, researchers, journalists and official representatives; they would ensure that EU actions are given a high profile in Third World Mediterranean countries through the organization of specialized seminars and conferences; the group would also be accountable to European authorities for anything that is written on or debated in Mediterranean countries on Euro–Mediterranean relations.

The core group could include experts in the following fields: geopolitics, economics, sociology and Islam, assisted by a secretary and a researcher. The setting up of the group would highlight the interest shown by the EU in the development, follow-up and monitoring of its Euro–Mediterranean policy in all its aspects.

In conclusion, then, Europe's support for the Euro–Mediterranean partnership should not stem only from arguments in favour of security by controlling political imbalance, social tension and immigration flows, but rather from a true conviction that a strong, stable, prosperous and dynamic Mediterranean would provide Europe with 'support for a geopolitical assertion of itself'.[18] Europe will not be able to assert itself in Asia, Latin America or Africa if it is unable to assert itself in its own immediate vicinity.

Financial aid is certainly a useful lever, but not necessarily the most significant one, in this assertion of Europe's role and image. Cultural exchange, promoting peaceful coexistence, respect for difference, for pluralism and diversity are even more important. After all, the Mediterranean is too narrow to separate, and too wide to join.

Notes

1.   See Khader (1994).

2.   Arkoun (1988, 80).

3.   Ibid., p. 80.

4.   Köhler, Martin (1994) *Pour un cadre de négotiation politique globale de l'Union Européenne en Méditerranée.* This study was conducted for the General Directorate for Studies of the European Parliament, Doc. FR/DV/266/266628, 18 November 1994, p. 5.

5.   *Renforcement de la politique méditerranéenne de l'Union Européenne: propositions pour la mise en oeuvre d'un partenariat euro–méditerranéen,* COM (95), 72 final, 8 March 1995.

6.   See the round table discussion organized by the review *al-Mustaqbal al-ʿArabi* on the Euro–Mediterranean partnership: 'L'avenir des relations euro–arabes entre les projets du 'Moyen Orient' et du partenariat Méditerranéen', 3 (1996): 88–117.

7.   Regnault, Henri 'L'intérêt économique de l'Europe au développement des PSEM' (PSEM, Southern and Eastern Mediterranean Countries), presented at the colloquium held at the Arab World Institute on 28–29 September 1995.

8.   Kebabdjian (1994, 9).

9.   For further details, see Talha (1995, 39–57).

10.   League of Arab Nations, *Raport économique arabe*, 1994, p. 135. Table 11.

11.   In general, the World Bank estimates for the total outstanding debt (reference source) are lower than estimates provided by private banking institutions.

12.   Joan Prats Catalá, *Organization, Institutions and Governance. Some new foundations for Development Strategies in Latin America*, 1995 (May). Barcelona.

13.   Sid Ahmad (1995, 61).

14.   On 27 November 1095, Pope Urban II called on Western Christians

to aid their Christian brothers in the East. This marked the beginning of the epic of the Crusades.

15.   Jean Chesneaux, *Le Monde Diplomatique*, September 1993.
16.   Sami Nair, *Le Monde*, 28 February 1991.
17.   Khader (1990).
18.   Brik El-Hannachi (Tunisian Secretary of State) (1994, 24–5).

Part Two

Islam and the West: Concepts of Civilization

5

'Clash of Civilizations': The Relations of the Future?

MOHAMMED 'ABED AL-JABRI

The historic events of 1989 and 1990, i.e. the fall of the Berlin Wall and the collapse of the Communist Block, opened radical new prospects for thought and imagination. The famous speech by former US President George Bush announcing the 'end of the Cold War' and the birth of a 'new world order' gave an official aura to those prospects. Worldwide, a radical change in international relations was awaited with expectation. People voiced their hopes, indulged in joyful predictions and even proclaimed the imminent 'end of history', the final triumph of liberalism and democracy. The peoples of the Third World hoped the West would give up the 'war logic' which governed its relations with the rest of the world and apply another logic inspired by the values of the Enlightenment, 'liberty, equality and fraternity'. Many of the modern elites of those countries expected that the West, emerging as victor in the Cold War, would encourage democratic changes in the Third World. Some thought that the West would certainly not fail to demand a genuine, sincere respect for human rights and a real democratization of social and political life as a prerequisite of any cooperation with Third World governments. From the viewpoint of the peoples of the Third World, it was expected that the future of their countries' relations with the West would depend on the West's 'new foreign policy'. Would it continue to operate within the same war logic or would it rebuild its policy and strategy to allow its relations with the South to develop within the 'post Cold War' period?

65

What has become of those aspirations? How does the West today see its relations with the Third World in general and the Arab–Islamic world in particular?

At least in the political sphere, aspirations in the West have given way to scenarios developed by professors of 'strategic studies'. Observers not wishing to have their minds poisoned by the prejudices and uncontrolled reactions of fanatical and xenophobic right-wingers in Europe or America can find ample material to draw from in the (would-be learned) discourse of such professors.

The persistence of war logic

Since the collapse of the former Soviet Union, Western analysts have constantly asked the question: after communism who is the enemy of the West? It is as if the end of one war, in this case the Cold War, only served to unleash another or, in philosophical terms, as if the Western ego could only assert itself in the negation of 'the other'. Before looking at the epistemological basis of such an attitude, let me first try briefly to review the principal theses of the authors who conceive the future relations between Islam and the West in this way.

In his July 1991 article, Barry Buzan[1] sets out to 'sketch the main features of the new pattern of global security relations emerging after the great transformations of 1989–90.' The key changes which have occurred at the 'Centre' (industrialized countries) and which, in Buzan's view, constitute the basic characteristics of the new type of relations between states, are four in number: the appearance of multipolar power structures instead of the bi-polar centre which existed during the Cold War, a lesser degree of ideological division and rivalry; the tendency to international dominance of a group of capitalist states concerned with the problem of security and a fourth change which, Buzan says, is less certain but is a logical consequence of the preceding three, namely a consolidation of the power of international civil society.

These changes at the Centre will have direct and indirect consequences for the political, military, economic and social security of the Periphery (non-industrialized countries). The consequence which concerns us directly here is what Buzan calls 'the clash of rival civilizational identities' which he sees as being 'most conspicuous between the West and Islam. ... this is partly to do with secular versus religious values, partly to do with the historical rivalry between Christendom and Islam, partly to do with jealousy of Western power, partly to do with resentments over Western domination of the post-colonial political structuring of the Middle East, and partly to do with the bitterness and humiliation of the invidious comparison between the accomplishments of Islamic and Western civilization during the past two centuries.' According to Buzan,

> In the case of Islam, this threat is compounded by geographical adjacency and historical antagonism and also the overtly political role that Islam plays in the lives of its followers. Rivalry with the West is made more potent by the fact that Islam is still itself a vigorous and expanding collective identity.

Furthermore, with the 'danger' which immigration represents, adding to that of the 'conflict of civilizations', it is according to the theory easy to conceive of a kind of 'societal cold war' between the centre and a part of the periphery, in particular between Islam and the West. Europe, we are told, will occupy a prominent position in such a war which, according to Buzan, 'would help European political integration, by providing a common foreign policy issue on which a strong consensus would be easy to find.' In short 'a societal cold war would serve to strengthen the European identity at a crucial time for the process of European union.' The author concludes: 'For all these reasons and others, there may well be a substantial constituency in the West prepared not only to support a societal Cold War with Islam, but to adopt policies that encourage it.' Given this approach to the relations between Islam and the West, we are justified in asking whether this is an analysis of the facts and their possible development or a direct incitement to hostility.

'Clash of civilizations'

Two years after the publication of Buzan's article (which passed almost unnoticed, perhaps because of its academic-sounding title and its cool, detached style), the same thesis was taken up again by Mr Samuel Huntington,[2] but this time under the sensationalist title 'Clash of Civilizations', written in provocative language and using a multitude of meticulously chosen examples, all of which caused a considerable stir around the world.

Huntington presents his thesis in unflinching terms: 'It is my hypothesis', he writes, 'that the fundamental source of conflict in this new world will not be primarily ideological or primarily economic. The great divisions among humankind and the dominating source of conflict will be cultural. Nation states will remain the most powerful actors in world affairs, but the principal conflicts of global politics will occur between nations and groups of different civilizations. The clash of civilizations will dominate global politics.' Thus:

> Civilization identity will be increasingly important in the future, and the world will be shaped in large measure by the interactions among seven or eight major civilizations. These include Western, Confucian, Japanese, Islamic, Hindu, Slavic–Orthodox, Latin American and possibly African civilizations. The most important conflicts of the future will occur along the cultural fault lines separating these civilizations from one another.

According to Huntington's article, Western civilization may seem today to be 'the universal civilization that fits all men' but it is only superficially so. Under the surface things are quite different. The concepts prevailing in Western civilization differ from those predominating in other civilizations. Individualism, liberalism, the constitution, human rights, equality, freedom, democracy, secularization, etc. are concepts which in general have little validity or intelligibility in the Islamic, Confucian, Japanese, Hindu, Buddhist and other non-Western civilizations. In light of this, Huntington believes that countries belonging to these civilizations will have to choose from three possibilities. Countries like Burma or North Korea may choose 'to pursue a course of isolation to insulate their societies from 'corruption' by the West, … The costs of this course, however, are high and few states have pursued it exclusively.'

Other countries will prefer to throw in their lot with the West and follow its example in every sphere, opting for complete Westernization. For Huntington, such countries will include Japan, Russia, the countries of Eastern Europe and Latin America.

But many countries will seek rather to achieve a certain balance between them and the West. They will aim to develop their economic and military potential, to cooperate with other non-Western countries against the West and to preserve their local values and institutions. In other words, they accept modernization but refuse Westernization.

According to Huntington, these are mainly the countries which form the 'Confucian–Islamic connection that has emerged to challenge Western interests, values and power.' To meet this Islamic–Confucian 'challenge', Huntington (in what is the aim of his article) calls on the West to:

> promote greater cooperation and unity within its own civilization, particularly between its European and North American components ... to limit the expansion of the military strength of Confucian and Islamic states; to moderate the reduction of Western military capabilities and maintain military superiority in east and south-west Asia; ... to strengthen international institutions that reflect and legitimate Western interests and values and to promote the involvement of non-Western states in those institutions.[3]

It is necessary here to stress the openly political nature of the 'clash of civilizations' thesis. Well-informed circles in the United States do not hesitate to argue that this kind of militant discourse geared to proving the existence of a new danger and a new 'enemy' is necessary in order to convince the American people and its representatives of the need to maintain the 'defence' budget at its current level.

The 'ideological conflict'

'Thus "civilizational clash" is not so much over Jesus Christ, Confucius or the Prophet Muhammad as it is over the unequal distribution of world power, wealth and influence and the perceived historical lack of respect accorded to small states and peoples by larger ones. Culture is the vehicle for the expression of conflict, not its cause.' This view is argued by Graham Fuller[4] in an article published two years after Huntington's. But we must not delude ourselves. This is no outright renunciation of the 'war logic' which underpins the thesis we have been analysing. Rather the 'enemy' is quite simply given another name.

For Fuller, the future conflict will be ideological. The feature characterizing the world after the fall of communism is the domination of the Western world view in the political and economic spheres. It is based on three fundamental principles: capitalism and the market economy, human rights and secular liberal democracy, and the nation state as the framework for international relations. These principles, which have favoured the progress and emancipation of Western societies, are, however, a source of tension and destabilization in the countries of the Third World and this will lead these countries to adopt other principles and build other world visions which do not match that of the West.

According to Fuller, we should expect to see the emergence in the Third World of an ideology opposed to Western values. The way in which this 'up and coming ideology' confronts the West will depend on the type of leaders emerging as defenders of these countries' interests. The countries who are candidates to play this role are those which possess the necessary qualities, namely those countries with roots in a historic civilization, those that have a sense of cultural supremacy and of continuity in the role played historically, an uncontested regional role, plus experience in applying ideologies for change, and those who feel particularly frustrated by the inability to fulfil a historical and cultural vocation due to Western colonization.

The author places China, India, Iran, Egypt and Russia at the head of the list of countries destined to play a 'pilot' role in the ideological struggle against the West. He also mentions others, such as Brazil, Indonesia or South Africa, which he believes could play a significant role in the ideological conflict, while stressing that it is not his intention to draw up 'the list of enemies' of the West. His professed aim in the article is restricted to 'making us aware' of the nature of the problem so that we can seek ways to avoid the formation of a block hostile to the West.

An epistemological model

It is not our aim here to engage in polemics with analysts and professors of 'strategic studies'. Huntington answered criticism of his thesis by arguing that his purpose was to put forward a 'model' and that this model cannot be dismissed as questionable until it is replaced by another more suitable one — to sound a warning for the West! This is the logic of the scenarios in the sphere of 'strategy': the 'act-against' strategy. But we can, and must, take another approach to the problem: the 'act-with' scenario. In this case the first critical question to ask is: what leads us to think about relations between two or more parties in 'act-against' terms? To answer, we have to switch our attention from politics to epistemology.

Despite their apparent differences, all the theses set out above are built on the same epistemological model, which has dominated Western thought for centuries. It is the model of a subject, an 'I' which knows and recognizes itself through 'the other', an 'other' which it selects and shapes to fulfil the assigned function, that of confirming the 'I' and structuring its 'being'. The roots of the epistemological model in Western rationalism go back to the beginnings of history. Since the ancient Greeks, affirmation in Western thought has only been possible through negation. The philosopher Parmenides, for example, could only discuss 'being' by postulating 'non-being' or the 'finite' by postulating the 'infinite'. When his disciple, Zeno of Elea, sought to defend his master's theses, he founded his arguments on the axiom that 'all determination is negation'. In modern times, Spinoza affirmed the contrary: 'all negation is determination'. The great philosopher of history, Hegel, combined the ideas of Zeno and Spinoza to found his dialectics and concluded 'all determination is negation and all negation is determination'. This explains the importance of negation in Hegel in particular and in European philosophy in general. In this tradition affirmation always involves negation and the European 'I' can only recognize itself reflected in the mirror of 'the other'. The well-known contemporary philosopher, Jean-Paul Sartre states this clearly: 'To obtain any truth about myself, I need the other. The other is indispensable for my existence and for the awareness I have of myself.'[5] In another work[6] he adds, 'I need the mediation of the other to be what I am.' In general 'preoccupation with the other is a cardinal feature, perhaps the most essential feature, of contemporary thought.'[7]

In the socio-historical sphere this 'preoccupation with the other' is even more manifest. We can recall Cato's question: 'What would Rome be without its enemies?' Inside the 'city' Greek and Roman individuals asserted their identity as 'citizens' by opposition to the slave, and outside the city by opposition to the 'barbarians'. In the middle ages, Islam (Muhammad and the Saracens) played the role of the 'other', permitting Christian Europe to recognize itself. In modern times, the East–West duality forms the basis of Europeans' discourse about themselves. This duality is rooted so deeply in European consciousness that an English poet resorted to the following definition: 'East is East and West is West/And never the twain shall meet!' The East at that time covered the geographic area which Western rationalism would later divide into Near, Middle and Far East (relative to Europe).

When the former USSR replaced the East as the 'other', Europe had found its required opposite – this time in the economic sphere. The communist world reaching as far as Eastern Europe became the new 'East'. Once again, the West could define itself by opposition to the East (the USSR and Eastern Europe). Since the collapse of the USSR a new North–South duality has emerged to replace the former East–West confrontation after the category 'East' had lost its function as 'the other' essential for Western self-definition. Besides these geographic oppositions, the West has never hesitated to use colours to define 'the other', e.g. 'the *red* menace' for communism, 'the *yellow* peril' for Asia, and 'the *green* peril' for Islam. White, being the colour seeking to find its own definition, is never used in these comparisons.

Balance of interests and cultural specificity

Are we doomed to remain prisoners of the war logic which cannot conceive of relations with others except in terms of hostility and the vocabulary of peril, clash, conflict, threat, etc.? Voices are being raised around the world, even in Western countries, against this conception of relations between the West and other countries. People are wondering about the real meaning of the ill-fated dichotomy and the reality it aims to conceal. What is the meaning of the East–West duality down the centuries of European expansion from Rome to the modern colonial empires? And what is the meaning of today's version of it, the North–South divide?

The term 'North' obviously denotes a geographic area including Europe, but how do we define 'Europe' itself? Since it is 'neither a geographic entity, a historical or political entity nor an economic entity', can it be defined in terms of civilization? European historians dispute the possibility, arguing that at the end of the Ancien Régime 'we do not find one European civilization but three main, clearly determined projects of civilization, none of them coinciding with the conventional limits of Europe: a Mediterranean civilization, a continental civilization and an Atlantic civilization.'[8]

And how are we to define the 'South', that highly varied,

fragmented, divided and unstable area? Does it really exist as an entity in its own right? How do we define the term 'Islam' in the expression 'Europe and Islam' which pairs two radically distinct realities, one geographic (Europe) and the other religious (Islam)? Even assuming that 'Islam' refers to the countries professing that religion, do they constitute a coherent whole? What is it that makes Iran, or Pakistan or even Egypt, the presumed ally of Sudan, or Indonesia or Morocco against Europe? Are relations between these countries not characterized by their almost total independence from each other, while all of them are connected to the West by ties of dependency and neo-colonial exploitation?

Considered objectively and free from egocentric logic, North–South relations today clearly constitute a system of capitalist-type hegemony on a global scale. The attitudes and behaviour of Western countries and the world economic order they impose on the countries of the Third World (both bilaterally and through international organizations) create a relationship of exploitation which turns these countries into proletarian nations united almost exclusively by their condition of being exploited. 'Conflict of interests', and not 'clash of civilizations', is the most appropriate term to describe the antagonisms generated by this situation.

What is the difference between the two expressions? Leaving aside political and moral (or ethical) considerations, let us consider the question from the epistemological viewpoint. Contrary to what one might expect, the expression 'conflict of interests' offers prospects for a rational handling of the conflict. The 'conflict of interests' is an intelligible fact. It can be defined, its causes can be understood and controlled, consequently it is amenable to a rational solution by achieving a minimum balance between the opposing interests. A solution is possible and there is no need to resort to threats or hostilities. The best illustration of this is that within their own societies, the industrialized countries have achieved a lasting dynamic balance between classes by means of social legislation: sliding wage scales, social security, unemployment benefit, etc. These countries have got the better of the Marxist theory of the 'class struggle', 'absolute poverty' and the 'inevitability' of the revolution in Europe.

On the other hand, the expression 'clash of civilizations' denotes something unintelligible, resistant to rational treatment and it is quite simply based on false premises. Today as in the past, relations between civilizations are not a case of confrontation but of interpenetration. The confrontations and conflicts within a given civilization, e.g. Europe, are more frequent and destructive than those between countries belonging to different civilizations. Proof thereof is the fact that the two world wars which humanity has endured this century were waged within Western civilization and were due to conflicts of interests.

But, one may object, what about 'Islamism' as the Western media dub it? We first need to analyse what the term means exactly. We all agree on the need to distinguish religion (Islamic or any other) and the uses made of it for political purposes. But we must also distinguish between extremism as a normal socio-cultural phenomenon occupying its usual place on the outer margins of society and the extremist currents which, at any given moment, can spread widely to engulf entire populations. In the latter case, socio-economic factors predominate. Islamists in Egypt, Algeria and elsewhere represent, or at least claim to speak on behalf of, populations with legitimate social and economic grievances. They are, in fact, elites who have emerged from these populations and are searching for their place within authoritarian systems based on social injustice. Such systems leave no room for frank and open political discourse and by their very nature they spawn extremism and the general use of a symbolic capital which is accessible to everyone, i.e. religion. If this 'Islamism' attacks the West, it is because it sees the West as a protector, if not a promoter, of such systems, a view that is not entirely devoid of truth. Western countries with influence and 'clout' around the world accord priority to their material, economic and strategic interests over the values they preach. To a certain extent, Islamism today is one of the consequences of a neo-colonialist world order.

These remarks should not, however, close our eyes to the cultural differences which exist even within a given civilization. Such differences are even greater between cultures not belonging to the same civilization, but in any event there is no justification for the argument that confrontation is inevitable.

Today, as in the past, two types of relations dominate on the world scale. One is the interpenetration of civilizations based today more than in the past on the circulation of manufactured goods, scientific knowledge and the means of communication and trade. The other is a relation of conflict of interests which can always be overcome by achieving the necessary balance in order to ease divergence and open up prospects of world cooperation within a framework of genuinely peaceful coexistence.

We must therefore approach the future of relations between Western countries and Arab and Muslim countries from two different angles: that of the conflict of interests and that of cultural specificities. As regards the conflict of interests between states, solutions can be found by the honest and sincere application of the method known as 'games theory'. The main rule governing this method is that the players must be on an equal footing. Western countries must put an end to their colonialist behaviour and be aware of their relationship of interdependence with under developed countries and the need for an attitude other than that of master and servant.

Cooperation and participation are only meaningful if based upon a balance of interests and free from hegemony. If, in addition, provision were made for economic and technical development aid, a level of cooperation should be rapidly achieved which would dispel misguided hypotheses such as the 'clash of civilizations'. Experts analysing the future of our planet and the relations between countries with a vision of peace and prosperity have shown scientifically that if the industrialized countries were to re-allocate 10 per cent of their defence and arms budgets to development projects in what we previously described as 'proletarian nations', the problem and the future of poverty and inequality in the world would be radically altered.

I am convinced that the spectre of looming confrontation could thus be banished, making way for a historic process of interpenetration and inter-cultural growth which could become the hallmarks of our era.

Obviously, we should not try to brush aside the differences that exist between cultures (even if that were possible). The aim should be to develop a process of inter-cultural growth based on mutual respect and the right to be different. The model I am putting forward here draws its inspiration from our great 'Arab European' philosopher, the famous Andalusian philosopher Ibn Rushd (Averroes).

The rules of Rushdian (Averroist) dialogue

During the Spanish prime minister's last visit to Rabat (7–10 February 1996), the governments of Morocco and Spain decided to create the 'Ibn Rushd (Averroes) Commission' with the purpose of improving mutual understanding between the two peoples and preventing misunderstanding between the two countries. To hail this commendable initiative and to give this book the historic dimension it deserves, recalling the founding role which Toledo, the first 'city of light'[9] played in the building of modern civilization, I would like to conclude by briefly outlining what I consider to be the 'rules of dialogue between cultures'. These rules come from the great Andalusian philosopher, Ibn Rushd, whose works were first translated here in Toledo shortly after his death, giving rise to the Averroist doctrine expressed in Latin, which proved to be a ferment of modern, or Western, civilization.

The philosopher lived in a situation analogous to that of our present-day world, a situation in which relations of opposition and difference predominated, relations between the Arab 'I' and 'the other'.[10] After the *fuqaha*, the doctors of Islamic law, had decried the 'sciences of the Ancients' which they branded as 'intruder' sciences, 'harmful' and 'contrary to Islam', the great Muslim theologian al-Ghazali began to campaign against philosophy and its sciences, accusing Muslim philosophers of 'innovation' and impiety.

Ibn Rushd, perfectly versed in Muslim law and Greek philosophy and aware of the political circumstances which had led to al-Ghazali's condemnation, resolutely set about clarifying the relation between religion and philosophy. As a legal counsellor he attempted first to determine the position of Islamic law regarding 'the ancient sciences' and then to re-establish the relation between religion and philosophy and 'dispel the confusion' surrounding the discourse of Aristotle and his translators. Ibn Rushd's intention was to redefine the relationship between the Islamic 'I' and the philosophical 'other' and to this task he devoted several works, including the famous *Tahafut al-Tahafut (The Incoherence of Incoherence)* in which he sets out to achieve the negation of negation and to go beyond the fallacious reasoning of a discourse which classifies as contradictory and antagonistic things which are simply marking their difference. To underline the importance of the Rushdian achievement and its striking relevance today, let us look at the epistemological principles on which the philosopher based his thesis. These principles have a universal value. They can be invoked by any cultural community locked in adversity and hostility, as is the case today with Europe and the Arab world, in order to rebuild their relationship.

Understanding 'the other' in his own system of reference

The first principle translates into the language of today as 'the need to understand 'the other' in his own system of reference.' In the case of Ibn Rushd, this is expressed in the application of an axiomatic method in interpreting the philosophical discourse of the Ancients. Addressing al-Ghazali who was determined at all costs to show the 'incoherence' of the discourse of the 'philosophers', Ibn Rushd writes:

> All those seeking the truth ... are recommended, when they confront statements which seem perfectly inadmissible to them, to avoid reject-ing such statements out of hand and to attempt to understand them by following the path which their authors claim is that of the search for truth. To achieve conclusive results, they must take all the time necessary and follow the order imposed by the nature of the question being studied.

By following this method, the philosopher will succeed in under-standing the religious questions within the religious discourse and the man of religion will understand the philosophical theses within the system where they appear.

When discussing with my Arab fellow-countrymen, I have al-ways stressed the need to respect this principle in our attempts to re-establish the dialogue between our cultural tradition and contem-porary thought around the world and to define a way of accepting our relationship with each. One has to note, however, that the West also fails to abide by that methodological principle and for that rea-son is unable to comprehend Arab reality in its particularity and specificity.

Both Europeans and Arabs, therefore, should borrow Ibn Rushd's axiomatic method to come finally to an understanding of 'the other' in his system of reference. Only such an inter-cultural approach can bring about deep mutual understanding, allowing us to see *both* banks of the Mediterranean as the banks of one 'river', as was the case in Ibn Rushd's day. At that time, the expression 'the two banks' applied both to the shore of the sea, e.g. at Tangier and Gibraltar, and to river banks, e.g. those of the Oued (river) Fès dividing the town of the same name into two banks, one inhabited by Andalusies and the other by Qayrawans, people from Kairouan in Tunisia which was then known as Ifriqiyya, as if Europe and Africa were simply opposite banks of the same river.

The right to be different

The second principle we should borrow from Ibn Rushd to recreate a fertile relationship between Europe and the Arab world could be expressed today as recognizing people's right to be different. The philosopher followed this principle in his attempt to redefine the possible relationship between religion and philosophy. He reproached Ibn Sina (Avicenna) with causing great harm to both religion and philosophy by his syncretism, which involved incorporating the principles of religion into those of philosophy. This was bound to have serious consequences, either sacrificing the principles of religion or those of philosophy or eliminating both, leaving only the dead end of skepticism. Ibn Rushd strongly defends the view that no contradiction exists between religion and philosophical truths because, as he writes, 'one truth does not contradict another but rather is in harmony with it and testifies in its favour.' However, harmony does not mean equivalence and to testify in favour of something does not mean to be identified with it. The right to be different must be respected.

Understanding, tolerance and indulgence

That brings us to the third principle of Rushdian epistemology which needs to be stressed. It is both methodological and ethical, and refers to understanding in the sense of tolerance and indulgence. Our philosopher reproaches al-Ghazali in his objections to the philosophers with not respecting the rules of a dialogue aimed at seeking the truth. Al-Ghazali said 'my aim was to question their (the philosophers') theses and I succeeded.' Ibn Rushd replies: 'that is not worthy of a learned man because the aim of a learned man can be no other than to seek the truth and not to spread doubt and leave minds confused.' Replying to those learned Muslim men who saw in the sciences of the Ancients opinions which were not in harmony with the spirit of Islam, he writes:

> When we encounter in our predecessors in the ancient nations a carefully considered theory of the universe conforming with the conditions required for sound demonstration, we must examine what they have said and written about it. If their views correspond to the truth, we should welcome them with joy and be grateful for them. If they do not correspond

to the truth, we should point this out and advise people of this, while excusing their authors.

This, he adds, is because 'doing justice consists of seeking arguments in favour of one's adversary just as one does for oneself.'

In my view, these are the main elements of epistemology for a Rushdian dialogue. An essential characteristic of this epistemology is that it defines a way of overcoming, or at least easing, the antagonism in relations of difference, in the relation between the 'I' and 'the other'. At a time when post Cold War ideologists would have us believe that the 'clash of civilizations' is the reality looming over tomorrow's horizon and Islam the most appropriate candidate to fill the role of 'the other' for the West, its future enemy after the collapse of communism, it is the duty of all defenders of peace in the world to fight such a mind-set which can only sow the seeds of mistrust and inflame hostility.

In light of the Western mind set and what one could call the 'psychology of the colonized peoples vis-à-vis their former colonizer' (sustained by the hegemonic behaviour of many Western powers), it is beyond doubt that peace, stability and especially trust will depend greatly on the blossoming of a dialogue based on the epistemology of mutual understanding which I have been outlining and whose founding father is no doubt the great Andalusian philosopher Ibn Rushd.

Notes

1.   Barry Buzan is professor of international studies at Warwick University. His article 'New patterns of global security in the twenty-first century' was published in the American review *International Affairs*, July 1991.

2.   S. Huntington is director of the John Olin Institute of Strategic Studies at Harvard and the Eaton Professor of the Science of Government. He has devoted his entire career to the study and teaching of military strategy, comparative studies of politics in America and politics in developing countries. The article in question appeared in the famous American review *Foreign Affairs* 72, no. 3 (1993).

3.   In a recent interview, Huntington stressed the demographic 'danger' of Islam, claiming that the 'most global threat for the West lies in the demographic expansion of the Muslim population'. It is a curious conclusion. Is such a claim meaningful at a time when ballistic missiles and supersonic aircraft have taken the place of the 'countless armies' of the past? See *La*

Croix, 21–2 January 1996. Paris.

  4.   Fuller (1995).

  5.   *L'existentialisme est un humanisme*.

  6.   *L'Etre et le néant*.

  7.   D. Lagache, *Encycl. médico-chir*. Ale 5, 1955. Quoted by P. Foulquié (1968). For further details see the interesting work by Theunissen (1984).

  8.   Philippe Ariès, *Contradiction de l'Europe*, quoted by Domenach (1990, 72).

  9.   Paris is known as the 'City of Light' (Ville Lumière).

10.   Here I should like to quote passages from the paper presented at the colloquium *Rencontres d'Averroès* held in Marseille on 10–11 November 1994, and organized by the Institut du Monde Arabe. The proceedings of the seminar were published under the title *L'Héritage Andalous*.

6

Cultural Dialogue and 'Islamic Specificity'

MAURICE BORRMANS

Before looking at Muslim reactions in favour of an 'Islamic specificity' in the cultural dialogue, the field and manifestations of such specificity should first be defined. Many would welcome a historical revision of 'Euro-Islamic relations' and rightly wonder about Islam's relationship with modernity. In both cases, what is meant by 'Islam'? Is it a religion, i.e. first and foremost a creed, a form of worship and a morality, a culture which shapes and molds customs, literature and the arts, or a political doctrine determining law, economics and politics? The context of our book on Europe and Islam would seem to ascribe primarily cultural and political dimensions to both the terms, while focusing attention on Arab and Turkish Islam in the Mediterranean Basin, the historical partners of Europe where Christianity is the main religion. Europe engendered and entered the age of modernity, even though modernity has extended today to include America and the Far East. It would seem that we inevitably overlook the non-Arab Muslims (80 per cent of the Islamic world) as well as the Christian Arabs in the Middle East who form dynamic minorities and were recognized as such by the Arab Nahda (renaissance) at the beginning of this century. Are the cultural and political dimensions in the Middle East therefore exclusively Islamic? If so, in what sense?

I think these preliminary remarks are necessary to relativise the absolute nature of the subject under consideration. That being said, however, the issue remains essential. This is underscored by a book published last year by the Moroccan thinker Abdelhadi Boutaleb, *Le Monde Islamique et le Projet du Nouvel Ordre Mondial*.[1] He writes, 'In conclusion, we can say that the Islamic world and the Western world find themselves today at a dangerous crossroads. By its abuse of

81

rationalism and secularism, the West has left progress, which was intended to lead to an improvement in the human condition, devoid of its spiritual content. Mankind no longer has its due place and has been sacrificed on the altar of profit. Most countries in the Islamic world tried to accept the liberal or socialist models of the North but have suddenly become aware of the failure of both systems while at the same time facing a kind of 'religious' implosion. Since no clearly defined social project is available, Islamic countries are in the throes of a conflict with opponents of the status quo, which is generating instability and anarchy and recalling a past era known as the *jahiliyya* (the pre-Islamic period).[2] Abdelhadi Boutaleb's meaning is clear and requires no further explanation. It must, however, be borne in mind as the starting point of our reflections. And that is why this article, which restricts itself to analysing parts of the issue, will address the following three questions: What has become of the cultural dialogue? What is the situation regarding 'Islamic specificity' which is very often equated to 'application of the *shari'a*'? and is it possible to 'redefine' the 'actors' participating in the dialogue, especially on the Muslim side? These questions should help complete our information on the subject, define our hypotheses and propose solutions before beginning our debate.

The cultural dialogue: welcome turns to rejection

Without reiterating the long history of cultural relations between the Muslim world and Western Europe since the early nineteenth century, we may summarize by saying that it began with a very long period in which Western modernity in its technical, economic, legal and political aspects was welcomed by the Islamic world, usually willingly and sometimes even admiringly. Countless 'missions' were sent out by Egypt and the Ottoman Empire. We are all familiar with the Ottoman *tanzimat* of the last century and the reforms of the khedives in Egypt or the beys in Tunisia. Although it went through different phases and adopted different forms and channels, in every country the phenomenon led to a modernization of the apparatus of the state, of civil society and of local culture. Administration, the education system and the economy also benefited. Shortly before the Second World War, in 1938 Taha Husayn, the reformist minister of education in Egypt, published *Mustaqbal al-thaqafa fi Misr (The Future of Culture in Egypt)* rooting the culture of his country in Greco-Mediterranean civilization. Later, in 1952, Abbas Mahmud al-Aqqad published *al-Dimuqratiyya fi l-Islam (Democracy in Islam)*, demonstrating that democratic values had been promoted by Islam from its very beginnings. In the same mood of welcome, thinkers of the period attempted to show that everything modern was based on forgotten - but retrievable - values of classical Islamic civilization and that feminism, nationalism and the reform of the social, legal and cultural systems had been possible thanks to Islam.

Times changed, however, after the Second World War and more especially after the 'Six-day War' which left the Middle East with the 'Palestinian problem' unsolved and widespread suffering in its wake. There was a further change after the unkept promises of the leaders of national independence movements from Morocco to Kuwait. Besides the sectors of Arab and Turkish societies who are bilingual and have adapted reasonably well to modernity, be it imported, naturalized or assimilated, there is another sector - not necessarily only Arabic - or Turkish-speaking – which refuses modernity wholly or partly in the name of a religious or cultural identity often known in Arab countries (in a curious hotch-potch) as an 'Arab-Islamic personality'.

In certain cases, has there not been an unconscious but real convergence between the official charters of single parties such as the FLN (National Liberation Front) in Algeria, the published writings of intellectuals such as Hichem Djaït *(cf. The Arab-Islamic Personality and Future)*[3] and the topics discussed during numerous 'weeks on Islamic thought' organized in certain countries? For some twenty or thirty years, a whole series of writers have devoted themselves to placing the great authors of the *nahda* or the Reform 'on the scales of Islam' *(fi mizan al-Islam)* because of the generous welcome they accorded to the culture of others and to denouncing what they see today as an 'invasion' or 'cultural aggression' *(ghazw thaqafi)*. These views are voiced in the writings of Muslim fundamentalists (radical or not) and in reviews published by the League of the Islamic World (Rabita) which is based in Mecca and aims to guide the Muslim *da'wa* around the world.

Perhaps at this point, it is worth making a tentative remark about the various processes of cultural dialogue in the Mediterranean basin, in particular those discussed during a recent colloquium organized by the Department of Arabic and Islamic Studies at the Ca'Foscari University in Venice. A brief survey of the material available to an average Italian reader wishing to inform himself honestly about the reality of the Arab and Muslim worlds showed that hundreds of books have been published in Italy in recent years and that the sources of Islam (Koran and *sunna*), the classics of religious thinking (al-Ghazali, etc.) and the works of great contemporary writers (e.g. Nobel prize winner Naguib Mahfuz) have been translated into Italian and are available to the general public. Italians thus have access to this different culture in its own texts without, I believe, any risk of Arabizing the Italian language - which could be perceived as 'cultural aggression'. It must be noted that in the other direction, the phenomenon is reversed: Egyptians, Tunisians, Moroccans, etc. have access to the great works of Italian (or French, English, etc.) literature and the essential works of European/Christian thought in the European languages, which thus compete with literary Arabic (the *fusha*) which already has to contend with the bilingualism or the *diglossia* of those who understand it (any lively spontaneous debate between Arab intellectuals quickly switches into the local dialect). Why are the great works of European thinking not, or no longer, translated into Arabic, whereas they were for the most part during the initial, welcoming phase in the nineteenth century? One professor pointed out in Venice that many Christians had translated the Koran and the great works of Islam into the European languages, whereas it is difficult to find a Muslim who has translated the Bible or any of the key works of Christianity into Arabic.

But beyond this cultural remark, which is not 'innocent', there is the more basic problem of what can be described as the transition from the 'national cultural sphere' to the 'Islamic cultural sphere', or what some consider to be the emergence of an 'Islamic nationalism' quite far removed from the 'pan-Islamism' advocated by Jamal al-Din al-Afghani in the late nineteenth century. In the name of 'rebuilding an identity' any input or influence from other cultures is rejected in order to rediscover Islamic models from the recent or distant past. Rashid al-Ghannushi, spokesman for the 'Islamist tendency' in Tunisia which became the (banned) party of Renaissance (Nahda), is an emblematic witness to this. Discussing the 'brutal metamorphosis' he went through during 'his night of 15 June 1966', he writes: 'It was during that night that I took the final decision to move from the world of Nasser-style Arab nationalism to that of Islam. The awareness came to me quite brutally that what I was and what I was experiencing had absolutely nothing to do with Islam. I realized that I was not a Muslim, that I was alien to Islam.'[4] This led to al-Ghannushi's rejection of Bourguiba and his 'victory over Arab-Islamic civilization in Tunisia' and to his condemnation of 'France's Tunisian sons'. For him, the Westernization of Tunisia was experienced as an act of violence.

The same applies to Tariq al-Bishri in Egypt for whom 'the idea of political and economic independence predominated until the defeat of 1967. That defeat was of crucial importance ... I gradually became convinced that the Islamist movement was a prolongation in the sphere of civilization of the political and economic independence movement ... I realized that Muslim thought provided the means of forming institutions at all levels.' Another Egyptian, Adil Husayn, followed a similar intellectual path, in his case moving from communism and anti-imperialism to Islam: 'The more I studied, the more I discovered the sources of Islamic culture and the more I realized that it was true ... Islam forms the very identity of this nation ... Islam is the creator of this Arab nation. That is a historical fact.' Lastly, one can cite the Muslim Brothers, the supporters of Nasser and many others who all agree that they have something in common and 'that something is Islam'.[5]

All these voices reflect a growing tendency which in the course of events has been encouraged by state structures everywhere, e.g. by Iran and the Khomeini revolution or by the Wahhabite regime in Saudi Arabia. It has been welcomed by those left by the wayside in a process of selective modernization which favoured some and neglected many. A new word has appeared in the vocabulary of the media: '*aslama*' (to Islamize). Newspapers, reviews, preachers, etc. all insist on the need to Islamize everything: Islamize the teaching of culture, Islamize dress and behaviour, Islamize banks and the economy. Furthermore legislation is placed 'on the scales of Islam' and accused of not conforming adequately to the *shari'a*. In the flush of excitement, the qualification 'Islamic' is even applied to military strategy.

One can ask whether there is not a danger in deliberately ignoring or neglecting the alien in order to exalt or justify the 'Islamic vision' of people and things. In any event, many leaders and decision makers have opted wholeheartedly for this approach. The tendency has crystallized around the issue of 'total application of the *shari'a*' aiming thereby to Islamize the entire society and bring it into conformity with the will of Allah. In September 1984 the Sudanese capital, Khartoum, hosted the First World Congress for the Application of the Shari'a. Many thus hoped to achieve the often repeated ideal, namely that Islam is *din, dunya wa-dawla* i.e. religion, worldly order and state. But what is the exact nature of the 'Islamic specificity' thus defined? Is it a dynamic concept or does it remain static?

Application of the shari'a and Islamic specificity

The *shari'a* is a multi-secular accumulation of varied interpretations of the founding texts of Islam (Koran and *sunna*) and has very often addressed and reflected the social and legal problems of the peoples and cultures of Islam in the course of its long history. For example the Ja'fari school of the Shi'ites and the Maliki, Hanafi, Shafi'i and Hanbali schools of the Sunnis are venerable, respected witnesses of this and have developed a wide variety of local traditions, many of which have been the inspiration for modern national legislations.

Never codified, the ideal *shari'a* purported, during the golden age of the Abbasid Caliphate in Baghdad or later during the Ottoman Empire, to govern all sectors of the public and private lives of Muslims: their creed, acts of worship, morals, personal and family law, economic transactions and political order. History shows that the *shari'a* was rarely applied in its entirety. It tolerated many exceptions and at times was divided into a religious sector and a profane sector. Contemporary Muslim fundamentalists insist exclusively on the *hakimiyya* (temporal domain) of Allah, seeing in it the total, global and perfect expression of divine will regarding all aspects of human reality. They consider the *shari'a* valid 'for all places and all times' instead of distinguishing between immutable principles and applications relative to different socio-cultural contexts. The debate thus remains open as to its real content and its full application.

The number of those in favour of full application has grown considerably over recent years. In 1951, for example, in his book *al-Islam wa-awda'u-na l-qanuniyya* (Islam and our Legal Institutions), Abd al-Qadir Uda exalts the superiority of this *shari'a*, divine in origin, over all human laws, which are the work of imperfect, transitory powers: 'The Islamic *shari'a* is the fundamental constitution of Muslims.

Everything in conformity with that constitution is good and everything opposed to it is null and void, regardless of the epoch and regardless of the development of thought on legislation.'[6] In his book *Ma'alim fi l-tariq* (Landmarks on the Road) (1965), Sayyid Qutb, the author of a 'revolutionary commentary' on the Koran (*fi zill al-Qur'an*), writes: 'Behind this cosmic existence, there is a will conceiving it, a decree moving it, an "order" harmonizing it ... Man is part of that cosmic existence. It was God who created that cosmic existence ... who established a "Law" for mankind ... a cosmic "Law" bound up with the order of the world. That is why it is compulsory to conform to the Law of God to achieve that harmony, besides our duty to give concrete expression to the doctrine of Islam ... because the opposite of the Law of God are the passions of men.'[7] These texts reflect an intransigent 'Islamic specificity' and views widely expressed on the subject. For example, Saudi Arabia boasts that it enjoys unparalleled stability and security because it applies the *shari'a* as a 'system of life' which 'commands good and bans evil'. The merits of this were proclaimed during the Khartoum congress.

Whether inspired by the Pakistani al-Mawdudi, the Muslim Brothers in Egypt or Ayatollah Khomeini, Muslim fundamentalists concentrate their efforts on enforcing strict compliance with, and full application of, the Islamic Personal Statute (family and inheritance laws) and the Koranic criminal code (on the one hand the 'lex talionis' and on the other the *hudud Allah*, crimes for which God has established the penalty, viz. fornication/adultery, false accusation of fornication, theft, banditry, consuming fermented beverages and apostasy). Not to be outdone, the official representatives of national Islam have often made these claims their own. In Egypt the rector of al-Azhar, Shaykh Abd al-Halim Mahmud, did not hesitate in his day to propose a 'standard Islamic constitution' for all Muslim countries,[8] as well as submitting a proposal for a Koranic criminal code to the Egyptian National Assembly[9] (the latter proposal was withdrawn after mass demonstrations and a general fast by the Coptic community). It is well known, however, that Sudan and Mauritania, as well as Saudi Arabia, have a criminal code quite in keeping with this 'Islamic ideal'.

Of course, many Muslims in government office or in civil society, advance different interpretations of the *shari'a*. In his book, *Imra'atu-na fi l-shari'a wa-l mujtama'* (Our Women in Religious Law and in Society) (1930),[10] Tahir al-Haddad from Tunisia distinguished between 'the permanent and the transitory' elements in the shari'a. Bourguiba's reforms of 'family law' (cf. *Majalla*, 13 August 1956) were inspired by this principle which has been reiterated by the Tunisian review *15–21* which is determined to accord due importance to both divine Law and human law. In Egypt, Husayn Ahmad Amin published his 'Mulahazat hawl al-da'wa ila tatbiq al-shari'a' (Remarks on the claim to apply Islamic law)[11] in *al-Musawwar*, distinguishing clearly between the role of divine Law and that of human laws, showing that in a number of its legal provisions, the *shari'a* is quite simply the work of human beings, and recommending the need to place the founding texts and the jurisprudence of the schools in their context as part of socio-cultural development. Even Fahmi Huwaydi in his book *al-Qur'an wa-l-sultan: humum islamiyya mu'asira (The Koran and Power: Contemporary Islamic Concerns)* (1981), does not hesitate to raise the same question. Convinced that the *shari'a* should be applied, he adds: 'The question is not whether, but rather where, when and how do we begin? We should ask: Is it only the application of the "*shari'a*" which creates the Muslim society? Is the *shari'a* all of Islam? Or is it its foundation?'[12] Adopting the teachings of Shaykh Mahmud Shaltut, he recalls that 'the *shari'a* without Creed is tantamount to a building without foundations.' Where then does 'Islamic specificity' lie in this case?

The question is made more difficult by the fact that many articles in the preamble to Civil Codes are far from clear on the matter, even when the constitutions explicitly state that the *shari'a* is a source, or *the* source, of the legislation. The first article of the Egyptian Civil Code of 1948 states that 'where no provision is made in the present text, the Judge must have recourse to custom *('urf)*, then to the principles *(mabadi)* of the *shari'a*, then to natural law *(qanun tabi'i) and then to equity ('adala).'* These are indeed strange divergences about the sources of legislation or jurisprudence, especially when the survival of the principle of *hisba* (control of markets, the police for repressing vice and the 'commanderie de bien') encourages the supporters of a strict application of the *shari'a* to go so far as to declare 'apostate' *(murtadd)* anyone criticizing the Koran, Islam or the Prophet. This was the basis which recently allowed Shaykh Yusuf al-Badri to ensure that a decree of divorce from his wife was pronounced on the writer Nasr Hamid Abu Zayd after his court conviction for apostasy.

Thus the debate is ongoing between advocates of a strict application of the *shari'a* considered untouchable (*usul* and *furu*) whose detailed contents are only known to specialists (*fuqaha*) and those who recommend *ijtihad* taking into account the immutable principles and their application which always depends on circumstances. Reached here Islamic specificity can be either static or dynamic. It can look to the past or it can invest in the future by updating 'the message'. Those are the alternatives. The question still remains buried under the formulation and interpretation of the various Universal Declarations of Human Rights in Islam, e.g. that of the Islamic Council of Europe submitted to UNESCO at its Paris headquarters in 1981, or the three successive drafts of the Organization of the Islamic Conference (1979, 1981 and 1990).[13] Constant reference is made to the *shari'a* as a 'limit not to be exceeded' or a 'framework to be respected' thus apparently making all of these texts 'confessional declarations' although Muslims themselves are unable to overcome divergences of opinion and develop an orthodox commentary on them.

The actors in the cultural dialogue and their ultimate identity

It seems therefore that the cultural dialogue has shifted in focus. It is no longer a dialogue between Europe with its Christian tradition and the Arab world with its Islamic culture, but amongst Muslims themselves trying to redefine their identity as they face the challenges of modernity and its achievements in the world (liberal or socialist economy, technology, democracy, secularism, etc.). This is where the profound divisions lie, not only for socio-cultural or socio-political reasons but rather for religious motives because Muslims ascribe widely diverging contents to 'their' Islam. Traditionalists, reformists, modernists or fundamentalists - all of them declare themselves Muslims and seek to give an 'Islamic specificity' to their position in the modern world, although for each it has a different content. Their capacity to fit in and be assimilated often depends on their own roots in the fourteen centuries of Arab-Islamic culture which has modeled their societies which today have a more or less firmly established national character. But is the dialogue between all the tendencies in contemporary Islam really profound and loyal, peaceful and constructive?

All too often the constraints placed on free expression of ideas and freedom of the press, as well as the limited means of social communication available, make such a dialogue difficult. Censorship imposed directly or indirectly by certain institutions (e.g. al-Azhar's condemnation of certain books on display at the Cairo Book Fair and its doubts about the new edition of Ibn Arabi's *Futuhat Makkiyya*) or by the Ministries of Information and Culture in many countries hardly facilitates such dialogue. A terminological rift opens up very quickly between those who talk of the *shari'a* and others who refer to the *musharri'* (national legislator). Sometimes the prestige of certain *'alim* threatens to remove any serenity or objectivity from the dialogue, as in the case of certain testimonies in the trial of the murderer of the Egyptian writer Farag Foda. As a result, in recent years many intellectuals and believers have asked the question: who represents Islam and can speak on its behalf? Who is truly Muslim?

The answers to such questions draw the dividing line today between Muslims wishing a static or a dynamic 'Islamic specificity' for their societies. Some share the view of Muhammad Sa'id al-Ashmawi that 'Islamism is against Islam.'[14] A reigning prince offered a timely reminder that as one well known *hadith* says, anyone practising the five pillars of worship is a Muslim. For other Muslims, 'Islamic specificity' requires full application of the *shari'a* and they seek to achieve this by an 'awakening' (*sahwa*) of religious consciousness or by political violence, some even denouncing the injustice of regimes in power. The real problem is precisely the content of this 'Islamic specificity'. What is the ultimate identity of the *umma*, the home of the 'actors' in the cultural dialogue amongst Muslims themselves?

Judging by the opinions of those advocating application of the *shari'a* and the leaders of radical or fundamentalist movements and by the views of their models, i.e. al-Mawdudi, al-Banna and Imam Khomeini, 'Islamic specificity' can be equated with the historical achievements of the *umma*, especially during the reign of the 'well directed Caliphs' (*al-khulafa al-rashidun*) in Medina (632–661). It appears to be based essentially on a secularization of the global society as it was later codified by Mawardi (991–1031) in his *Ahkam sultaniya (Government Statutes)* and by Ibn Taymiya (1263–1328) in his *Siyasa shari'iya (Politics Obeying Islamic Law)*. However, this essentially backward looking view of 'Islamic specificity' might appear too static and not sufficiently religious since its spokesmen make scant reference to God or the religious experience of believers. The supporters of a more dynamic view of 'specificity' point out precisely that

Islam needs to be freed from its historical accomplishments which were often a function of their spatio-temporal context. Syed Z. Abedin, an Indian Muslim and for many years director of the Jedda-based *Journal of the Institute of Muslim Minorities*, has frequently pointed out that one third of Muslims today live in societies which are (and always will be) non-Islamic and that they can be perfectly good Muslims even in such a society.[15] In this he is questioning one of the fundamentalists' criteria and redefining the *umma* as a supra-national community whose members, in the words of the Koran, are 'those who believe and who encourage each other mutually to exercise patience and indulgence' (Koran 90,17: *alladhina amanu wa-tawasaw bi-l-sabr wa-tawasaw bi-l-marhama*). Mahmud Mohammad Taha was sentenced to death and executed in January 1985 in Khartoum for declaring that the political and military dimensions of Islam in Medina only had substitute value, that Islam does not require the detailed application of the *shari'a*, and that it should return to its 'second mission', i.e. that of Mecca itself.[16]

The work of the renowned Tunisian thinker, Pr Muhammed Talbi, follows similar lines. In his latest book *'Iyal Allah, afkar jadida fi alaqat al-Muslim bi-nafsi-hi wa-l-akharin (The Family of God: New Reflections on the Muslim's Relationship with Himself and Others)* (1992), he argues that 'the Islamic *umma* never was a political unit. It was always founded on spiritual unity, the unity of witness and adoration *(wahdat al-shahada wa-l-'ibada)*. Its unity was never political. On the political level there have constantly been conflicts and wars, right from the moment of the 'great sedition' (*al-fitna l-kubra*) to the present day.'[17]

In light of the diversity of references, opposing interpretations, different 're-readings' of history and contrasting approaches to the founding texts, we are all inevitably bound to reappraise the methods we employ in reading and understanding the Holy Book of the Koran and the *sunna* of the Prophet who transmitted its message to Muslims. No one is exempted from the task of carrying out a thorough, sound process of hermeneutics. But this is where the difficulty lies given that the renewal of exegesis today is hardly on a par with the gravity of the problems we all face. Is it not true that events such as the recent 'war of *fatwas*' in Cairo between the Grand Mufti of the Republic and the rector of al-Azhar have only contributed to spreading confusion in the minds of many believers?

Conclusion

That ultimately is the question we all face and which I have tried to address in this brief paper. I have attempted to show how, in the minds of many, there has been a gradual and imperceptible shift from an attitude of welcome to one of rejection vis-à-vis the dialogue between Europe and the Arab-Islamic world. This is due to the need to redefine the notion of 'Islamic specificity' and the fact that many want to include application of the *shari'a* as an essential element in such a notion. Judging by the varying definitions they give of the *umma*, Muslims themselves seem far from unanimous on this matter. It may be precisely those who reject (either partly or totally) the application of the *shari'a* who impart a certain dynamism to 'Islamic specificity' by freeing it from reference to historical achievements of Islamic civilization and rechanneling it to an essentially spiritual and cultural project. This is the question we should return to in our debate, trying to define the elements involved and bring out the positive and enriching prospects for the future of us all.

Notes

1. Boutaleb (1995).
2. Op. cit., p. 151.
3. Djaït (1974).
4. Quoted by Burgat (1995, 48–60).
5. Op. cit, pp. 44–8 and pp. 60–8 for Tariq al-Bishri and Adil Husayn respectively.
6. Translated in 'Débats autour de l'application de la *shari'a*', *Études Arabes-Dossiers* 70–1 (1986): 23, (PISAI), Rome.
7. Ibid., pp. 29–35.
8. Arabic text and English translation in *Majallat al-Azhar* 51, no.4 (1979): 1092–1110 (Arabic version) and pp. 1118–26 (English version).
9. Arabic text and French translation in *Études Arabes-Dossiers*, op. cit., pp. 87–109.
10. Ibid., pp. 113–20.
11. Ibid., pp. 137–80.
12. Ibid., pp. 181–98.
13. See special issue of *Islamochristiana* 9 (1983) on 'Human rights in Islam'. (PISAI), Rome.
14. See his book *al-Islam al-siyasi* (*Political Islam*) (1987), partly translated into French as *L'islamisme contre l'islam*, p. 106: 'God wanted Islam to

be a religion, but men have turned it into politics.'
15. See Abedin (1990).
16. Arabic text and French translation in *Études Arabes-Dossiers*, op. cit., pp. 215–37.
17. Talbi (1992, 98).

7

'Clash of Civilizations'? Contemporary Images of Islam in the West

JOHN L. ESPOSITO

The dominant factor affecting contemporary images of Islam and the West is the impact of political Islam or what is more popularly referred to as 'Islamic fundamentalism'.[1] A series of explosive events during the past two decades have not only dominated headlines but also provided the dominant images of a 'militant Islam': the Iranian revolution and 'Americans Held Hostage', the assassination of Anwar Sadat, kidnappings and hostage taking in Lebanon and the broader Middle East, the Salman Rushdie affair and assassinations of some of those associated with its publication, Saddam Hussein's call for a *jihad* against the West in the Gulf War, the World Trade Centre bombings and subsequent trial of Sheikh Omar Abdul-Rahman and others for conspiracy to bomb major sites in the United States, the killing of Coptic Christians in Egypt and the harassment and persecution of some Christian churches by the Islamic Republic of the Sudan.

In the post Cold War period, relations between the Muslim World and the West continue to be affected by the Islamic resurgence and the visions of those in government and the media who raise the spectre of the religious, political, cultural and demographic threat of 'Islamic fundamentalism' or of an impending clash of civilizations.[2]

We live in a world in which it remains common to speak or see headlines with – militant Islam, resurgent Islam, fundamentalist Islam, Islamic bombs, Islamic extremism, Islamic fanatics, Islamic guerrillas, and Islamic terrorism. The hysteria has created a climate in which the wearing of the *hijab* (a head scarf) is not only seen as a threat by the regime in Tunisia but also by France.

94

Many Muslim rulers have reinforced Western perceptions of an Islamic threat or impeding clash of civilizations. From Morocco and Egypt to Saudi Arabia and Malaysia, governments have denounced their religious opposition as extremist and warned of its international as well as domestic threat. Muslim rulers as diverse as Egypt´s President Hosni Mubarak and Libya's Muammar Qaddafi, Saudi Arabia´s King Fahd and Malaysia´s prime minister Dr Mahathir Mohamad, all challenged domestically by Islamic opposition, were critical of radical Islamist movements. Many have warned of the betrayal of moderate Islam by those who manipulated and distorted its true teachings.[3]

The continued violent revolutionary challenge of militants to Muslim governments and societies in the 1990s has reinforced fears of 'Islamic' extremism and terrorism. Radical Islamists in Algeria (the Armed Islamic Guard) and Egypt (the Gama'at Islamiyya) have been locked in confrontations with government military/security forces. In Israel and Palestine, attacks by Hamas and al-Jihad have threatened the PLO-Israeli Peace Accords and have been denounced by both Yasser Arafat and Shimon Peres. Radical groups from Algeria and Egypt to Israel/Palestine and Pakistan have waged battles in which other Muslims and non-Muslim citizens as well as Americans and Europeans have been victims, killed in streets and cafes, school and mosques.

In Europe and America, fear of the export of 'Islamic fundamentalism' and its threat to domestic security have captured media attention and at times reinforced the image of Islam as a demographic threat. Among the more prominent incidents have been: the convictions in the 1993 World Trade Centre bombing and the subsequent trial and conviction in New York of Sheikh Omar Abdul-Rahman and co-conspirators for plotting to wage a war of urban terrorism against the United States; bombings in Paris by Algerian extremists; and the arrest of some 50 activists, reputedly linked to Algerian extremists who 'were planning a terrorist attack somewhere in Europe'.[4]

Islam in the West

For some in the West, the nature of the Islamic threat is intensified by the linkage of the political and the demographic. Much as observers in the past retreated to polemics and stereotypes of Arabs, Turks or Muslims rather than address the specific causes of conflict and confrontation, today we are witnessing the creation of a new myth. The impending confrontation between Islam and the West is presented as part of an historical pattern of Muslim belligerency and aggression now viewed as a potential domestic threat, given the significant presence and growth of Muslim communities. Past images of a Christian West turning back the threat of Muslim armies seeking to overrun the West are conjured up and linked to demographic and political realities: images of Charles Martel who 'halted the first Mohammedan advance preventing the crescent from closing over Christian Europe', the Crusaders attempt to save Jerusalem and the narrow defeat of 'Islamic legions' at Vienna are linked to current realities and fears of the expansion of a resurgent Islam in Europe and America: 'Contagion is precisely what some European countries are starting to fear. With Islamic fundamentalism gaining strength at Europe´s doorstep, notably in Algeria and Turkey, they worry that it will spread to the large Muslim populations of Western Europe.'[5]

Serbian leaders have played on past history, portraying their genocidal war against Bosnian Muslims as a struggle to turn back the tide of radical Islamic fundamentalism and the creation of an Islamic state in the heart of Europe. Others observed that a 'cultural curtain is descending in Bosnia to replace the Berlin Wall, a curtain separating the Christian and Islamic worlds'.[6] The German magazine *Der Spiegel* reported, 'Soon, Europe could have a fanatical theocratic state on its doorsteps.'[7] France has reacted out of fear that Algeria´s crisis would lead to massive emigration from Algeria that would swell the ranks of its already sizeable (four million) and potentially combustible Muslim community, fostering a domestic fundamentalist threat. Some have warned that the combination of radicalism and spiralling population growth threaten to overrun East and West.[8]

The impact and assimilation of Muslims is a particularly contentious issue in countries such as Great Britain and France among others where earlier settled communities from the Middle East, Asia and Africa have become sizeable, dominating local politics in cities and towns like Bradford, England and Marseilles, France and asserting their rights nationally and locally. These communities are projected to grow significantly, supplemented by new waves of immigrants. The presence of significant Muslim minority populations puts strains on the social fabric of European societies like France where Islam is the second largest religion and Great Britain where it is in third place. Anti-Arab/Muslim sentiment in Western Europe is part of a growing xenophobia. Muslim communities and indigenous groups have clashed over questions of continued immigration, citizenship and the accommodation of Muslim belief and practice.

In England, debates, from the Rushdie affair to local politics and school issues, have raged. Muslims have demanded that Muslim schools be allowed to receive state subvention, such as is allowed for Catholic and Jewish schools. Such events have contributed to British Muslim politicization as well as highlighting the diversity of Muslim responses. While some British Muslims created a Muslim Parliament of Great Britain, which included a speaker and four deputy speakers (including two women), there has been considerable dissension within Muslim ranks in Britain. Some have charged that creating a Muslim parliament is merely playing the Western game (i.e. 'parliament') while others have charged that it constitutes a form of 'apartheid'.[9] Still other Muslim leaders have objected to any notion of separatism as an alternative to their integration into British society.[10]

In France, calls for the expulsion of foreign workers have been accompanied by celebrated cases in which Muslims girls in schools and universities have been prohibited from wearing a *hijab* in school. The *hijab* issue 'exemplifies the widening gulf between French society and its Muslim minority. Nearly thirteen centuries after Charles Martel halted the Muslim conquest of Europe at this city, the new battle of Poitiers encapsulates the growing suspicion of – and sometimes hostility to the Islamic faith in Europe.'[11] Ironically, political demagogues in France, for example, play on many of the same cultural fears of foreign cultural penetration and loss of identity that are so prevalent in the Muslim world: 'Europeans now feel threatened by so many things … The 'Americanization' of our culture, the drift to the left, a loss of identity, the rise of an ugly populist response to things foreign.'[12]

Western European fears often express themselves in religio-cultural as well as economic and political terms. While assimilation of other Europeans occurred in the past, many today doubt the possibility or desirability of absorbing the new immigrants, especially Muslims who are both nationally and religio-culturally alien: 'Our former immigrants were Europeans; these are not. Arab girls who insist on wearing *chuddars* (chador, veil or covering) in our schools are not

French and don´t want to be … Europe´s past was white and Judaeo-Christian. The future is not. I doubt that our very old institutions and structures will be able to stand the pressure.'[13] In one survey, three out of four French people interviewed 'thought that the word "fanatical" best applied to Islam.'[14] Some observers have seen the outcome of the current debate in potentially cataclysmic terms: 'While Europe has overcome the Cold War … it now risks creating new divisions and conflicts, such as a white, wealthy and Christian "Fortress Europe" pitted against a largely poor, Islamic world. That could lead to terrorism and another forty years of small, hot wars … '[15]

While French Interior officials have identified fundamentalism as a domestic threat and arrested Islamic militants suspected of supplying arms to Algerian Islamists, the more complex reality of Muslims in France was revealed in Lyon in 1994–95. The building of the Grand Mosque in Lyon reflected the fears of some but also hope for the future. The mosque was initially resisted by those who feared that it would become a breeding ground for extremists, especially by the extreme-right National Front who called for 'active resistance against the danger of Islamic colonization'.[16] However, within a short period after its opening, the mosque emerged as a symbol of reconciliation. As its Algerian-born grand mufti declared 'The protest have completely disappeared because we have shown that French Islam can be a force for moderation and integration … Iran, Algeria, terrorists all blend into a simplistic and ignorant view that Islam means violence and fanaticism. I´m afraid we have a long, slow education process ahead of us.'[17]

The Muslim presence in Europe or North America does pose a challenge, though not in the sense that some have predicted. First and foremost, the challenge is to distinguish between the majority of its Muslim citizens and a minority of violent revolutionaries. Like many before them, the vast majority of Muslims who immigrate to the West come to escape authoritarian regimes or to seek a better future economically and educationally for themselves and their families. They are and wish to be loyal citizens. However, this does not take away the challenge that all minorities have faced, namely assimilation versus total integration. Jews and Roman Catholics, like many ethnic and religious groups, have faced the problem of assimilation without a loss of identity. Responding to these concerns led to the construction of a vast educational system by Roman Catholics and

Jews as well as religious and ethnic fraternal and social welfare societies. How to be American or British while retaining one´s sense of ethnic origins or faith is not a new issue. It is particularly acute for minorities. Indeed, the problem of national identity and multiculturalism and pluralism remains a contested issue, particularly in France.

The situation of Muslims in the West at first seems quite different from others (immigrants or indigenous converts) who however ethnically diverse possessed a shared Judaeo-Christian culture. Muslims, like Jews in the past, find themselves in Western cultural contexts where they are often regarded as completely 'other'. This is caused not only by an ignorance of Islam or by its equation with extremism and terrorism but also by the failure to appreciate the extent to which Islam is part of a Judaeo-Christian-Islamic tradition. Too often, categories that pit Islam against the West have been reinforced by an intellectual and religious outlook that privileged a Judaeo-Christian tradition over and against the 'other' world religions. Islam, despite its monotheism and prophetic tradition was grouped with 'foreign religions' (Hinduism, Buddhism, Taoism, etc.) in our scholarship, university curricula, libraries and bookstores. While there are significant differences among the three great monotheistic faiths, there is also a common theological outlook or shared ethical monotheism which can be a source of mutual respect and cooperation rather than confrontation.

The demonstrations, violence and death threats that accompanied the Salman Rushdie affair in Europe, charges that Muslim citizens in Britain, France and America have formed radical networks with international connections, the World Trade Centre bombing and other conspiracies to blow up major buildings and tunnels in America – have all reinforced the image of a militant Islam and raised questions about national security and immigration policies. Concerns are reflected in headline stories in major newspapers and the media such as: 'Holy war comes to America', 'Islam under siege', 'The new dawn For Islam: The global campaign against the secular state', '*Jihad* in America'.[18] Some warn that 'Britain and the US have become the bases for extremists seeking to turn Islam into an aggressive political movement ... Since the World Trade Centre, the FBI is playing catch-up, even utilizing CIA connections in meeting what is belatedly seen as a domestic threat.'[19]

For some, the question: 'Can they accommodate or assimilate?' is often joined to another, 'Can they be loyal and trusted citizens?' While these are legitimate questions, the tendency has been to exaggerate the magnitude and extent of the threat as well as to place these questions within an 'us' and 'them' context. This approach risks painting all Muslims and indeed Islam itself, as violent rather than carefully distinguishing between a radical fringe and the mainstream, those who manipulate and distort religion to justify their actions and the Islamic tradition itself. The carefully nuanced distinctions made by many in the West between religious and ethnic communities and a minority of their members when judging the activities of the Jewish Defence League, the IRA, Mafia or Christian extremists calling themselves 'The Army of God', who bomb abortion clinics, as well as distinctions between liberation or resistance movements and terrorist organizations, are not as sharply drawn when dealing with Muslim extremism. The situation is compounded by those who sharply contrast the Judaeo-Christian tradition with Islam on such issues of peace, violence, holy war, and revenge or those who speak not only about religious and cultural differences but also about diametrically opposed and thus irreconcilable differences in principles and values. This tendency fosters a sense of alienation, marginalization, and radicalization on both sides. As one Muslim leader noted in France, 'Our only ambition is to become at the same time good Muslims and good French citizens ... But as long as people wage campaigns on the peril of Islam, as long as we let rancour and frustrations accumulate, we will encourage all forms of radicalization.'[20]

Democratization

Integral to the view of the Islamic threat is the belief that Islam is inherently anti-democratic and intolerant or that, at best, it is 'not hospitable to democracy'.[21] Lack of enthusiasm or support for political liberalization in the Middle East has been rationalized by the claim that both Arab culture and Islam are anti-democratic and the fear that Islamists will use the electoral process to seize power.

The democratization movement in the Middle East and the participation (and successes) of Islamic movements in electoral politics both raise the question of the compatibility of Islam and democracy.[22] Among the arguments proffered by those who fear the promotion of a democratic process in the Muslim world is that it risks the 'hijacking of democracy' by Islamic activists and further Islamic inroads into centres of power, threatening Western interests and fostering anti-Westernism and increased instability.

Today in most Islamic countries, free elections would produce fundamentalist victories and validate the imposition of theocracy.

> ... They have pressed for free elections in several Arab countries. Presenting themselves as the protectors of the oppressed, they have done quite well in these elections as they knew they would. But it is questionable that their real aim is to promote democracy ... Islam draws no line between religion and politics. As undemocratic as the present Saudi regime is, a total Islamic one – even with broader political participation – would be less free. It would have no neutral public space where people´s views are treated as opinions, not as truth. Elections would become trivial in that environment.[23]

Many argue that Islamic values and democratic values are inherently antithetical, as seen in issues like the inequality of believers and unbelievers as well as of men and women. History has shown that nations and religious traditions are capable of having multiple and major ideological interpretations or reorientations. The transformation of European principalities, whose rule was often justified in terms of divine right, into modern Western democratic states was accompanied by a process of reinterpretation of reform. Indeed, democracy itself has had multiple meanings; it has meant different things to different peoples at different times from ancient to modern notions of democracy, form direct to indirect democracy, from majority rule to majority vote.[24] The Judaeo-Christian tradition, while once supportive of political absolutism and divine right monarchies, was reinterpreted to accommodate the democratic ideal. 'Islam' also lends itself to multiple interpretations; it has been used to support democracy and dictatorship, republicanism and monarchy. The twentieth century has witnessed both tendencies.

Islam and Islamic movements are often portrayed as incapable of tolerating diversity and political dissent. The record of Islamic experiments in Pakistan, Iran and the Sudan raises serious questions about political and religious pluralism, the rights of women and minorities under 'Islamically' oriented governments. The extent to which the growth of Islamic revivalism has been accompanied in some countries by attempts to ban political parties or limit opposition, to restrict women's rights, to separate women and men in public, to impose and enforce veiling, and to restrict their public roles in society strikes fear in some segments of Muslim society and challenges the credibility of those who call for Islamization or re-Islamization of state and society. The record of discrimination against the Baha'i in Iran and the Ahmadi in Pakistan as 'deviant' groups ('heretical' offshoots of Islam), against Christians in Sudan and Pakistan, and Arab Jews in some countries as well as communal sectarian conflict between Muslims and Christians in Egypt and Nigeria pose similar questions of religious pluralism and tolerance.

If many Muslims ignore these issues or talk of tolerance and human rights in Islam in a facile way, discussion of these questions in the West is often reduced to two contrasting blocks, the West which preaches and practices freedom and tolerance and the Muslim world which does not. Muslim attitudes towards Christian minorities and the case of Salman Rushdie are marshalled to support the indictment that Islam is intolerant and anti-democratic.

Muslim demands for independence are regarded as deceptive and a threat to minorities: what is being pursued, therefore, is not Wilsonian self-determination (though many of these *intifadas* have adopted its language), because in the Islamic world self-determination is permitted only to Muslims. What instead is being pursued is a pan-Islamic demand for sovereignty over any territory where Muslims form a local majority.[25]

The charge of intolerance is supported by statements from some Christian church leaders. Muslim fundamentalists have no use for ecumenism or dialogue which is a 'betrayal to Allah ... For Islam, there is only one revelation, the final word has been spoken in the Koran, and Muhammad is the final Prophet.'[26]

Issues of interpretation

At the heart of Western misinterpretation, stereotyping, and exaggerated fears of Islam is a clash of viewpoints. Older stereotypes of 'the Arab' and Islam in terms of bedouin, desert, camel, polygamy, harem, rich oil *sheikhs* have been replaced by those of gun-toting *mullahs* or bearded, anti-Western fundamentalists. Western fears and antipathy are fed not only by media reports and headline events but are also rooted in a secular outlook on life which we understand. The nature of religion and the relationship of religion to politics and society greatly determine our presuppositions, expectations and judgements. Modern, post-enlightenment secular language and categories of thought often prejudice and distort understanding and judgement. The modern notion of religion as a system of personal belief makes an Islam that is comprehensive in scope, in which religion is integral to politics and society, 'abnormal' (insofar as it departs from an accepted 'modern' secular norm) and nonsensical. Thus, Islam becomes incomprehensible, irrational, extremist and threatening. What most forget is that all the world's religions in their origins and histories were fairly comprehensive ways of living.[27] While the relationship of religion to politics varied, religion is a path or way of life with a strong emphasis on community as well as personal life: the way of the Torah, the straight path of Islam, the middle path of the Buddha, the righteous way (*dharma*) of Hinduism. They provide guidance for hygiene, diet, the managing of wealth, stages of life (birth, marriage, death) as well as for ritual and worship. The modern notion of religion has its origins in the post-enlightenment West. Its restricted definition has become accepted as the norm or meaning of religion by many believers and unbelievers alike in the West. Bereft of a sense of history, few realize that the term 'religion' as known and understood today is modern and Western in origins. Similarly, it was the West that then set about naming other religious systems or 'isms'. Christianity and Judaism were joined by the 'newly named' Hinduism, Buddhism, and 'Mohammedanism'. Thus, the nature and function of other religious traditions were categorized, studied, and judged in terms of a modern Western, post-enlightenment secular world view with its separation of church and state.

As most forget or are ignorant of the fact that our concept of religion is a modern construct, so too there is a tendency to forget that the Western notion of separation of church and state is relatively new. Historically, the dividing line between faith and politics among the Abrahamic faiths (Judaism, Christianity, and Islam) had been blurred from the biblical conquests and the early Jewish kingdoms to imperial Christianity. As the Christian empires and Crusades demonstrated, while church and state were distinct, they were not always separate in Christianity. However, modern notions of religion as a system of belief for personal life and separation of church and state have become so accepted and internalized that they have obscured the beliefs and practice of past history and come to represent for many a self evident and timeless truth. As a result, from a modern secular perspective (a form of 'secular fundamentalism') the mixing of religion and politics is regarded as necessarily abnormal (departing from the norm), irrational, dangerous, and extremist. Those who do so are often dubbed 'fundamentalists' (Christian, Jewish or Muslim) or religious fanatics. Thus, when secular-minded peoples (government officials, political analysts, journalist, and the bulk of the general public) in the West encounter Muslim individuals and groups who speak of Islam as a comprehensive way of life, they immediately dub them 'fundamentalist' with the connotation that these are backward looking individuals, zealots who are a threat. The attitude of many governments and secular elites in the Muslim world is often similar. Images of militant *mullahs* and the violent actions of some individuals and groups are then taken as representative and proof of the inherent danger of mixing religion and politics.

The dangers of secular fundamentalism

Secular presuppositions – which inform our academic disciplines and outlook on life, our Western secular world view – have been a major obstacle to understanding and contributed to a tendency to reduce Islam to fundamentalism and fundamentalism to religious extremism. For much of the 1960s, the received wisdom among many, from development experts to many theologians, could be summarized in the adage: 'Every day in every way, things are and will continue to get more and more modern/secular'. Integral to definitions of modernization was the progressive 'Westernization' and secularization of society: its institutions, organizations and actors.[28] Religion and theology reflected the same presuppositions and expectations as theologians spoke of demythologizing the scriptures, of a secular gospel for the modern age, of the triumph of the secular city (as distinguished from Augustine's City of God), and a school of theological thought emerged which was dubbed the 'Death of God Theology'. [29]

Religious faith was at best supposed to be a private matter. The degree of one´s intellectual sophistication and objectivity in academia was often equated with a secular liberalism and relativism that seemed antithetical to religion.

Acceptance of the 'enlightened' notion of separation of church and state and of Western, secular models of development, relegated religion to the stockpile of traditional beliefs, valuable in understanding the past but irrelevant or an obstacle to modern political, economic and social development. Neither development theory nor international relations considered religion as a significant variable for political analysis. The separation of religion and politics overlooked the fact that most religious traditions were established and developed in historical, political, social, and economic contexts. Their doctrines and laws were conditioned by these contexts.

The post-enlightenment tendency to define religion as a system of belief (restricted to personal or private life), rather than as a way of life, has seriously hampered our ability to understand the nature of Islam and many of the world´s religion. It has artificially compartmentalized religion, doing violence to its nature, and reinforced a static, reified conception of religious traditions rather than revealing their inner dynamic. To that extent, a religion which does not seem to do so (a religion that mixes religion and politics) appears necessarily retrogressive, prone to religious extremism and fanaticism and thus a potential threat.

Edward Said´s critique of Orientalism, though at times excessive, was insightful in identifying deficiencies and bias in the scholarship of the past as well as in media coverage of Islam.[30] However, new forms of Orientalism flourish today in the hands of those who equate revivalism, 'fundamentalism', or Islamic movements solely with radical revolutionaries and who fail to focus on the vast majority of 'Islamically' committed Muslims who belong to the moderate mainstream of society rather than a radicalized minority. Too often academia, government and the media have focused on crises and headline events and then a violent radical fringe and, failing to see the forest for the trees, not studied sufficiently both moderate political and non-political movements and organizations. This trend (and deficiency) has been reinforced by the realities of the market place. Publishing houses, journals, consultancy firms, and the media all too often pander to that which captures the headlines and confirms fears of extremism and terrorism and reinforces stereotypes.

Islamic revivalism has challenged many of the presuppositions of Western liberal secularism and development theory: modernization means the inexorable or progressive secularization and 'Westernization' of society. Too often analyses of policy making have been shaped by a liberal secularism which fails to recognize that it too represents a world view which, when assumed to be a self-evident truth, can take the form of a 'secular fundamentalism'. Secularism or liberal democracy is no longer regarded as 'a' way (one of many possible paradigms albeit for some the best way) but 'the' way, the only true path for political development. In the name of enlightenment (reason, empiricism, pluralism) a new absolute, a new norm is posited. Alternative paradigms, especially religious ones, are necessarily judged as abnormal, irrational, retrogressive.

This secular bias blinds many to the force and role of religion as a source of faith and identity. Political economy is essential in understanding the rise of social movements. However, the force of political Islam can not be simply reduced to the socioeconomic failures of societies. We cannot simply portray 'fundamentalism' as the child of poverty and unemployment. While FIS support came in large part from Algeria's unemployed younger generation, the membership of Egypt's and Jordan's Muslim Brotherhoods, while also attracting disaffected youth, consists in large part of middle and upper middle class professionals (teachers, doctors, lawyers, engineers).

Focus on 'Islamic fundamentalism' as a global threat has reinforced a tendency to equate violence with Islam, to fail to distinguish between the illegitimate use of religion by individuals and the faith and practice of the majority of the world's Muslims who, like believers in other religious traditions, wish to live in peace. To uncritically equate Islam and Islamic fundamentalism with extremism is to judge Islam only by those who wreak havoc, a standard not applied to Judaism and Christianity. Fear of fundamentalism creates a climate in which Muslims and Islamic organizations are guilty until proven innocent. Actions, however heinous, are attributed to Islam rather than to a twisted or distorted interpretation of Islam. Thus, for example, despite the historic track-record of Christianity and Western countries in conducting warfare, developing weapons of mass destruction, imposing their imperialist designs, Islam and Muslim culture are portrayed as somehow peculiarly and inherently expansionist and prone to violence and warfare (*jihad*). The risk today is that exaggerated fears will lead to double standards in the promotion of democracy and human rights in the Muslim world. Witness the volume of Western democratic concern and action for the former Soviet Union and Eastern Europe compared with the muted and ineffective response with regard to the promotion of democracy in the Middle East or the defence of Muslims in Bosnia-Herzegovinia.

We live in a period of significant change. Our challenge today is not simply to focus on the dangers of an impeding clash of civilizations but rather to engage in a civilizational dialogue. While profound differences exist, there is a 'common ground' – shared beliefs and values as well as common political and economic interests – which offers a basis for mutual understanding and cooperation. As Anwar Ibrahim, deputy prime minister of Malaysia and a Muslim intellectual has noted: 'Enduring peace and security of the world must be built not upon religious, cultural, economic and political hegemonies but on mutual awareness and concern. For understanding brings respect, respect prepares the way for love. Love, like truth, liberates and takes us onto a higher kind of loyalty. What is true, just and virtuous.'[31]

Notes

1.   For studies of the Islamic resurgence, see Haddad, Voll & Esposito (1991); Esposito (1991) and (1987); Voll (1994); Piscatori (1983) and Ayubi (1991).

2.   For an analysis of the demonization of Islam, see Esposito (1995), upon which this study is based, and Hippler & Lueg (1995).

3.   'PM: Be wary of fanatics', *New Straits Times*, (Malaysia) 3 March 1994.

4.   'Muslims Activists held in London', *New Straits Times*, (Malaysia), 3 March 1993, p. 22.

5.   Thomas Kamm, 'Clash of Cultures: Rise of Islam in France Rattles the Populace and Stirs a Backlash', *The Wall Street Journal*, 5 January 1995.

6.   R. D. Kaplan, 'Ground Zero: Macedonia: the Real Battleground', *The New Republic*, 2 August 1993, pp. 15–16.

7.   Lueg (1995: 9).

8   Buchanan, 'Rising Islam May Overwhelm the West', *New Hampshire Sunday News*, 20 August 1989.

9.   Tariq Azim-Khan, a member of the Muslim Forum as quoted in *The Independent*, 209 October 1991.

10.   Dr Hesham El-Essawy, Chairman of the Islamic Society for the Promotion of Religious Tolerance, as quoted in *The Independent*, ibid.

11.   Kamm, loc. cit.

12.   Dominique Moisi of France's Institute of International Relations, as quoted in Judith Miller, 'Strangers at the Gate: Europe's Immigration Crisis', *The New York Times Magazine*, 15 September 1991, p. 86.

13   Ibid., p. 80.

14.   Lueg (1995: 16).

15.   Ibid., p. 86.

16 William Drozdjak, 'Once Feared, Lyon's Mosque Emerges as a Symbol of Tolerance', *International Herald Tribune*, 6 March 1995, p. 2.

17.   Ibid.

18.   Lisa Anderson, 'Holy War comes to America', *Chicago Tribune*, 12 July 1993; William Safire, 'Islam under Siege', *The New York Times*, 18 March 1993 & 'The New Dawn for Islam: The Global Campaign against the Secular State', *El País*, reprinted in *World Press Review*, June 1993, p. 19.

19.   William Safire, 'Islam under Siege'. *The New York Times*, March 18, 1993.

20.   Kamm, 'Clash of Cultures'.

21.   Amos Perlmutter, 'Wishful Thinking About Fundamentalism' and Hungtinton (1984: 26).

22.   For an analysis of this issue, see Esposito & Piscatori (1991: 40–2); Voll & Esposito (1994b: 3–11) with ripostes, pp. 12–19 and Voll & Esposito reply (1994b: 71–2); Monshipuri & Kukla (1994: 29–39); Wright (1992: 131–45).

23.   Leslie Gelb, 'The Free Elections Trap', *The New York Times*, 29 May 1991.

24.   John O. Voll & John L. Esposito, (1994b).

25.   Charles Krauthammer, 'The New Crescent of Crisis: The Global Intifada', *The Washington Post*, 16 February 1990.

26.   Buchanan, 'Rising Islam … '.

27.   For an early and insightful analysis of the origins of the modern construct of religion, see Smith (1962).

28.   Lerner (1958) and Halpren (1963). For an analysis and critique of the factors which influenced the development of modernization theory, see Mehden (1988).

29.   See, for example, Cox (1965) & (1984); Bonhoeffer (1967); and Hamilton & Altizer (1966).

30.   Said (1979). For coverage of Islam specifically by the media and experts, see his (1981).

31.   Ibrahim (1995: 6).

8

Citizenship and Human Rights in Some Muslim States

ANN ELIZABETH MAYER

Few members of Muslim societies enjoy the full rights of citizenship, which entail political participation on a basis of equality within a modern constitutional system that recognizes popular sovereignty and respects human rights. The claims of non-citizens, which are grounded in their humanity as opposed to their nationality, are likewise given short shrift.[1]

If one generalized from the Saudi Arabian example, one might conclude that, where Islamic specificity is the basis for a polity, this precludes both citizenship rights and human rights. Commenting on the 1992 Basic Law, King Fahd posited a conflict between rights and freedoms and Islam, defending the lack of democracy by appealing to 'our Islamic beliefs that constitute a complete and fully-integrated system,' maintaining that democracies were not suited to his region or to the 'unique qualities' of the Saudi people.[2] However, the problems of citizenship and human rights cannot fairly be blamed on Islamic specificity, since actual denials of citizens' and human rights seldom conflict with the relevant Islamic precepts or, at least, have little connection to these. Other forces, like struggles to establish a basis for national unity and to shore up the authority of regimes, may be degrading rights.

Saudi Arabia

In Saudi Arabia citizenship is merely nominal. The 1992 Basic Law affirms in articles five, six and seven that the Koran and the *sunna* support the rule of the Saudi clan, as if the warrant for the Saudis' absolute monarchy were set forth in the texts of the Islamic sources. Article six includes a provision that 'citizens,' *al-muwatinun*, are to pay allegiance to the king in accordance with the Koran and *sunna*, admonishing them that they are to do so 'in submission and obedience.' Calling for Saudi 'citizens' to render the kind of obedience that was formerly exacted by traditional *amirs* and *sultans* of their subjects is anomalous; in reality, Saudi nationals are merely *ra'aya*, or 'subjects.'

Abdelrahman Munif explores how dramatic economic shifts transform culture and the ruler-subject relationship in *Cities of Salt*. One character from an idyllic Arabian oasis jeopardized by development protests to the *amir* bent on bringing in Americans for oil exploration that 'money is not everything in this world. More important are honour, ethics and our traditions'.[3] Presciently, another character comments: 'You are the government, you have the soldiers and the guns, and you'll get what you want, maybe even tomorrow. After the Christians fetch the gold for you from under the ground, you'll be even stronger.' The *amir* cuts off the objections with the assurance: 'My friends, the government knows better than you and is stronger. As I told you, as to morals and faith, we're the ones who safeguard morals and faith for you'.[4] The rulers in Munif's tale unite with the Western oil industry to plunder resources and ruthlessly to crush all resistance to their increasingly tyrannical domination of their subjects, revealing that the *amir*'s guardianship of morals and faith amounts to nothing more than fancy rhetoric. Munif's caustic novel implied that, to understand the essence of the Saudi system, one needed to grasp not some unique morals and faith but, rather, the politics of untrammelled greed pursued under the auspices of Americans backing the supposedly 'traditional' ruler. Munif was punished by being stripped of his Saudi citizenship and now lives in exile, proving that he was a mere national, never a real 'citizen'. The current heavy-handed efforts to quash the abrasive attacks of the Committee for the Defense of Legitimate Rights betray how nervous the Saudi royals really are about whether their claims to govern in accordance with an Islamic mandate are convincing.

In addition to mentioning 'citizens', the Basic Law uses an equally incongruous term, 'human rights', in article 26, which is out of place in a system deliberately structured to stifle human rights. The Saudi royals seem to have concluded that, as of 1992, any document like the Basic Law would have to include provision for citizenship and human rights, even if they had no intention whatsoever to allow their subjects to enjoy these exotic concepts. Having invoked human rights, the Basic Law omits one of the most contentious issues in Saudi society, the rights of women. The official use of supposedly 'Islamic' criteria to keep them as a subjugated underclass is not a subject that the regime feels comfortable about putting in writing this foundational document. Thus, even in this supremely retrograde law, there were indications that new values and concepts had percolated through Saudi culture, registering even on the rulers' consciousness. These adjustments suggest that ideas about whether an Islamic specificity could or should determine rights are in flux, even in Saudi Arabia.

Kuwait

The peculiar hierarchy of rights in neighbouring Kuwait should disabuse one of the idea that Islamic specificity drives denials of rights.

Kuwaiti parliamentarians do not conduct themselves meekly like the subjects of an all-powerful monarch; they act with the confidence of citizens mistrustful and even disrespectful of the prerogatives of the ruling Sabah clan, vigorously asserting their parliamentary prerogatives and lambasting their rulers for their misdeeds.

However, the relatively open Kuwaiti system is fraught with paradoxes, including *de jure* distinctions between first and second class citizens. Under Kuwait's arcane rules, only the small class of men who qualify as first class citizens may vote. Kuwaiti women, despite their heroic sacrifices during the Iraqi occupation, are still not allowed to vote, even though they may share identical lineage with the men who qualify for first class citizenship. Thus, where voting rights are concerned, all women and most men are placed in one, subordinate category, which has no parallels in Islamic jurisprudence. The peculiarity of Kuwaiti standards is brought home by comparisons. Living under a theocratic Shi'i regime, all Iranian men and women have the right to vote. Ruled by an absolute monarchy, Saudi subjects, both male and female, are all denied the right to vote. Where is the Islamic specificity?

Kuwaiti nationals are still seeking the equal rights of citizens, but aliens are exposed to special risks of discrimination and harm. Iraqis, Palestinians, stateless Gazans, and other Muslim aliens have been deprived of basic rights and are subject to arrest, imprisonment, and sudden expulsion. The old concept of an Islamic *umma*, often rhetorically invoked, does not deter Kuwait and other nation-states from mistreating fellow Muslims who are non-citizens.

The hapless plight of the *bidun* of Kuwait provides a telling example of how the technicalities of nationality override former ideas of communal and religious solidarity.[5] There is no reason either in terms of Islamic law or the traditions of the region to treat the *bidun* as alien beings devoid of rights. The *bidun* are not ethnically or religiously distinguishable from Kuwaiti citizens – indeed, many have close relatives who are Kuwaitis. The *bidun* have wound up as stateless aliens because of their non-compliance with bureaucratic formalities imposed by the alien institution of the nation-state, which now has imposed rigid territorial boundaries and citizenship requirements. Being denied civil identification cards, driver's licenses, and travel documents, the *bidun* are compelled to live virtually under house arrest. *Bidun* are not permitted to travel abroad, even for medical emergencies and religious pilgrimages, unless they accept never to return to Kuwait. In the case of the suffering *bidun* population, where reverting to Islamic categories like common membership in the *umma* would enhance rights, one sees a notable disinclination to appeal to Islamic specificity.

Focusing on the rights of citizens can distract one from the question of the rights owing to persons by virtue of their humanity. In this regard, the exploitation and abuse of impoverished Third World migrants who work in Kuwait merits attention. These migrants may be treated no better than slaves, with the predicament of Asian women in domestic employment being particularly grim. Is the dehumanizing exploitation of domestic servants from distant lands in Kuwait a relic of the medieval Islamic tradition, when non-Muslims from the *dar al-harb* were enslaved? Or, is it simply the product of the same egregious economic disparities that result in migrants in Europe and the USA working under awful conditions that mimic the rigours of slavery?

Iran

Iran considers itself the Islamic state *par excellence*, but in Iran's Islamic constitution, modern notions of equality for citizens that have no counterparts in the Saudi Basic Law intermittently surface. For example, article 20 guarantees for 'all citizens of the nation' equal protection of the law – here, the secular law, or *qanun* – and article 3.14 aims at 'securing the comprehensive rights of all citizens, both women and men, and the establishment of judicial security for all, as well as the equality of all before the law' – again, the secular law or *qanun*. However, other provisions hint, albeit only to the careful reader, that Iranian women and non-Muslims do not enjoy equality. For example, article 19 asserts that 'all the people of Iran enjoy equal rights, and factors such as color, race and language do not bestow any privilege.' The omission of sex and religion is designed to allow the perpetuation of the old hierarchy approved by Islamic law, according to which Muslim males ranked above both women and non-Muslims. A creative tension results from the constitutionalization of modern egalitarian ideas alongside provisions designed to accommodate the discriminatory features mandated by Iran's reactionary Islamic ideology.

Significantly, Iran does not want to admit to having a policy of discriminating against its nationals based on their religion. Thus, in contrast to Kuwait's overt segregation of citizens into two classes, Iran's religious minorities are not defined in terms assigned to second class citizenship. Instead, in article 13, Zoroastrians, Christians and Jews are euphemistically called 'recognized minorities'. In article 14, Iranian Muslims are enjoined to treat recognized minorities 'in an ethical fashion and in accordance with Islamic justice and equity and to respect their human rights', the need for such an injunction indirectly betraying the subjugated status of these minorities. Article 14 suggests that, where non-Muslims suffer, it will be due to their proclivity to engage in political conspiracies. 'This principle (of good treatment) applies to all who refrain from engaging in political conspiracy or activity against Islam and the Islamic Republic of Iran'. This gives the regime a secular basis for explaining away persecutions of religious minorities on grounds that are accepted in Western laws, such as treason. The drafters preferred this formulation to openly resuscitating *dhimmi* status, which they seem to have realized, would be anachronistic in the context of a nation-state – especially since Iran has discarded Islamic principles according to which all believers belong to a single *umma*. (Iranian laws differentiate between Iranians and Muslims who do not qualify as Iranian nationals). That is, although discriminatory Islamic categories are being employed, Iran seems rather reluctant to highlight this – or to admit its shameful policies vis-à-vis the Baha'is. As if embarrassed to acknowledge that, because of their belief in a prophet who succeeded Muhammad, Baha'is in Iran are no better than outlaws, the constitution prefers to remain entirely silent on the Baha'is' status.

Since Iran espouses an exigent Islamic ideology, nationals who do not adhere to the ideology cannot be citizens on par with those who do. The Constitution in its preamble asserts that Iran's Islamic government involves 'the realization of the political ideal of a nation which shares the same customs and way of thinking,' implicitly rejecting the liberal idea that governments should be tolerant of the different and often antagonistic convictions of their citizens. Of course, this sets the stage for political repression and the attendant denials of human rights to Iranians whose perspectives deviate from the officially approved way of thinking and winds up being destructive of the rights of the Shi'i Muslim majority, whose members are punished if they question the state-imposed orthodoxy.

Dissident Iranian Shi'is have learned the hard way that their being theoretically entitled to full citizenship is no guarantee of their rights and freedoms. Iranian Shi'is are among those who have been prohibited from running for political office, censored or subjected to harassment, arrest, torture, and even murder for ideological deviations. In the wake of arrests of many *ulama* in November 1995, one could wonder: When a Shi'i theocracy arrests Shi'i clerics for deviant ideas, is it not time to discard the idea that 'Islam' is driving Iran's policies on rights? On a more positive note, one could speculate: Is it not inevitable in these circumstances that Iranians will be prompted to appraise critically the use of 'Islam' as a pretext for denying them civil and political rights?

The Iranian Constitution does not expressly stipulate that men are a degree above women; with deliberate vagueness, article 21 of the Iranian Constitution provides women rights 'according to Islamic standards.' The preamble to the Iranian Constitution also pretends to have a positive message, advising that the revolution will resurrect the noble and respected function of motherhood. The innuendo of this was actually quite sinister, since after the revolution, in the guise of fostering Islamic morality, efforts were made to curb women's professional and educational opportunities, to press girls into early marriages, and to promote the idea that women's true function was attending to their wifely duties and producing offspring with the right ideological orientation.

Although the Iranian Constitution does not call on women to obey the ruling clerics 'in submission and obedience', in practice it turns out that all women are expected to dress alike as a token of their submission to the official Islamic ideology. The uniform dress requirement flows from the determination to stanch all signs of resistance. Women who do not follow Islamic dress requirements are vilified and punished, not simply because of the actual dress infractions, but because they reveal subversive attitudes. Like non-Muslims, women, having been assigned inferior status, are assumed to be rebellious and ill-disposed towards the regime, which in turn suggests that the regime is uncertain how well their subjugated status can be reconciled with the premises of citizenship in a modern nation.

Turkey

Before one concludes that it is Islam that dictates Iran's policies on interfering with women's attire, one might turn one's gaze westward towards Ankara. In fiercely secular Turkey, governments view any deviations from their commands for how Turks are to dress as political insubordination. For example, Turkey has banned the wearing of Islamic head scarves by women in government institutions. From the standpoint of Turkey's secular regime, the Islamic head scarf is as much an affront to its ideology as omitting the head scarf would be to Iran's ruling clerics. So great is the symbolic capital invested in officially prescribed modes of dress that in neither system are women free to dress in accordance with their personal convictions and preferences. Significantly, women in both societies have come to perceive the imposition of both of these officially approved modes of dress, one secular and one Islamic, as human rights problems.

The Turkish example helps distinguish regional trends affecting citizenship and human rights from those shaped by Islamic values.

The problems facing Turkey's Kurdish minority are not identical with those of the Baha'is in neighbouring Iran, but both face harsh consequences if they embarrass the states involved by reminding them of their existence. According to the 1982 Turkish Constitution, Kurds do not exist. The Preamble makes the counter-factual assertion that all inhabitants of Turkey share the same ideal of a strong nation with a Turkish identity. The chilling effect that the policy of disappearing the Kurds has on political debate was felt in March 1994, when thirteen duly elected parliamentarians were stripped of their parliamentary immunity and were tried and imprisoned or obliged to flee to exile because of links to the cause of Kurdish separatism. Their fate demonstrated that a secular government could be as aggressively intolerant of a suspect minority as Iran's theocracy was. Again, one sees that acts and ideas jeopardizing the ideological orthodoxy that glues the nation together are criminalized. That there is no Islamic particularism behind making minorities disappear is also shown by Bulgaria's treatment of its large Turkish minority shortly before the collapse of communist rule, when Bulgarian Turks had their ethnicity and Islamic identity forcibly obliterated by a state determined that all Bulgarians should be Slavs. Ironically, the large Alavi minority in Turkey has long felt obliged to try to disappear itself. Just as all Turkish nationals are meant to be Turks, according to Turkish officialdom, Islam is Sunnism, the sect sponsored by the secular republic. Recently, Turkish Alavis have become more assertive and in March 1995 won a significant concession, that Alavi Islam and history would for the first time be taught in schools, this recognition constituting an important step towards inclusion. By manifesting their conviction that they had a right to recognition on a par with Sunnis, Alavis were claiming the equality owing to citizens.

Meanwhile, Turkish women, despite benefiting from many opportunities and freedoms, have been discriminated against in matters of personal status under Turkey's imported European laws, which reminds one that secular laws, as well as Islamic laws, could deny women equality. In 1992 Turks discovered the potential of constitutional equality provisions that were buttressed by international human rights norms when Turkey's constitutional court used these to invalidate a law requiring a wife to obtain her husband's permission to work on the grounds of its conflict with women's right to equality.[6]

Egypt

In Egypt, as in most Muslim countries, it remains impossible for a Muslim woman legally to marry outside her faith, a prohibition that relates to the inferior status that Islamic jurists traditionally assigned to both women and non-Muslims. In this, there is an element of Islamic specificity, but the pattern of barring women from the dominant group marrying men belonging to a minority or subjugated group is not unique to Islam. Moreover, Muslim countries like Egypt discriminate against women based on purely secular categories, as well. Thus, for example, Egypt refuses to allow Egyptian nationality to be passed on by an Egyptian woman who marries a non-Egyptian, whereas an Egyptian man who marries a non-Egyptian wife can pass on his Egyptian nationality to his offspring. Both the Islamic prohibition of a Muslim woman marrying a non-Muslim and the secular nationality rules, which have been borrowed from Europe, assume that women are – and should be – subordinated to their husbands, so that it is the husband's religion or nationality that is controlling. If Egypt clings to both of these discriminatory rules, one religious and one secular, is the determinative factor perhaps ingrained sexism rather than Islamic specificity? Significantly, when entering its reservations to the women's convention (CEDAW), Egypt vigorously defended its discriminatory nationality rule, but it made no mention of barring marriages between Muslim women and non-Muslim men.[7] Egypt's unwillingness to acknowledge and defend a marriage ban that was strongly supported in Islamic law revealed that Egyptian officialdom was not confident that appeals to Islamic specificity justified breaching a principle of human rights law, setting the stage for rethinking this question.

Muslim converts to Christianity are punished by the security forces, being harassed, threatened, and even tortured to compel recantation,[8] which might be attributed to Islamic teachings forbidding apostasy. However, 'apostates', Copts, and converts to Christianity are not treated worse than Egypt's most militant Muslims, who have been ruthlessly suppressed and persecuted. Even members of relatively moderate Islamist factions have fallen into the maw of military justice.[9] Since the recent convictions of Islamists precluded them from running for parliament as members of the opposition, their real crime may have been mobilizing challenges to Mubarak's military dictatorship. In any event, the persecution of converts and mistreatment of religious minorities in a modern nation-state like Egypt, where Islamic law has for the most part been abandoned and where the government has for decades been dominated by a secular-minded military clique, is only tenuously connected to Islam *per se*; a policy of using religion as a mechanism of control seems to be the driving force.

Finding no way to defend its discriminatory treatment of non-Muslims, the regime pursues the line that there are no minorities in Egypt – again, the popular strategy of disappearing oppressed groups. Of course, such cover-ups eventually unravel. In June 1995 the notorious case of Nasr Hamid Abu Zayd exposed Egypt's discriminatory laws affecting women and non-Muslims and the disinclination of Egypt's courts to protect citizens' rights or human rights. This Muslim academic was ruled by a court to have become an apostate from Islam – tantamount to being declared a non-person or an outlaw – by reason of allegedly heretical ideas presented in his literary scholarship. Officially reclassified by the court's ruling as a non-Muslim, Abu Zayd found his marriage to his Muslim wife dissolved, a nullification that one might have expected in Iran but that was jarring in the context of a French-inspired legal system run by a regime that Islamists lambasted as heathen for its failure to apply Islamic law. The wishes and feelings of Abu Zayd's wife about her marriage were, naturally, treated by the court as completely irrelevant.

Ultimately, the human rights of Egyptian Muslims are not significantly better protected than are those of Egypt's Christians in a system where any dissenting or independent thought exposes people to prosecution or worse. Islamic specificity is inadequate to account for Egypt's pervasive human rights violations.[10]

Accommodating difference

The triste spectacle of Quebec separatism enables us to separate threats to human rights and citizens' rights that come with identity politics and nation-building from any Islamic specificity. To win support, Quebec separatists pretended that their goal was a multicultural and multilingual nation based on ideals like democracy, tolerance and equality of the sexes.[11] However, occasionally they revealed their true colours, as when Lucien Bouchard lamented that French Quebecers were among the white races that had fewest children, indicating that steps needed to be taken to correct this 'problem'. The racist implications was that in Quebec libre it would become the duty of women to bear children to prevent French Canadians from losing ground demographically to non-white races. After the October 1995 referendum, the tribalistic and exclusionary dimensions of Quebec separatism sprang to the fore. Provincial Prime Minister Jacques Parizeau angrily called out for revenge, blaming the loss on 'money and the ethnic vote'. What Parizeau objected to was not ethnic voting per se, of course, but any group daring to obstruct the realization of a state with a French Canadian identity. His attitude by itself explained why minorities feared to live in a sovereign Quebec pervaded by a primitive ethnic nationalism.

According to the mentality of the Quebec separatists, all who do not espouse the national ideology are demoted to the status of outsiders and women serve as vehicles for producing children to serve an ideological cause. This mentality has, unfortunately, many analogues in other North Atlantic countries, where ideologues have won wide followings via discourses inimical to human rights and full citizenship for all. Managing the dynamics of using specificities like ethnicity and religion to build meaningful political communities without infringing on human rights and citizens' rights turns out to be a problem facing the West, as well.

The realities of our contemporary global society, where peoples of different kinds no longer can live separately and isolated from each other but are forced to reach accommodations with difference, present challenges that did not have to be addressed in the past when people still lived in intact, traditional societies. Accommodating our increasing exposure to diversity necessitates adjustments – although these adjustments are not unprecedented. (After all, in the multicultural Habsburg Empire, Emperor Franz Josef used to address his subjects as 'my peoples', and, in the same era, on the shores of the Bosphorus, the ideal of Ottomanism was espoused by leaders like Prince Sabah al-Din, who likewise aimed at an inclusive definition of citizenship that recognized difference.) These adjustments will not come without difficulty for those who cling to models of ethnic purity and cultural uniformity. Reacting with shock to the disruptive impact of immigrants in Britain, the Tory extremist Stuart Milson recently protested: 'We have had an unnatural multicultural society imposed on us.'[12] Milson's mistake was assuming that multicultural societies are unnatural in present circumstances, when, in reality, the integration of different peoples into a single global community means that henceforth no culture can live in isolation from others. Among other things, Muslim and European cultures must learn to coexist and interact – and to come to terms with the fact that, increasingly, they will be overlapping.

Given this reality, trying to maintain or construct polities based on the notion that difference is illegitimate and should be stamped out can only perpetuate barriers to realizing human rights. In both Western and Muslim countries people need to abandon ideas that all citizens should be compelled to think and act according to a uniform, ideologized version of the national culture. The West is certainly ahead at the moment in terms of accommodating difference where expressions of political dissent by citizens are involved, an area where reforms are urgently needed in Muslim societies. However, both sides need to commit themselves more fully to the principle of equality for all citizens and decent treatment for the non-citizens who often for reasons beyond their control find themselves far from their home countries and dependent on others recognizing the claims of humanity.

Notes

1.   See Mayer (1991) and Martín Muñoz et al. (1994).

2.   See Middle East Watch, 'Saudi Arabia's new Basic Law', 1992, (May), p. 2.

3.   Munif (1989, 85).

4.   Ibid., p. 89.

5.   See Human Rights Watch. Middle East, 'The Bedoons of Kuwait: Citizens Without Citizenship', 1995.

6.   See Mayer (1995, 444).

7.   The Egyptian CEDAW reservation can be found in *Multilateral Treaties deposited with the Secretary-General: Status as at 31 December 1994*. UN Doc. ST/LEG/SER.E/12 (1995), p. 163.

8.   Human Rights Watch. Middle East, 'Violations of Freedom of Religious Belief and Expression of the Christian Minority', 6, no. 2, pp. 20–34.

9.   'In the Face of Criticism, Egypt Sentences 54 Muslim Leaders', *New York Times*, 24 November 1995, p. 12.

10.   The reports by the beleaguered but immensely courageous *Egyptian Organization for Human Rights* provide valuable documentation.

11.   'Adieu Liberal Nationalism', *New York Times*, 2 November 1995, p. A27.

12.   'Wretched Refuse Is Just the Start', *New York Times*, 10 March 1996, p. 4E.

Part Three

The Dialectics of Reason and Faith:
Secularism and Islamism

9

Islam and Secularism

ABDOU FILALI-ANSARI

The relation between Islam and secularism (or Islam and laity) has been debated with surprising regularity over the past century or so. The question is addressed either directly or via related issues. Frequently, comparisons are made between pairs of concepts, e.g. 'Islam' and the 'West', 'Islam' and 'Modernity', 'Islam' and the 'Modern State', etc., in which 'Islam' is a constant that is contrasted with realities taken to be opposed to it. In a certain way, the constant presence of the question of Islam and secularism, or its repeated return to the fore, constitutes a phenomenon worth analysing in its own right. It appears necessary today to analyse both the reasons for the persistency of this question and the build-up of different approaches which it has generated.

This paper does not aim to take stock of the bibliographic material devoted to the question. Neither does it attempt to add new material, data or considerations to the existing debate. More modestly, the aim is to analyse certain approaches to the subject and to initiate an appraisal of certain hypotheses and views adopted by analysts of the question, regardless of whether they come from within the Islamic faith or not.

The Islamic attitude to politics

The most remarkable fact about the different approaches recorded to date is the apparent convergence of the conclusions reached and set out by writers of highly varying backgrounds. Most writers underscore the particularity of the relationship between religion and politics in the Islamic context. Islam is considered almost unanimously as a religion encompassing both the spiritual and the temporal, in which religious piety and the establishing of a given social and political order are thought to be inseparable. According to Abdelmajid Charfi, the most widely held view on this matter is that, unlike Christianity, 'Islam does not recognize the distinction between the sacred and the profane, between the spiritual and the temporal. It is both *din* (religion) and *dawla* (state) without distinction.'[1] For Yadh Ben Achour:

> Islam is a religion of the two cities. It determines a constitutionality in which there is no rift between the political and the religious. It unifies norms and institutions. The law is the embodiment of the faith. The state directs prayers and protects religion, as well as administrating secular society.[2]

Bernard Lewis adds:

> The distinction between Church and State, so deeply rooted in Christianity, did not exist in Islam, and in classical Arabic and other languages drawing their intellectual and political vocabulary from classical Arabic, there are no pairs of words reflecting the distinction between the spiritual and the temporal, the lay and the ecclesiastic, the religious and the secular.[3]

An initial reaction to this could be to ask whether this view stems quite simply from the fact that one particular religion, Christianity, or a certain vision of Christianity, has been set up as a norm or standard by which other religions (including, but not exclusively, Islam) are to be judged. Thus piety considered as something strictly personal and the acceptance that the social and political order is not to be established on the basis of religious concepts are considered *a priori* as normal characteristics of religion and any deviation from the norm is taken *ipso facto* as requiring explanation. In any event, even if such a reaction may appear justified, this in no way diminishes the perceived gulf between the ultimate aim of any religion, viz. providing a system of beliefs and practices geared to the salvation of the soul, and the supposed peculiarity of Islam which is thought to combine this aim with a pre-established conception of the social order. In other words, the model or norm of the religious is indeed present, and the fact of relativizing it or treating it from a historicist standpoint in no way removes the need to address the questions raised by the deviation from the model or norm.

This leads us to the following question: if such a characteristic has been peculiar to Islam since its origins, why has it been necessary to recall, reformulate or indeed rediscover it from new standpoints and in new terms throughout the course of the twentieth century? Could it be that the public to whom such discourse on Islam is directed has difficulty in understanding a system alien to it, because Western society which has established different types of relationship between religion and politics feels a constant need for an explanation of what is perceived as an insurmountable difference? Or could it be that the conditions which prevail at present in Islamic societies raise problems for establishing such a relationship because (expressed in different terms) the (social, political, etc.) environment has become hostile to maintaining a system combining politics and religion? Or should the constant re-occurrence be ascribed to the fact that something does not quite ring true in the perceived image, that some paradox appears to be present which the various attempts at formulating it have been unable to pin down?

To progress in our examination of these questions, it seems necessary to re-appraise our actual concept of Islam. We should not overlook another remark which also arises with striking regularity, i.e. that the concept 'Islam' simultaneously encompasses highly varying elements. Islam refers both to religious beliefs and to a history, i.e. both to a religion and to a civilization. As Mohammed Arkoun notes 'the confusion between Islam as a religion and Islam as the historical framework for the development of a culture and a civilization, has been perpetuated and compounded right up to the present day.' The same author asks: 'Who would dare to describe all European societies under the heading "Christianity and its Civilization" or "The Civilization of Classical Christianity" [the titles of two widely-read works on Islam]?'[4] Thus in discussions of Islam it is clear that the term does not always denote the same reality. There is often indeed a constant, albeit unwitting, to-ing and fro-ing between the two meanings (viz. religious belief and historical reality).

The question which this immediately raises is the following: how far is this point related to the first? How far is the link usually perceived between Islam and politics the consequence of a fact of language, i.e. that people habitually associate the term 'Islam' both with the beliefs constituting the Islamic faith and the actions of those who have adopted such beliefs down the ages? Are we in fact dealing with some sort of 'Kantian category' of the mind, i.e. not merely a question of language but a factor determining *a priori* our perceptions in this field whether we are directly involved (Muslims) or observers (Muslims or non-Muslims)?

Several studies have been undertaken by writers and analysts down the years to show the complex relationship between concepts associated with Islam and the numerous problems (theoretical, social and historical) they raise. Among the attempts to disentangle what appears a highly complex knot of problems, it is worth mentioning one study dating from the beginning of this century which is remarkable for its open, direct approach to a problem which is both simple and yet portentous in its scope, namely: is the association between the religious and the political due to the influence of Islam as a set of beliefs or as a civilization? The Egyptian theologian, Ali Abd al-Raziq (1888–1966) is the author of an essay[5] whose publication marks a major event in contemporary Islamic history and which is considered by most analysts today to be an attempt to address directly the implicit postulate of the 'total continuity' or the 'profound unity' between the principles of the Islamic faith and the historical practices generated by Muslims in the name of those principles. For the first time in the twentieth century Ali Abd al-Raziq questioned the prevalent view that the Prophet created and governed a state during his lifetime, thus establishing a system in which 'politics are practiced in and as part of religion'. How did Ali Abd al-Raziq proceed? What are the possible consequences of his work today? And is his work a marginal contribution to the debate or a key element in the mainstream?

The domains of faith and of history

It is remarkable that this author, unlike most theologians, from the outset avoided any attempt to use verses from the Koran or turns of language to justify *a posteriori* an established fact or more exactly 'fait du prince'. He immediately set out to produce a conclusive demonstration, a genuine *'fasl al-maqal'* in Ibn Rushd's expression, to settle once and for all a question dogged by ambiguity for centuries.

Ali Abd al-Raziq set out initially to review the corpus of sacred texts defining the Islamic creed, viz. the Koran and the *hadith*. His conclusion is very clear and has been known to Muslims from the outset: those texts contain *no injunction* or *any indication whatsoever* for Muslims about any political system or order they should adopt. All one finds in the texts is a certain number of recommendations about morals in the widest sense, but no principles of political life. For example, the texts call for obedience to people in positions of authority, consultation between Muslims, etc.

As Ali Abd al-Raziq notes, theologians down the centuries have had to resort to sometimes highly intricate argumentation to read meanings into the Holy Scriptures and the words of the Prophet and thus try to underpin their theories in the uncontested sources of the faith. Ali Abd al-Raziq then tackled another problem of the Islamic religious heritage stemming from the sacred texts: the practice of the Prophet. As already mentioned, one major argument in favour of a 'political' content of Islam is the reference to the experience at Medina where the Prophet is said to have given an example of an ideal Islamic community which later generations supposedly aimed at (or dreamed of) recreating. To dispel the confusion which is frequent on this subject, Ali Abd al-Raziq analyses one particular – and basic – aspect of any collective experience: the nature of the authority exercised. In a highly original conclusion (which has not received the attention it merits), he proposes a theory of prophecy and its role in history, casting new light on the experience of Medina. The Prophet, we are told, has a kind of authority over his adepts which is quite different from that exercised by temporal potentates, however they accede to power. One could almost speak of a 'prophetic regime', just as one refers to a monarchical or republican regime, were it not for the fact that these latter are geared to self-perpetuation in their established form, whereas the former, by definition, cannot last and aims instead to endure in its substance, or rather to ensure that its message endures.

Similarities between the practice of the Prophet and the political models are, therefore, simply formal or apparent: they indicate absolutely no identity of kind nor indeed the slightest relationship. The early Muslims understood this perfectly. On the death of the Prophet they fully understood that they were beginning a new stage in their collective life and that they faced numerous choices. They actually considered several feasible possibilities which have been recorded in history (a type of monarchy with Ali, a changeover of political power between parties based on the proposal of the *ansars*, an oligarchy in line with tribal customs, etc.), but also other possibilities which have been forgotten and which Ali Abd al-Raziq reminds us of, namely: the separation of the religious and the temporal, and the figure of Malik Ibn Nuwayra, a tribal leader wholly won over to Islam but rejected the very idea of an Islamic state, and who can be considered the first advocate of secularism in Islam.

Ali Abd al-Raziq returns to these crucial moments in Islamic history and beliefs and presents them in a new light. He shows firstly that the problem of power arose within the framework of the *history* of Muslims and not of their creed, and that it refers to historical practices which began *after* the Prophet's death and does not arise from teachings during his lifetime.[6] He shows in particular how a strictly political, temporal power (the power set up immediately after the Prophet's death) literally *annexes* religion and proceeds to invent (or re-invent) a political system which encompasses religion, converting it into a reserved domain under its own control and for its own purposes, as existed in the ancient societies of the Middle East.

Breaks in the history of the Islamic community

Besides these questions, Ali Abd al-Raziq draws our attention to a key aspect of the problem, namely the breaks and turning points in the history of the Islamic community. After the end of the Prophetic message, the history of the Muslim community was experienced not as a uniform continuum but rather as a succession of distinct stages, each with its own meaning. This organization of past time plays a crucial role in determining Islamic consciousness. It must be reconsidered if deep-rooted questions of Islamic awareness are to be understood.

The main turning point in the history of the founding community (the first community or paradigm community) in the awareness of Muslims corresponds to the end of the reign of the so-called 'virtuous caliphs' (*khulafa rashidun*) and the beginning of the first dynasty (the Umayyads). The transition from an order of things where the caliph was co-opted from the Companions of the Prophet to one in which he acceded to power by hereditary transmission was seen by Muslims as a fall, as the loss of what they considered the crux of Islamic legitimacy. The impact on Muslim consciousness was so profound, as Fahmi Jadaane[7] stresses, that it gave rise to a feeling of the equivalent of original sin, a sense of the tragic. It was loss of both innocence and the hope that the promise offered by religion might be realized on Earth. It was the birth of a distinction, of a division, which was to last right up to the present day, the gulf between legitimacy and legality. One monarchical caliphate duly succeeded another, each being accepted as the de facto power, i.e. legal though not genuinely legitimate, thus falling short of authentic Islamic power. Theologians of subsequent generations worked on defining the theoretical framework which would render this situation both intelligible and legally valid.

Ali Abd al-Raziq addresses the problem of the imagined continuity between the Prophet's 'regime' and that of the 'virtuous caliphs' and shows that the political era begins with the death of the Prophet, thus taking away the sacred aura from a period enshrined as a golden age and subsequently converted into a myth and a rallying cry to stir people into action. Thus according to this author, to use the term 'Islamic political regime' is a contradiction in terms: there never has been and never could be such a thing. The break internalized in Muslim consciousness between a legitimate regime and regimes which are merely legal is thus unfounded. From the point of view of religion, the 'religious caliphs' were no more legitimate than their successors. The very idea of political legitimacy based on religion is groundless. It leads to the sacralization of the 'worldly' power of certain men and the mistaken belief that Mohammed's prophecy could somehow be extended beyond his lifetime.

By taking so novel and radical a perspective, Ali Abd al-Raziq highlights a process that has profoundly modelled and shaped the consciousness of Muslims, without their being fully aware of it. He shows that, with Muslims, historical awareness has had a disproportionate, even devastating, effect on their religious faith.

Unfortunately Ali Abd al-Raziq was unable to pursue his research because of the major upheaval his essay caused. He nonetheless opened up a vast field for subsequent study and mapped out the terrain for important future investigation, namely the historical consciousness of Muslims. Such investigation involves a vast re-structuring and in-depth re-organization to show up the main historical turning points in their true light and recognize them as such, that is, as historical transformations which have shaped the contents of Muslim doctrine, and not vice versa.

Implicit constitution and socio-political balance

The work carried out since Ali Abd al-Raziq, from the compendium by Ahmad Amin in the 1930s and 1940s[8] up to the critiques of Arab and Islamic reason and the projects to renew Muslim theology in the 1970s and 1980s, have concentrated on this aspect of the subject, namely how the historical experience of Muslims has changed and shaped their religious views. This has permitted a further achievement: the rediscovery, the recovery by memory, of another major turning point in Islamic history, a turning point which has had the greatest impact on how Muslims conceive and maintain their basic beliefs about the social and political order. I refer to the major controversy or the so-called great discord about the creation of the Koran and the elimination of the Mu'tazilist current which ensued. Mohammed Abed al-Jabri has highlighted the political stakes involved in what might appear to be a purely theological controversy.[9] Marshall Hodgson has shown how society, faced with a political system which seemed to be getting beyond its control, opted for a sacralization of its own norms.[10] The idea of the unconceived Koran which won through as the orthodox vision (or which the masses finally imposed as the only acceptable vision) was a way of freeing the system of norms from manipulation by a political power devoid of genuine legitimacy. By a quirk of history, Mu'tazilism which was most sensitive to the 'rational injunctions' of the Koranic text and the most attached to what constitutes the novelty of the Islamic message compared to other monotheistic revelations, was evinced because it was suspected of being a vehicle of external influences. The opposing conception, on the other hand, adopted because of its alleged 'authenticity' or its faithfulness to the religious heritage, was a direct adaptation of the Platonic doctrine of an eternal archetype of the world. As E. Gellner suggested: 'Plato divinized the word; Islam attributes the word to the deity. This has proved to be socially more effective.'[11] It was during this specific turning point in the history of the Islamic community which saw the birth and the spread of the idea of an 'implicit constitution' of Islam and when the consecration (or sacralization) of the vast corpus built up by the first generations of theologians during the first three centuries of Islamic history occurred. A purely philosophical doctrine, Platonism, thus infiltrated theological notions and, thanks to changes in a society trying to achieve autonomy vis-à-vis the political authority, shaped religious doctrines so far as to become their sole acceptable expression.

Was this a balance characteristic of a strictly medieval society? Was it a redistribution of power whereby religion, initially annexed or expropriated by the political authority, was subsequently retrieved or recovered by society trying to achieve some degree of autonomy? In any event, that balance would be maintained for several centuries until the next major historical break, namely that of modernity, occurred, with the forceful encroachment of an entirely different world causing the strongest impact and posing the most serious challenge which such a system had ever had to face.

The series of transformations which Muslim societies have undergone since the end of the eighteenth century culminate in the triumph of the modern state and the establishment of a vast process of dismantling of traditional structures born out of the medieval balance. In one way, as Abdelmajid Charfi points out, secularization is already an established fact in Muslim societies today.[12] It is already a fact as regards mentalities and as regards the institutions which define the social and political order. Today, no field of practical life is still subject to religious-based norms (with the possible exception of the 'statut personnel' currently under keen debate). As regards perceptions, even the emergence of Islamic fundamentalism can be considered as the expression of secularization, as E. Gellner notes, insofar as it consecrates the elimination of popular religiousness and all the attitudes through which it manifested itself. This can be seen as the end of religion as a body of myths and celebrations often linked to *local* saints and its replacement by religion conceived as a doctrine and rituals with a *universal* validity. Certain observers see in this process a striking similarity with the initial period of the Reformation in the context of Christianity.

Can the elimination of the mythical contents of religion be seen as an initial step towards the adoption of the values and concepts of the modern world? One is tempted to think so. In fact, what we are witnessing today may be the reverse of what has happened in Europe since the sixteenth century. Even if secularization is already a *de facto* reality, the equivalent of the Christian Reformation (understood as an updating of religious perceptions and concepts in line with the requirements of rationality and modern science) is far from having been achieved. The situation is reversed, one could say, if we take the development of modern Western society as a model. Secularization exists, but *without* the Reformation making it acceptable for people's consciousness. This may account for the depth and intensity of the rift felt in contemporary societies on the southern rim of the Mediterranean. On the one hand, the idea of religion as an implicit meta-constitution remains present and active. Today it is generating ideologies of political contestation in ways which recall the medieval cycles described by Ibn Khaldun with a succession of 'revolutionary' regimes fired by the determination to establish a moral and religious order and regimes which have relinquished moral responsibility and aim only to preserve their vested interests. On the other hand, the modern state, the modern economy and the new social strata generated by them are unable to provide themselves with constitutions which would convert them into systems governed by the rule of law. State and economy operate as harsh mechanisms imposed on society.

Medieval constitution as opposed to modern anarchy: is this too schematic a presentation of the situation? The most serious danger in the present context seems to come from spheres currently generating and disseminating views which influence events in the real world, namely areas of research shaping the views of the media and decision makers. A Platonism is at work there in a covert manner. The Islamic community at one point in its history has sacralized concepts and norms based on its religious and political practices. The research community seems in part to be perpetuating this situation even today. It is striving to establish the equivalent of a specific Islamic 'essence' instead of trying to reveal the mechanisms of the transfer from historical practices to the creed. It continues to talk of Islam (with a capital I) as an ideal archetype outside space and time, as an unchanging model influencing or determining reality without being affected by that reality. The extent of the transformations, contradictions and problems endured by societies, of which religious formulations are no more than a reflection, has been forgotten. Here may lie the paradox of current concepts and the reason why they need to be constantly reiterated, reformulated and, possibly, refurbished.

Notes

1. Charfi (1982, 59).
2. Ben Achour (1992, 15).
3. Lewis (1988).
4. Arkoun (1989, 18 & 31).
5. *Al-Islam wa-sul al-hukm.*
6. W. C. Smith has some interesting remarks on this subject: 'We would suggest ... that the historical process in general is special for Islam: the Islamic conception of history is unique, and in some ways history is more significant for Muslims than it is for almost any other group.' He adds, 'As we have said, the truth has been disclosed before. What was momentous, superbly creative in this instance, was the event plus its sequel: the application of the truth, its living embodiment in human history from this point. Here was not a restatement of what God has to say to us, but a society developing around that restatement: a society that, grasping firmly the injunctions which are there revealed, dedicates itself to living up to them, and thereby sets forth on the reconstruction of human life on earth', (1957, 6 & 14–15).
7. Jadaane (1981).
8. Amin (1929, 1933–36, 1945–52, 1952).
9. Abed al-Jabri (1990b).
10. Hodgson (1993).
11. Gellner (1981, 22).
12. Charfi, op.cit.

10

Relations Between Europe and Islamists

TARIQ RAMADAN

The end of the twentieth century is a time of considerable upheaval and the signs are that we are heading towards a new kind of conflict between Western and Islamic civilizations. Writers and analysts have developed various theses to describe this balance of power, or state of war, and to many the future seems grim. A more optimistic view is feasible, however, and it is to be hoped that, instead of conflict, the two civilizations will develop both a genuine dialogue and a constructive relationship. But the fact remains that today there is little to convince us that such hope is well founded.

It is essential to follow the path of dialogue and develop possibilities for mutual encounter and recognition. The task is demanding and requires from both the West and the Muslim world the acceptance of the presence of the other, the recognition of its own specificity and especially the need to overcome prejudice and caricatures which are projected on to the other culture.

The awakening of Islam

The West is witnessing the 'awakening of Islam' with certain trepidation. Bombarded with pictures of the Iranian Revolution, events in Algeria, the bombings by the Palestinians and daily news coverage of Muslim worship we tend to lose our bearings and find it difficult to analyse this 'new phenomenon'. This is clear from the terminology we use. Since 1979 the terms 'fanatics', 'fundamentalists' and 'Islamists' are used almost daily by the media without any clear understanding of their meaning. We no longer know, for example, whether the

Muslim who prays five times a day or the veiled Muslim woman are practising believers or potential extremists. Confusion reigns, concepts get muddled and sweeping generalizations take over.

Islam in general and Islamism in particular appear as a threat because all too often the West does not understand the forces traversing the Muslim world. Superficial analysis is all too common and the mobilization of Muslims is all too frequently reduced to its most radical manifestations. No mention is made of the development of reformist thought over the last century. The works of philosophers and thinkers are rarely read. Little is known about the underlying debates currently taking place in the Muslim world. Emotional reactions take the place of considered analysis. The dictators in Islamic countries have no difficulty in using this for their own ends, portraying their opponents as extremists hostile to Western values, thereby attempting to legitimize harsh repression. The West, meanwhile, turns a blind eye.

The stated intentions and actions of radical movements do give genuine cause for alarm. It is essential that violence in all its forms be condemned: both the violence of radical movements and of the regimes in power must be condemned outright. But condemnation alone is not enough and our analysis must go beyond this and attempt to further our understanding of what is known as 'Islamism' today. This involves not only analysing present-day reality but also the historical background.

The historical background

To understand the phenomenon of what is termed 'Islamism' today requires making a reappraisal of history, at least since the end of the nineteenth century when the movement called the Nahda (renaissance) was born. Certain philosophers of this movement were to exert considerable influence on the development of political thought in the twentieth century. This is the case with Jamal al-Din al-Afghani (died 1897) who, in the course of his frequent exiles and travels, called for a far-reaching reform of Islamic thought as well as the social, political and economic structures in Islam. With the Ottoman Empire in decline, al-Afghani's aim was to devise specifically Islamic answers to the questions of modernity and in this sense attain liberation from both institutional and cultural influences from the West. In his day, Jamal al-Din al-Afghani had to face criticism from the pillars of 'official Islam' who were submissive to the Powers and defended a traditionalist Islam. His disciple and companion Abduh (died 1905) and then Rashid Rida pursued his work defining the factors involved in the contemporary problem of Islam. The aim was to develop a new reading of the Koran and the traditions of the Prophet (*hadith*) and liberate the dynamic forces of Islamic renaissance and independence.

The contribution of these intellectuals is essential reading for anyone aiming to understand the true nature of the re-awakening of political Islam. While Europe at the time reigned supreme on all fronts, they called for mobilization against imperialism and for a two-fold liberation: a total liberation in the field of politics and a selective liberation in the cultural sphere. They affirmed the need to keep what was compatible with the references of Islam considered as a religion and a civilization. Accordingly, the mobilizing verse of the Koran (13–11) was 'God changes nothing in the state of a people before the people change what is within themselves'.

This question was taken up by Muslim thinkers in the early twentieth century, setting the debate clearly on the intellectual plane as well as in the social, political and economic spheres. After returning to India after a stay in Europe, Muhammad Iqbal (died 1938), published a highly critical analysis of the Turkish options at the beginning of the century, reproaching them for their 'slavish imitation' of the West. He distinguished, as most Islamists would do subsequently, between the struggle for independence and nationalist aspirations. This latter was seen as an imported Western concept: 'Turks, Iranians, Arabs, all intoxicated by Europe'. It was essential to create solidarity on a transnational basis. In Algeria, Ibn Badis (died 1940), having visited Egypt at the age of 24 and after several years working as a teacher and journalist, took the path of the reformists and proposed a new, more easily accessible commentary of the Koran. As the prominent leader of the independence movement, he sought to create a party, the 'Hizb al-Islah' ('Party of Reform') and in 1931 finally founded the 'Association des Ulémas'. Between 1931–40 he launched an elementary religious education programme, organized literacy campaigns and a vast social action movement throughout Algeria, setting up local committees of the 'Association des Ulémas'. Subsequently considered a threat by France because of his calls to resist French colonial occupation, this religious activist was placed under house arrest by the Algerian administration acting on the orders of Paris and his newspaper banned. He died in mysterious circumstances in 1940.

In Egypt, the Muslim Brothers spread the word of reformist Islam most widely. This movement, set up in 1928, developed very quickly in the Egyptian countryside before its founder, Hasan al-Banna, moved to Cairo. Taking up the thought of the founding intellectuals of the Nahda, al-Banna attempted to spread the idea of a return to Islamic values while, at the same time, undertaking educational and social work throughout Egypt. In the 1930s the political strategy of the Muslim Brothers, based on Islamic references, crystallized and went on to become highly effective in the early 1940s. Certain aspects of the Brothers' creed, which still make up their platform today, may be highlighted: Islam is both a 'religion' (in the sense Christianity is) and a 'civilization' (in the sense of a culture). The Koran and the *sunna* are its main points of reference providing the sources for the *shari'a*. It is important not to 'sacralize' the work of the wise men of Muslim *fiqh* (jurisprudence) who were responding to the circumstances of their time.

The Koran and the *sunna* only provide the major outlines of legislation, or more exactly indicate the spirit for updating legislation. The application of the *shari'a* (literally meaning 'the way') entails a very broad view of social reality and cannot fail to take into account time and place. This principle of adaptation is recognized in the *ijtihad* (effort of judgment) to which the wise men, specialists and politicians must apply themselves by a new reading of the Koran and the *sunna* and real knowledge and awareness of the societies in question.

The first phase of applying the *shari'a* should involve a process of social reform with the aim of restoring very basic rights to the people. Education, together with the need for involvement in the struggle for social justice, is the watchword of the Muslim Brothers. There was never any question in al-Banna's texts of reducing the *shari'a* to the status of a criminal code. The application of this code has several prerequisites, primarily that a society has reached a sufficient level of social justice and individual responsibility.

Starting from a clearly reformist stance, this view of Islam determined the political options of the Muslim Brothers. Commitment is first and foremost social. The members of the association were organized in sectors and carried out multiple actions at local level, preaching, educating and fostering social solidarity. Around 1945 no less than forty members' cooperatives had been formed, operating as service providers or associations to avoid interest-bearing loans. On the political front the Brothers organized the movement against British colonial rule. Following al-Banna's first arrest in October 1941, there was a crackdown on the association which for the first time had to reconsider its social action strategy. In 1943, district networks were set up working with a lower profile.

This was the beginning of a crackdown which was tightened under post-independence regimes. The various processes leading to the anti-colonial struggle were misinterpreted in Europe and the main actors involved were not properly identified. The history books have dated the events and listed the main actors in the power struggle – Nasser, Bourguiba, Ben Bella, etc., whose names were synonymous with the liberation of peoples under colonial rule. Clearly, the reformist Muslim leaders succeeded in mobilizing the key sectors of the population who would prove the most active. The Muslim Brothers and the Association des Ulémas (the *mujahidun*) are the two most striking examples, though not the only ones. Once it became clear that independence was inevitable, Britain and France sought out interlocutors in the respective countries and did not hesitate to participate in the campaign of mystification to thwart the pretensions of leaders and movements judged 'too Islamic' who had fought both for political liberation and for just recognition of their Muslim identity (they were 'Islamists' in the current meaning of the word). It soon became clear to the Islamists that the so-called 'liberators', while laying claim to the benefits of the struggle for independence, were betraying the initial objectives of the movement.

A glaring example of this is the case of Egypt which saw the birth of a new Islamist political platform of the kind being updated today. In the 1940s Nasser espoused the views of the Muslim Brothers with whom he appeared in public and to whom he claimed to belong. He was aware that at that time the association was the most popular and best organized opposition force. Once in power, however, Nasser did not hesitate to re-establish contacts with the former British colonialists (1954 agreements) and to use exceptionally harsh methods to repress his former allies who for reasons of expediency he dubbed as 'terrorists jeopardizing the social order'. Despite his switching alliances in the international sphere, repression (including executions) was a constant feature of his domestic policy with the tacit agreement of the great powers who were quick to see where their interests lay.

The birth of radicalism

Radicalism was born out of this repression. Death sentences, prison and exile gave rise to the first signs of disagreement amongst Islamist militants. Very quickly two movements emerged with differing views on two key points: political strategy and the definition and application of the *shari'a*.

Noting that the new liberators of Islamic nations were even harsher and more unjust than the colonialists from whom they had struggled to free themselves, certain militants advocated, and used Islam to justify, the armed struggle to free Muslim countries from these despots. Small groups formed in Egypt and Algeria, for example, calling for an overthrow of the party in power. This political strategy frequently took root in the humblest sectors of society, e.g. in Upper Egypt. Its programme often took the form of a call for the immediate literal application of the criminal code of the *shari'a*. Today these groups account for a very small minority within the Islamist movement even if they and their high-profile actions make the front pages and obtain media coverage around the world.

The vast majority of socially and politically committed intellectuals have, however, remained true to the initial reformist line. They do not consider their social, political and economic activities to be directed against the West (many of them have lived in the West and know it well), even if they stress that they wish to build their societies differently and remain true to their religion, their culture and their civilization. They form the contemporary Islamist mainstream which is made up of various movements and a large number of independent intellectuals and is to be found in all Muslim countries today. Led by university teachers, the movement's popularity is undeniable and constitutes today the most credible opposition force in Indonesia, Syria, Iraq, Saudi Arabia, Jordan, Egypt, Algeria, Libya, Morocco, Tunisia, Turkey and in the Palestinian territories. Acting within the law, militants shun political violence, organize themselves in political parties if this is possible, and defend the idea of applying the *shari'a* in its progressive interpretation. The first stage of this involves improvement in standards of living (literacy, social justice, etc.), respect for the principle of general elections (*shura*) and the establishment in stages of an alternative basic economy with no speculation or interest.[1] Without exception they are opposed to the traditionalism of certain official Muslim scholars and state institutions.

Europe today should recognize the existence of these movements and avoid sweeping the condemnation and anathematization of those who take Islam as a reference for building their society of the future and who are indiscriminately labelled 'Islamists'. It is essential that all those wishing to build a decent future should study the terrain, consider the nuances in differing views and enter into discussion with Muslims determined to follow the legal course of action. For their part, Islamists must multiply contacts with people in positions of responsibility in the West by combating caricatures presenting the West as totally Machiavellian, which are all too widespread in the Muslim world.

What dialogue?

All too often Muslims confuse the West with the Christian world and consider pêle-mêle Humanists, atheistic Communists and virtually all intellectuals as the supporters, or indeed henchmen or disguised accomplices, of the strategy of the North. The countries of the South with a majority Christian population, Western non-governmental organizations, journalists or intellectuals – all are branded as suspicious and Islam is seen as the enemy of them all. Such sentiments are common in the Muslim world, as well as in minority Muslim communities in the West: they reveal a genuine misunderstanding of reality and a lack of maturity as regards the need for dialogue.

The same applies to virtually all alternative, so-called 'left-wing' movements in Europe and the United States. Militant Islam worries them. They were in favour of independence from colonial rule and frequently participated in the struggle for that independence with their socialist comrades south of the Mediterranean, with whom they share the same ideals, the same analyses and the same terminology. However, since yesterday's partisans have become today's dictators or have been eliminated, who is there now to support? The credible popular opposition no longer speaks the same language but refers to religion, morals and culture, using other words, other expressions and disconcertingly different turns of mind. Rather than seeking understanding of this within the references of the other civilization, Westerners make what seems the obvious comparison and infer that in religious terms the awakening of Islam is a return to our Middle Ages. Rejection soon ensues as well as mistrust and self-reassuring simplifications. It is difficult to expect anything else from committed men and women who have been working in grass-roots communities in South America and Africa: for some, the fear of Islam is ancestral and deep-rooted; for others, they are competing with Islam in the conversion of souls; for many, it is the Western media which almost exclusively shape their political views and their analysis of the situation.

All of this bodes a difficult relationship, a dialogue of the deaf. The responsibility for this is shared. We must, however, insist at this time on the need to build bridges between the varying experiences of popular movements in the countries of the South. Anyone who has worked in the field in grass-roots communities, developing social and economic strategies at local level, is bound to be surprised at the similarities they reveal with experiences in Muslim countries. The references vary, as do the fields of application, but the philosophy is the same and it derives its inspiration from the same source, that is, resistance to the blind interests of the major powers and the multinationals. This is not to assert the reality of some idealized, self-satisfied Islamic Third World philosophy echoing the northern version we have known for years. Rather, Islam, insofar as it is the point of reference for committed Muslims, expresses itself through the same demand for dignity, justice and pluralism that has shaped Christian and humanist movements. For this reason, therefore, if for no other, relations should be multiplied and exchanges of experience permanent. Since the 1940s Muslims have conducted a multitude of experiments in types of social integration and researched the feasibility of alternative local economies operating without interest or usury, e.g. partnerships; and in the late 1960s, the movement set up by liberation theology following on from Vatican II adopted the same lines. In both cases the aim is to defend an idea of the human being, his dignity, and his rights and duties. The writings of Cardinal Gutierrez and Leonardo Boff and the firm declarations of Dom Helder Camara, former archbishop of Recife, are bound to find a favourable echo among Muslims, if only they take the time to study them. Likewise, if liberation theologians and their Christian and humanist supporters in Europe were to take the time to study the formal claims of Muslims, they could not but share their aspirations. Are they familiar, for example, with the ideas of Sa'id al-Nursi in Turkey, Ibn Badis in Algeria, Muhammad Iqbal in India, Hasan al-Banna in Egypt, Abd al-Salam Yassin, Malik Bennabi, Abu'l-Hasan al-Nadawi and so many other Muslim intellectuals and militants who have defended the cause in countries ranging from Morocco to India?

Supporters of these views are responsible for this mutual ignorance. Links should be developed among theologians, intellectuals, associations, organizations and cooperatives. Scattered centres of resistance, unaware and mistrustful of each other, are in fact acting in an irresponsible manner. The wasted energy, pointless conflicts, the divisions allowed to persist, the ignorance that is perpetuated ignorance in such situations, are extremely harmful and only benefit the major powers and the dictators. Media coverage, tendentious and unfounded mistrust (denounced so often and by so many) eventually wear down our commitments just when most caution is required. All too often on both the Muslim and the Christian and Humanist side people take the easy option, turning in on themselves, and their precious certainties, abandoning any attempt to communicate and resorting to anathema and exclusion. This occurs despite calls for dialogue and the need to listen to each other. People speak at, not to, each other. In fact, however, genuine dialogue between Jews, Christians, Humanists and Muslims could not fail to generate a powerful movement of resistance to human folly, injustice and exploitation. Anything short of that would be 'parlour religion' or 'congress humanism'. Fine sentiments – in meetings, around dinner tables, or wherever – are empty words which are no credit to those voicing them. The human content is often forgotten whenever such sentiments are expressed.

Not mistaking the enemy

The aim is not to share the same ideals and the same hopes. God wanted diversity, and there must be pluralism and mutual respect. It is urgent that we clearly state what we refuse and define what we find unacceptable. This entails committing ourselves to ensuring that the unacceptable is not in fact accepted and does not end up becoming normal and commonplace. In a world in which the economic has gained the ascendancy over the political, where financial and commercial interests determine state policy, and where values are mentioned only if they do not stand in the way of deals or contracts, however dubious, we must not mistake our enemy. We must join forces with those for whom the life of an individual has both meaning and value, those who refuse to accept folly and murder and choose to defend faith, respect, dignity, fraternity and love.

This awakening of consciousness and the search for union should, however, be accompanied by greater vigilance. Until such time as people in the West seek to achieve a deeper understanding of Muslim claims for respect for their religion, their civilization and their culture and understand that to this end Muslims are endeavouring, albeit falteringly, to develop a blueprint for a society which is authentically their own. The chances of real cooperation are slim, as is the hope for a transition avoiding a clash between two civilizations. It is often the more 'progressive' sectors of society who are said to be most vehement in their views about Islam and what is commonly called the 'Islamic reawakening'. Their judgments are clear cut and free from nuance, often hasty 'black-and-white' pronouncements reflecting a lack of time devoted to studying the question or listening to people from other civilizations. Sweeping generalizations and indiscriminate judgments are commonplace. Committed Muslims are portrayed as necessarily armed and viscerally patriarchal terrorists and misogynists. It is inconceivable that there could be common ground, common demands or a similar respect for life and values. Playing into the hands of the major powers, the defender of justice, values and humanism identifies his enemy in the other civilization as someone who in fact defends the same justice, the same values and the same concept of mankind. Conflict arises where there should be dialogue. The same intellectual bankruptcy is present in Muslims who, as we have seen, treat the West as a monolithic block, a generator of conflicts, where not a single man or woman is untainted by moral perdition, materialism, violence or corruption. This view is not only exaggerated; it is erroneous, misleading and false. It fails to take into account the millions of men and women who give their time, energy and sometimes even their lives to change things and it overlooks the millions of human beings who suffer for the state of the world and in their solitude, helplessness and confusion, clutch at straws simply to survive. Furthermore, it ignores the rights, the areas of liberty and the recognition of dignity offered to citizens in the West and the fact that a tiny fraction of these would be welcome progress in Muslim countries. These realities have to be recognized and faced.

It is not possible for us to go on caricaturing each other and brandishing extremist simplifications. For sincere Muslims, as for Jews, Christians and humanists, the real struggle is against the concept of 'reason of State' and the inhuman economic strategies implemented by the industrial powers, the IMF or the Gulf States; it is against the dictatorships in Tunisia, Syria, Egypt and elsewhere, and against social exclusion, poverty, delinquency and drugs in the United States, France, Spain, Belgium, the United Kingdom, etc. We must not forget the need to recognize the right of others to decide on their faith, their values, their projects for society, and their legitimate wish to return to the living sources of their religion, to preserve their spirituality, their culture and their civilization and to live out their identity with full respect. To see others solely in terms of one's own set of references and consider differences as deviations is simplistic and dangerous. Prejudice is almost always worse than recognition of one's ignorance. To think one knows and to simplify is tantamount to an admission of self-satisfaction and laziness. It is perhaps our greatest common enemy.

Fears

It would be disingenuous to predict a better, safer future for us and our planet by blinding ourselves to the real state of the world and of relations between Islam and the West. We may not share Huntington's view but in any event we must be lucid. We are at a crossroads and our epoch is crucial. The tension is perceptible. Not a day goes by without reference being made to Islam, Muslims and the 'threat of Islamic fundamentalism'. We are justified in fearing the worst. The clash between civilizations is not simply theoretically possible, because the signs of potential rifts are already visible. This reality must be faced and we must be aware of the dangers at a time when being a Muslim, a practising Muslim, is almost a fault in itself in the eyes of Westerners. They have heard so much about the 'Islamic or the Islamist threat' (who would be capable of defining those terms exactly?) that the world of Islam appears as something suspect, troubling, hostile. The rift is just as much in people's minds as in the geo–political and economic arenas.

There is a real cause for concern. And over the coming decades, we will no doubt see a deepening of certain basic divisions between the two civilizations. The most striking aspect is certainly the different status accorded to religion in the respective societies. Western culture, which has done so much to free itself of dogma, finds difficulty in accepting the return onto the social and political stage of 'the religious'. When this phenomenon affects specific dependent ethnic groups (Yanomanis, Sioux, etc.), major upheavals are not to be feared. But when Islam is involved, things are different. Because of Islam's considerable influence, the number of Muslims, the strategic stakes involved, the balance of power and the historical legacy, religious manifestations in the Muslim world have other, objective consequences for the West. Of course, officially concern is expressed about 'extremism' but closer analysis reveals that the source of the problem is the religious frame of reference. To speak of God and seek to express the meaning of one's faith in one's life raises a problem of 'order' for many Europeans and Americans, especially if vast sections of the world's population express their *identity* in this way. This affirmation of the *tawhid* (transcendence) on such a large scale shakes the liberal universe to its roots.

The second focus of tension relates specifically to the hegemony of Western culture. The progress achieved (scientific, technical, etc.), the rights and 'universal values' recognized and the completed processes of secularization come face to face with a symbolic universe which *de facto* relativizes the extent of that achievement. Islamic civilization, with its references to the Koran and the traditions of the Prophet, its conception of the world and of mankind, cannot be reduced to the cultural, terminological or semantic categories of the United States or Europe. Of course, attempts have been made to inundate the countries of the South with productions from the North, but the populations involved – be they intellectuals educated in the West or the poorest of the poor – react very strongly when allusion is made to elements of their 'intuitive culture'. Deep down they remain attached in their highly specific way to their faith in God, their religion, their civilization and their culture. Attitudes obviously vary with levels of education. People from the humblest backgrounds tend to express their feeling of identity in the most forthright or even violent way, whereas people with a university background tend to manifest more subtle, nuanced or developed views. Across the board, however, religious and cultural references play a key role. For the first time in centuries it has even become possible to contest the culture based on science and material progress. The tension is well founded.

The same apprehension manifests itself at the political level. For some years, people have become aware of the transnational phenomenon of so-called 'Islamist' movements. Some thought they were groups manipulated by certain states such as Saudi Arabia or Iran which provide funding for 'fundamentalist' activities. However, serious analysis has shown this to be a simplification. There are indeed many Muslims today who echo Islamic political claims expressed by opposition groups who abhor violence and wish to use only legal methods. The regimes in power are aware of the fact that these movements are highly representative and use sweeping generalizations to confuse the issue and prevent their participation in genuine democratic elections. The phenomenon can be observed in virtually all Muslim countries. What was thought to be the awakening of the 'have-nots' is proving to be a broad-based movement of intellectuals with extensive popular backing opposed to the regimes in power but also to Western policies of supporting dictatorships and unfair management of resources. Today, in a quite concrete manner, South–South alliances centred on Islamic references have become feasible. The major powers are clearly aware of this and realize that major interests are at stake. To justify their policies, they resort to the strategy of satanization: Islam, allegedly, is a return to past ages, committed Muslims are considered obscurantist or suspect, and Muslim women suffer outright discrimination. The list is well known. But behind this portrayal of Islam, major interests are at stake and the intentions of those painting this picture are highly pernicious. The aim is to justify policies aimed at supporting dubious regimes and gaining spheres of influence. Wars are encouraged, breaches of law overlooked, etc. One is bound to recognize today that the strategy of the major powers has borne its fruits but no-one can be sure that the consequences can be controlled. The phenomenon of radicalization, which has been encouraged, promoted and used as a pretext to account for political decisions, threatens to get out of hand and generate confrontation in the future for which the West will bear the largest responsibility.

In this context one cannot overstress the key (sometimes dangerous) role played by the media. The control of information on a large scale constitutes a source of enormous power which today has fallen to a mere handful of news agencies, overwhelmingly Western, which inevitably present a certain viewpoint on the state of the world. Images, sound bites and speed have gained ascendancy over in-depth analysis and overall understanding. Simplification and caricature has taken over when there is an urgent need for nuance, level-headedness and balance to give account of a complex reality. The media shape public opinion and arouse fears. Today it is television which 'creates an issue' about which people, even university graduates, are called on to express their views. We are all aware of this and we all undergo the consequences. But very few people can get away from the pressure, indeed the oppression, of the media and think through their own analysis of the situation, with perspective and free from the imposition of 'topical issues'. Today tension between Islam and the West has become such a 'topical issue' about which sweeping statements are made. One ends up 'forgetting' that Islam is a religion, a spirituality, a universe of meaning and a philosophy of life, because the TV pictures do not show that. However, when we see threatening images and the commentator hints that Islam is above all 'a threat', we believe it (we *know* what we have *seen*). If Sufism is still today more or less 'in favour', it is because it is not really quite Islam: isolated and remote, it is not disturbing for anybody. Some journalists, to be fair, do attempt to provide a balanced, in-depth analysis. They are committed and understand what is at stake. The feeling that 'something is being hidden', that reality is not what the media coverage suggests and that collusion is frequent between the Western powers, the multinationals, the arms trade and the dictators in the countries of the South. It is not infrequent for shares in the media to be owned by arms manufacturers. The media' interpretation of the world is not 'innocent' and their commitments are not gratuitous. Certain journalists, analysts and intellectuals do, thankfully, spurn such cynicism and self-interest. When fears and retrenchment abound, such a stance offers a welcome glimmer of hope.

Reasons for hope

Reasons for hope exist, provided goodwill is forthcoming. Many concerns are shared by theologians, intellectuals and the population at large in both Western and Muslim countries. Without downplaying the differences between the religious frames of reference, cultural backgrounds and social, political and economic patterns in the respective countries, men and women of goodwill will find common ground for action allowing them to move beyond mere dialogue to adopt a common commitment and a common stance.

In the Muslim world, as in the West, one finds individuals, thinkers and politicians who are content with the present state of affairs who seek to justify such and such a policy by reference to the Islamic tradition or the liberal ideal, not baulking at justifying the worst horrors or the basest betrayals of the revealed message or egalitarian principles. Such people do exist and there are many of them. However, there are also men and women with a conscience and quite different aspirations, whose prime qualities are intellectual honesty and clear-sightedness about what we are being offered under the title of 'the new world order'. The forces in Western societies opposed to and struggling against 'scientism', 'economicism', the technological society and unbridled, aimless 'progress' will find partners in the Muslim world whose existence they had not even suspected. The need for a framework of references, values and purpose which forms the basis of Islamic culture centred on the notion of the *tawhid* is echoed in these times of crisis by Western questioning about meaning and ethics. The aim is not to find the same answers since, as we have seen, plurality is an objective element in creation and in the present state of the world. Rather, the purpose is to find a common front to resist soulless liberalism which considers it normal that today's world order imposes 'sacrifices' and that, accordingly, people will have to be sacrificed. After the hopes kindled by 'development' in the 1960s and 1970s, we have now entered the age of 'cynical realism' whose main characteristic is that it leaves no room for illusions. This fatalism and abdication of responsibilities, this grim colonization of people's minds is the real peril the West faces today, not communism or liberalism or the 'barbarians'. Progressive movements in the South, fired by faith and/or their belief in mankind and humanism, can join forces with those last voices in the North calling for an awakening. These sources of energy must meet and encourage and enrich each other.

Undoubtedly social justice must be the first field of action. Islam could not accept a world in which such deep rifts exist in society. And many social actors agree that such serious dislocation in society is not acceptable. Cooperation is possible in specific, concrete ways and relations between Muslims living in Western societies and Europeans and Americans should make a dialogue on the complex terrain of the South possible. The way forward is difficult and there is no place for naive optimism. Each day brings its share of disappointments and setbacks in the relations between the two civilizations. The gate is narrow, but anyone moved by religious faith or profound convictions knows that living means assuming this kind of challenge.

The West is experiencing a return to the question of meaning. The awakening of ethical concerns, ecological problems and recognition of the limits of progress and growth herald the advent of a new era. The manifestations of new forms of religiosity are multiplying: sects, mystical groups, conversions, the widespread presence of Oriental traditions, especially Buddhism, etc. Young people are expressing new needs and metaphysical and cultural concerns are back in vogue. The times are changing. Some have interpreted 'the extreme movements' in this direction as a 'revenge of God'. In any event it seems that in all societies it is the expression of something lacking. It is easy to see the extent of this phenomenon in our daily lives, regardless of whether we welcome it or decry it. The present world order, the current aimlessness and daily injustices are all crying out for an urgent reaction. If the current crisis and malaise generate a reaction, it can be hoped that the remedy will spring from the illness itself. Perhaps then people will look to 'other horizons', religious and cultural, to discover a universe with positive meaning and invigorating ethical challenges which in a spirit of plurality can help change the world. Islam is a civilization still fired by a feeling for the sacredness of the world, it is morally demanding, ecological in its essence, humanist by revelation, and present and meaningful in the hearts of more than a thousand million human beings. As we have said, it is a civilization ready to participate in the changing world of the future – a future that will be peaceful if the tendency to anathematize can be controlled and conflictual if arrogance, self-satisfaction and untruth persist.

For Muslims, being in contact with God means endeavouring day by day to give meaning to what Islam calls *rabbaniyya* (being for God).

It means working for peace – with all the force of one's being. And by the same token, it means resisting injustice and untruth. For those not satisfied with mere words, peace founded on injustice and untruth is not peace: it is an abdication of conscience. In the relations between the two civilizations it is not possible to settle for sham or pretence. Equity is essential and transparency a duty. One would like to believe that awareness will dawn, albeit faintly, before the catastrophe occurs. Our hope is based on minute signs, however rare. Our duty is not to abdicate. Plurality is a testing ground for mankind. It puts our faith and our consciousness to the test and it marks out the path of our dignity.

Notes

1.   An impressive number of studies have been conducted on these possibilities by Muslims around the world.

11

Islamism and Some of its Perceptions of the West

MOHAMMED TOZY

The phenomenon of Islamism has existed for almost twenty years. This is perhaps not a sufficient lapse of time for analysts to come to definitive conclusions about its theoretical characterization or to completely avoid errors due to fascination with the phenomenon on initial contact. Over the last 15 years the Islamist movement has offered analysts a fairly wide spectrum of sensitivities, development scenarios and doctrinal output. It is now possible to observe, describe and analyse Islamist movements in all their phases of development and in highly varying contexts ranging from authoritarian regimes hostile to all thought of progress to political systems where competition between parties is controlled. In certain countries, e.g. Iran, Sudan or Pakistan, they are actually in power, while in others they are more or less integrated into the political system and have their parliamentary representatives, e.g. Turkey, Jordan or Egypt.

Islamist literature provides a highly nuanced corpus of doctrine, allowing us to distinguish between political fundamentalism and the policy of the fundamentalists, that is, the positions adopted by fundamentalist movements in a particular historical context, geared to meet the challenge of the circumstances and, as an overriding priority, achieve power, as well as actual political practice once power has been achieved. The ageing of the movement comes across in the clearly noted transition from a 'prophetic', missionary type literature characterized by a total, radical and often simplistic view of the question of power to another view which is more nuanced and political as a result of the years spent learning the logic of political activism. Moreover, the natural position of these 'new ecclesiastics' freed from the heritage of traditionalist *ulama* places the clerics and the 'Islamist'

153

professionals of politics back in a position of leadership each time that established systems have integrated Islamists into the political sphere. The 'Thermidorization'[1] of the Iranian Revolution heralds the likely normalization of other movements of this type although we must not downplay the specific features of what is a new political culture or forget that the movement is being created by new generations whose characteristics it is difficult for their Western partners to understand and whose practices may appear atypical.

As time passes and the Islamist movement endures, it is taking its distance from part of its recent historical heritage, in particular that of the Muslim Brothers. It generates its own landmarks, its own references and its own heroes. It manifests thus a broad range of sensitivities shaped for the most part within national borders and on the basis of problems rooted in modern times.

A relatively large part of this study looks at the movement's relationship with the West in general and Europe in particular, and we will see the extent of this variety of sensitivities. The movement is becoming aligned on ideological forms of contestation and gradually proceeding to lose its original singularity and adopt a more serene approach.

Islamism: becoming part of everyday life

The phenomenon under consideration is a religious movement with unusual sociological characteristics (young people in schools, a recently urbanized population). It can provisionally be characterized as fundamentalist since it expresses itself either through an open prophecy or through an (equally prophetic) re-appropriation of original religions, that is, a solitary act renouncing links with the religious establishment.

North Africa has not escaped this intervention by men of religion in the running of the city. Paradoxically, it was the state which called on the *ulama* to legitimize the party or group in power.[2] Their appearance on the political scene in the early 1980s was no surprise. The clerics first occupied the mosques and used Friday prayers as a forum to denounce the inadequacies of the powers that be and harangue the crowds, then subsequently led the process of political change as in the case of (firstly) Egypt, then Algeria, Morocco and Tunisia.

On the whole, analysts have been negative in their appraisal of this encroachment of the religious on the political sphere. Some considered it a return to obscurantism and fanaticism. But subsequently views have evolved. The resurgence of a rational, reasoned sacred sphere on the basis of highly developed religious expressions can no longer be seen as something archaic or a timid reaction to an irreversible process of modernization, but rather as a phenomenon accompanying the crisis of a state which has also failed in its function of allocating resources and regulating competing areas of interest.

The proliferation of religious movements and manners of expression is a partial consequence of this situation. More than any other factor, it reflects the widespread wish for a redefining of the boundaries of a new, modern political sphere to account for, and give meaning to, the survival strategies of new social groups frequently cut off from their community roots and subject to the requirements of social, spatial and economic mobility. The 1970s marked a watershed in the transition from an agrarian system based on a minority having the monopoly of writing[3] backed by a distinction between high and low culture, rigid social stratification, and the predominance of the rural life style to an industrial society characterized by compulsory education for all, a questioning of traditional social stratification as well as social and spatial mobility. As defined today, modernity is no longer an attribute of a disenchanted world but rather the object of a strategy of appropriation moving along prophetic paths opened up by Islamists amongst others.

If one takes the analytic approach of opposing disenchanted modernization with religious archaism, in other words, lumping together in the same category ideals of modernity and the work of modernity within social structures, data gathered sociographically are automatically disconnected from the instruments of interpretation. Most analysts of the religious revival face this problem. All of them find that the leaders of and actors in the renewal process and the populations targeted manifestly operate within the sphere of modernity, while at the same time designating it as the main enemy. Closer scrutiny reveals that their struggle is targeted more at the signs, rather than the content, of modernity and that they favour a reformulation/recreation of that modernity.

Islamism, rebuilding an identity, and modernity

The explanation in terms of an identity crisis as developed at length in François Burgat's thesis[4] is too enticing to be rejected out of hand. The idea of a 'third stage of the decolonization rocket', however, over-stresses a certain continuity and is incapable of taking into account the rift between generations. Furthermore, Islamism is seen as turning into a war machine to conquer an identity which has been lost or at least betrayed by politicians involved with the West. While it is difficult to deny the existence of a project to rebuild an identity, it is fairly obvious to all that there is a systematic opposition to the West, which may indicate a trend back to parochial culture, a turning inwards and a withdrawal from modernity.

While Islamism constitutes a frame of reference under construction, its doctrinal content is far from being complete. For some twenty years changes have been occurring within the Islamist corpus. Ideologues within this corpus have been drawing material from several sources to provide militants with a coherent archetype covering all sectors of life. Behind the uniformity of language used, there is an infinity of practical configurations matching different situations and the different capabilities of the actors involved. This faltering approach[5] nonetheless offers the best prospects for providing a structural framework for the rebuilding of an identity.[6]

The explanation of this phenomenon in terms of traditionalism through an excess of modernity[7] might have proved satisfactory but for the fact that it locks us into a negative evaluation of the Islamist exegesis. The concept of traditionalization has certain limits in that the political and even ideological work of these new groups is involved in recreating and interpreting the tradition with a view to appropriating modernity and legitimizing the assault of a new generation. The discourse of the leaders, revealing a desperate search for the original tradition, may deceive us and blind us to the highly modern aspects of this process of rebuilding an identity. We may overlook the diversity and multiplicity of the exegesis and the close link between it and the historical and political developments in each country.

In the space of 20 years several Islamist movements have distanced themselves from the traditional frame of reference. Qutb, Mawdudi, al-Ghazali, Shattibi and Ibn Taymiya are exemplary on this count.[8] Islamists are now presenting their own ideologists to negotiate on their behalf and ensure that the movement is firmly rooted in modernity (this is the case with Hasan al-Turabi, Rashid al-Ghannushi, Abd al-Salam Yassin, etc.). If Islamism is seen as one of the possible responses to a crisis of identity, this crisis is diagnosed in terms of its relation to modernity, not to the West; unless we are to accept the confusion made by Islamists themselves and argue that difficulties of adapting to the consequences of modernity do not affect Westerners. As Olivier Roy rightly recalls, Islamists constitute a phase in 'the disenchantment of the world'[9] insofar as 'they borrow from modernity the refusal to return to the real tradition in the name of a fantasy tradition: they reject popular religiosity, the village, Sufism ...'[10]

A study carried out in the 1980s clearly showed that the dividing line between Islamists and other young people was simply their militant commitment. Both categories share the same frame of reference and a common mindset. In a survey conducted among 400 students, 75 per cent were not hostile *a priori* to a discourse along Islamist lines and thought the *shari'a* to be the only solution to the problems of the day. The same respondents were in favour of co-education, against extra-marital sex and thought that respect for religion did not necessarily entail rejecting technical progress.

The idea that Islamism is a direct consequence of the processes of modernization merits further consideration. Islamism can be interpreted as the response at a given point in time to the need for social mobility and 're-localization' in an environment which is global in scale. As Giddens points out, worldwide 'we have entered into an acute phase of modernity, breaking with the re-assuring points of reference offered by tradition.'[11] The outer signs of this are rapid urbanization, mass school attendance, a questioning of traditional social strata and the demand for social and spatial mobility. But this groundswell movement has led to 'the removal of social relationships from local contexts of interaction and their re-structuring in undefined spatio-temporal fields.'[12]

This modern configuration of societies, regardless of whether they are Muslim or not, is having certain traumatic consequences on individuals because modernity entails the 'institutionalization of doubt'.[13] Radical commitment leading to an attitude of active contestation targeted against what is perceived as a source of danger constitutes one of the four possible forms of adaptation to this situation.[14] The other three are: 'pragmatic acceptance, dogged optimism and cynical pessimism.' Despite his scepticism, Giddens does not rule out the possibility of a resurgence of religion. In such an event, certain aspects of life would regain a new stability, similar in certain respects to that of tradition. This regained stability could form the basis of a feeling of ontological security under human control. The need for a re-deployment of identity applies to both 'the local and the global in a complex manner.'[15] It can be seen as a strategy of re-localization aiming at a re-appropriation or redistribution of roles in de-localized social relations rooted in local spatio-temporal contexts.

Islamism is characterized by the paradox of its extreme need for both spatial and social mobility and an apparently fixed frame of reference. The *tabligh* may be said to have inaugurated this migratory cycle. However, it is European Islamism which heralds what Islamism might have been in the Muslim world were it not for the compartmentalization caused by the existence of nation states and the difficulties of crossing what are often tightly sealed borders. The ease of movement which Islamists enjoy in Europe and their high degree of mobility reflect their pressing need to escape from a rigidly closed environment. Islamism offers, as it were, a means of escaping from a rural, agrarian culture and plays the role of what sociologists of modernity describe as an abstract system of reference capable of universalizing points of reference with a view to permitting extreme mobility while at the same time endowing them with a high localized content.

Islamism: the voice and the way for the young

The increase in population in the countries of North Africa during the 1960s was accompanied by a rapid – and uncontrolled – rise in investment in the education and training of an elite, despite the fact that the facilities in place were not ready to accommodate this.[16] The excessive hopes of achieving mobility through education confronted a system which was incapable of developing because of a lack of resources aggravated by widespread nepotism and 'clientelism'. It was an educational system built in haste with inadequate resources which soon began to fail.

It is in this context that the 'generation gap' phenomenon comes into its own. The process of renewal was indeed multidimensional and, as often underlined, expressed a revolt against injustice, despotism and moral erosion but also the individual's intense desire to assert personality in situations of social marginalization, sometimes accompanied by a fear of loss of self-esteem or, more widely, a profound identity crisis. Religious militancy provides the possibility of acquiring stable, positive and high self-esteem.

Brotherhoods and associations provide access to forms of fraternization which redefine social hierarchies in terms of criteria which are not necessarily those of society at large. Piety, militant commitment and work usually take precedence over considerations of age or social background, and allegiances are forged around charismatic personalities outside any hierarchy. The goal of seeking a new identity is strengthened by a principle of effectiveness. Once liberated from the guardianship of their elders who, according to social custom, are legitimately entitled to make public pronouncements, the Islamists undertake a patient labour of de-legitimization and subversion of mediation either by traditional or by post-independence hierarchies, thus becoming generators of meaning and opinion leaders.[17]

New strategies are developed, all geared to obtaining a position in the system, rarely to questioning or destroying it. The conquest of power, starting at the top,[18] is no more than a marginal element in this movement of young militants. Another way chosen to question prevalent values is that of promoting an edifying standard of morals and a work ethic, backed by options about dress and about marriage. The results are spectacular: a parallel society combining the power of denunciation and de-legitimization with that of an immaculate, exemplary militancy.

There are multiple scenarios as regards generational succession.[19] This depends on how a given society has negotiated the way in which young people are co-opted into the decision-making process. Algeria offers an extreme case of violent succession, and countries such as Morocco, Tunisia or even Nigeria or Egypt are not free from the risk of following a similar path. The generation gap is also a factor within Islamist movements. It partly accounts for the burgeoning of new sensitivities within these movements and the multiplication of groups proclaiming their allegiance to the Islamist cause.

The succession of new studies of the highly volatile Islamic

Salvation Front (FIS) highlights this predominance of young militants which has been as powerful a motive as state violence in the decision to opt for the zealous approach to the struggle for power. On this count, it should be noted that 'new generations of radical militants act within the framework of an *avant-garde* made up of intellectuals'[20] who have emerged from the ranks of the Islamic Salvation Front but have broken with Islamist leaders whom they accuse of playing a waiting game. They also include Arabic-speaking primary and secondary school teachers and young officers who have deserted from the army, such as Sa'id Makhlufi or A. Chbuti. The group of technocrats who have furthered their political cause within the Islamic Salvation Front are at the heart of the problems we are analysing. Most of them were born during the 1950s, and they are the first generation of university graduates since independence. Almost in their entirety they are French-speaking and have a scientific training. Their profile is that of a modern-minded, technological, upwardly mobile elite but often thwarted in their social ascendance by the logic of the 'apparatchniks'.

These young people were late converts to Islamism via the FIS, but their militancy very soon evolved towards radicalism/radicalization with the shift from militancy through religious expression in the mosque to action in the frame of 'maquis' and 'jihad'.

Developments within the FIS led to the eviction of the founding fathers from July 1991, that is well before the formation of the 'maquis'. The emergence of personalities such as R. Kebir, A. Haddam and A. Hachami heralded a 'total renewal of the FIS leadership'.[21] Even if one closely analyses the military expressions of the Islamist movement, viz. the Islamic Armed Groups and the Islamic Army of Salvation (close to the FIS), it is clear that the break is not simply between the extension of a political movement by an armed movement (the IAS) and a movement without the supervision of 'cadres', but rather a rift between generations of militants. The violent internal clashes reflect the particular background of combatants having suffered humiliation at the hands of their elders just as much as a predefined political programme.

Local news and gossip gathered by Myriam Vergés highlights the feeling all young people have of being in a dead end: 'When you stand back and look at yourself, you realize you have nothing to remember, you have done nothing and you have nothing. It's amazing. Where do

I live? What am I doing? What have I done to deserve this? In other countries people of our age are starting a career. Our heads are empty and it is better not to ask questions. Otherwise, we would go mad.' (Morad, aged 30, hairdresser); 'In other countries, people get fair treatment and people say 'Hello' in the street. If they weren't *kuffar* [impious] *they* would be the ones to go to Paradise.'[22]

There is nothing of fascination or resentment in this type of outburst, rather a cry of distress, a plea for a place in the sun gradually turning into a commitment to obtain a place in Paradise by attaining martyr status. This kind of testimony can be compared to that gathered by F. Burgat in an interview with a al-Gama'iyya al-Islamiyya militant in Upper Egypt: 'Back in Cairo we faced many adversaries. The Sufis were a very strong opponent as regards doctrine and they were very active. Families were also a major adversary. At Sa'id, for example, when people meet they usually say: 'Hello, is the news good? How are you doing? How is your health?' But in greeting someone or replying, we would say, 'Peace be on you.' Said at any time of day, that sounded strange to the locals. For example, a great-uncle of mine on my father's side once said to my father: 'If your son answers me in that manner again, I'll murder him! The youngster acts really weird.' And it's true. We did act strangely – in our prayers, for example, and in our doctrinal options. The people in Sa'id observe the Malekite rites. But al-Gama'iyya al-Islamiyya refuses to recognize differences in rites and preaches a consensus amongst everybody. We even met with physical aggression as if we were preaching a completely new religion that was not even Islam!'[23]

In Morocco, the young generation of Islamists have not adopted a stance hostile to the brotherhoods since that position had already been occupied by the *salafist* nationalists who made it their credo during the independence struggle. Since the state clamped down on the use of mosques and prayers for political ends by institutionalizing the clergy, a new generation of clerics has emerged usually working as part of an association or on a clandestine 'freelance' basis.

This new elite assumed the leadership of the process of religious renewal by promoting a new rhetoric and undermining traditional means of education. As graduates of modern universities, they give preference to education by the written word (newspapers, reviews, etc.) as opposed to sermons in the mosque.

The basis of legitimacy of these (often young) clerics is their ability to articulate the real problems of young people today. They consider compliance with traditional techniques of exegesis to be secondary. A study of some twenty such leaders was carried out by a group of intellectuals and Islamic militants (of which I was a member) to characterize this theological revolution which has developed in the framework of what an Islamist review calls the '*fiqh maqassidi*'. For these young Islamists:

> we must take into account both divine signs and signs of a reality in movement. The first thing people familiar with the *sunna* must understand is that the *fiqh* is not merely a memorization and an account of the texts, but also the full assimilation of their profound meaning so as to reveal their rationality. To absorb oneself in the texts and only concern oneself with their literal meaning without looking at the global aims of religion invariably leads to superficial understanding and sometimes to a total absence of meaning.[24]

This new generation of Islamists question the criteria of the exegetic competence of the clerics of the past and aims to undermine this function which is based on techniques of memorizing and a timeless solidarity with the ancients. At the same time, they stress the emergence of the individual as a responsible actor capable of assuming the function of exegesis. This is particularly important since the decision to join the movement implies a break with family solidarities.

The rift between Islamists and non-Islamists runs tragically right through the family. Adepts of al-Adl wa-l-Ihsan become *muhajir* once they are accepted into the movement, and this requires a severing of all previous ties. In practical terms, it means that new members leave their families and go to live in the *usra* of the *jama'a* and that their day-to-day habits and their militancy change.

The strategies in the three examples mentioned above are different, but in each case they aim to outflank former elites and promote the emergence of the individual as a producer and a beneficiary of the Islamist message.

In Algeria, the young militants ('les cadets') have taken over leadership of the Islamist movement through both electoralism and the 'maquis'. In Morocco, this has been achieved by taking control of the modern instruments of exegesis and consequently of a code of ethics suitable for a modern-day exegesis. In Nigeria, the emergence of new groups has been encouraged by adopting a new exegesis and by a series of breaks with ethnic types of grouping and community belonging characterized by rigid hierarchy according to age.

The traditional order is questioned by fostering a genuine counter-culture based on rigorous social morality and a highly effective entrepreneurial ethic. During Ramadan in 1991, FIS militants in Algeria set up 'Islamic *suks*' where scarce commodities and produce were available at wholesale prices. Two years previously (29 October 1989), after the tremendous Tipasa earthquake they had proved highly efficient in organizing rescue operations within 48 hours. In Morocco, al-Adl wa-l-Ihsan functioned as a credit company operating with 'associative capital' on the basis of a combination of commerce and contraband, thereby creating stable jobs for its militants. In the same country, large numbers of Islamist entrepreneurs have set up in the dairy and confectionery sectors where a reputation for hygiene and integrity is essential. In both cases, they have succeeded in equating an ideological, ethical and social choice with business success. During the floods in February 1996, the Islamists were the first to mobilize and provide assistance for the families of the victims. They were the first on-site to provide the inhabitants of Derb Carloti with their post-fast soup and offer first aid, whereas the state took almost 24 hours to react and when it did, it placed the region under quarantine preventing direct assistance to the victims.

Every sector of daily life is now covered by a close-knit network of associations which are not only highly efficient in themselves but show up the inadequacies of state policies. States often react to this situation by restricting public liberties. In late November 1992, after failing lamentably for weeks to provide assistance to the victims of a major earthquake, the Egyptian government issued a decree banning associations from fund-raising, even for humanitarian purposes. Likewise, since 17 February 1993, the validity of trade union elections is subject to a minimum turnout of 55 per cent in the first round and 30 per cent in the second, although participation is traditionally low. Failure to achieve the minimum threshold means the organizations are placed under control of the judiciary.[25]

Education is the first of these strategic objectives for the men of religion, be they Islamist or Christian:

> It is not possible to talk of development without a concomitant policy.
> The regimes in power in Islamic countries do not try to harness and

develop the creative potential of the various sectors of society. Rather they shore up their position by security measures based on conservatism and on the accentuation of existing inequalities ... This leaves ample leeway for education as a channel for political action.[26]

Moroccan Islamist groups, for example, have taken a two-pronged approach to achieving this objective. Firstly, they have set up private schools linked to various groups starting from kindergarten level. e.g. the network of schools established in the mid-1970s by Jama'at al-Tabligh encouraged by the existence of a lively private education sector promoted by the Nationalist movement from the mid 1940s but which grew exponentially as the public education system deteriorated. A second approach involves focusing conversion campaigns on the educational sector. The university has been a priority target for groups like al-Adl wa-l-Ihsan in Morocco, Nahda in Tunisia and Hamas in Algeria. These groups currently dominate the students' union movement. The first indication of an organized Islamist presence on a university campus appeared in the council of student halls of residence around 1979–80. At the same time the first Islamist cultural week was held after Abd al-Salam Yassin devised the holding of similar events as part of a – still immature – activist movement.[27] The mosque within the halls of residence became the nerve centre for the movement, which was beginning to distance itself from the Islamic *shabiba*. By the mid 1980s the structure of Islamism in universities centred on three movements, namely al-Islah wa-l-Tajdid, al-Adl wa-l-Ihsan and the former *shabibists* who were split between activist options and a more political, Ghannushian option (Rashid al-Ghannushi was the leader of Nahda in Tunisia).

At present all the leaders of the student movement in Casablanca are Islamist according to the findings of a survey in early 1995, i.e. a population of 64 students from Casablanca University's Faculties of Law, Arts and Science.[28]

The Islamist population is relatively young. Less than 12 per cent were born before 1970. Their average age is 23. No woman is present among the leaders, although there is a large number of women students on the campus and in the lecture halls. The student leaders appear to have quite normal study records, i.e. their average time at university is just over five years for a four-year course. This applies to 75 per cent of the population. Less than 20 per cent have repeated more than one year, even in the case of science studies. This relatively high rate of academic success reflects the values defended by the movement, with its insistence on performance and its union activity geared

The language option does not seems to affect the students' militancy. In the Law Faculty, the breakdown between economists and jurists among militants reflects the overall situation, i.e. 55 per cent economists (this may be the result of negotiation). The only anomaly which could bring out the language factor is the absence of jurists and publicists studying in French. In the Arts Faculty, 75 per cent of students are enrolled in Arabic language courses, i.e. Islamic studies and Arabic literature. While this is hardly surprising, it is striking to note that 25 per cent of student leaders are studying English Literature.

In addition, constant efforts are directed to cultural activism in primary school teacher training colleges and in 'lycées'. Islamist teachers do not hesitate to promote after-class activities to make up for deficiencies in the state education system.

Remedial classes provided free of charge as well as collective revision groups help Islamists mark themselves out from the rest and recruit massively among future students and teachers. As M. Yatin notes, Islamic associations originally considered cultural activism simply as a means of providing outlets for action by militants without a place in the movement's political structure, but they are now treating it as an *avant-garde* activity since it is a means of forging direct links with society.[29]

The scope for action is enormous given the deterioration in quality of the state education system with its overcrowded classes and unmotivated teachers. In a 'lycée' in a working class suburb of Casablanca, an Islamist group has infiltrated the administration and part of the teaching staff. With the complicity of these latter, special classes are organized for Islamist pupils who receive special training and emerge as the best students in the school. Comparisons indicate that there is a correlation between their academic success and their religious commitment.

In working class districts of Cairo, the Gama'at have opened surgeries where doctors provide medical care on a charity basis. The service is of good quality and virtually free of charge, contrasting sharply with the run-down national health service and the exorbitant prices of private health care.

In Morocco the pietist group Jama'at al-Tabligh, which devotes its attention mainly to preaching, has organized a permanent structure for hospital and prison visits. Other Islamist groups, e.g. al-Islah wa-l-Tajdid, are developing specific action targeted at state hospitals that are being abandoned by doctors setting up in private practice. More and more, doctors who are adepts of al-Islah or al-Adl wa-l-Ihsan are providing medical attention with a quite noteworthy degree of devotion. In this context, the 'Islamist' label has frequently become a hallmark of conscientiousness, competence and high levels of moral integrity.

Europe in the discourse of Islamists

It is very difficult to define the relationship between Islamism and Europe. In their own writings Islamists find it difficult to agree on a clear, common-sense position. Without doubt, Europe in the geographic sense is a keenly sought after destination and all means are used to try and gain access. To cite only one example, the '*tabligh*' made Europe their secret garden for many years and outside their Indo–Pakistani birthplace, really only thrived in Europe (in the United Kingdom and Belgium). Islamists have at no time denied themselves access to Europe on doctrinal grounds. There would have been no shortage of possible arguments given the number of temptations and risks of corruption. Another sign of change is that for contemporary Muslims, time spent in Europe is no longer perceived as a period of exile as it was for the first generation. Sayyid Qutb's journey to the United States or even Abd al-Salam Yassin's stay in France were perceived at the time as an ordeal. In the case of Qutb, a hagiography of temptation has stressed the miracle of the Koran's protection. In any event, Qutb's master work *Fi Adhilal*[30] was born out that encounter with total difference. The author seeks by an extreme aestheticization of the Koranic contents to defuse the risks of his guilty pilgrimage and express explicitly the impossibility of 'transplanted' experience.

At present the satanization of the West for its culture or its religion is, paradoxically, less and less in evidence in combative Islamist literature. From time to time, inflammatory sermons do appear decrying the watering down of morals (*tafassukh wa-l-inhilal*) and/or associating AIDS with civil weddings between homosexuals. But this is not a main theme. The combat is seen as more political than religious. On this count Islamists often share the views of other currents of opinion, especially the political left. In Islamic writings the references are less and less to societies and more to states. Europeans are criticized as groups of states in collusion with the USA and Israel, as a Christian civilization tempted by missionary zeal or as imperialistic nations.

The relationship of Islamists in general and Moroccan Islamists in particular with Europe has recently undergone a number of major historical vicissitudes, e.g. the war in Afghanistan, the Gulf War, the Serbo–Bosnian conflict, etc. Apart from Afghanistan, where Islamists temporarily aligned with the American camp (which deserves due recognition for its support of the *mujahidin* in their fight against the atheistic regime in Kabul) and hence distanced themselves from the local opposition elites, the position of Islamists regarding major conflicts and their reading of the geo-political situation and upheavals in the world political order since 1990 do not differ from other currents of opinion.

Islamic literature of the last decade, which we will now consider, offers few specific themes not found in Third World discourse generally and apart from a few exceptions, doctrinal statements on the relation with Christian Europe are based on the ideas of thinkers who are not necessarily Islamists. Two main themes occur frequently either by way of explanation of the historical conflicts between Muslim and Christian countries or as an assessment of the possibilities of better understanding and dialogue between the two civilizations, the arguments for both theses being drawn from the same framework of reference.

The new international economic order after the Gulf War

The Gulf War caused a deep trauma and an intense feeling of injustice, aggravated by comparisons between the handling of that conflict and the one in Bosnia. These sentiments were not peculiar to Islamists but were shared by all the Muslim intelligentsia, including Euro–Muslim intellectuals.

The adoption by Islamists of the book *Guerre des Civilizations*[31] by

Mahdi el-Manjra (1992), a Moroccan economist, former civil servant at UNESCO and founding president of the OMDH, helped them out of the impasse caused by the assimilation of the Gulf War to a confrontation between religions since the American camp included some major Muslim countries. In the course of time and with the advent of the Bosnian conflict, they have developed a highly convincing discourse on the new international order, the weakness of Europe vis-à-vis the USA giant and the failure of the United Nations system.

> With the collapse of the Soviet Union, a new 'unipolar' world is emerging headed by the United States. The Gulf War has to be seen against this backdrop as a way of ensuring oil supplies and teaching a lesson to all those attempting to escape from the circle of US influence. The Americans succeeded in mobilizing the Europeans and other industrialized countries on their side. All this means that the struggle for energy resources in Latin America and Africa is an important stage in the consolidation of the new world order and a key element in the strategic redeployment of the USA which is endeavouring to confine these partners/adversaries in secondary economic roles. This is the overall background against which current events should be interpreted. The contradictions within the Western camp should not blind us to a reality which emerged at the end of the Gulf War: the main contradiction is between two blueprints for civilization, the Islamic and the Western.[32]

Some Islamists have already made the conceptual leap from a war of interest to a war of religion, using the writings of Islamist Muslim thinkers,[33] non-Islamists (Abed al-Jabri, el-Manjra) and Westerners (Huntington).[34]

The Bosnian conflict, which led to an extensive mobilization of Islamists in the framework of an association providing support and organizing fund-raising,[35] crystallized the confrontation around the theme of religion. It should be noted, however, that commentators have frequently been perplexed by the impossibility of treating the question in a Manichean, black and white manner, since the Bosnian camp includes major Christian powers. Many studies have shown an acceptable degree of nuance and the quality of geo–political analysis has improved accordingly.

'We have heard about the setting up of a new world order now that the West has overcome the internal struggles between East and West and has become united around values consciously founded on its Judaeo–Christian heritage which structures its relations with others

... This reunification has occurred to the detriment of the South whose main assets lie in the Muslim countries. The West has forgotten that the peoples of the South now make a distinction between their interests and those of the former colonial power. This is generating a crisis of consciousness in a civilization based on the exploitation of the wealth of others, war and the eradication of cultures, while at the same time proclaiming the values of fraternity, liberty and equality. How is it possible to reconcile these values with the practice of racism and the existence of a crusading mentality? The strange thing is that this aggressive attitude has given itself the drapings of legality within the framework of the new world order. We must stress the importance of religious factors and civilization besides the other elements at play in this war against the South, insisting on the differences of civilization between the West and Islam which have led to 'cold wars' and also to 'hot wars' and which express the depth of Christianity's hostility towards Islam and Muslims, a hostility which is deeply rooted in the European sub-conscious ... To insist on this point is not to make sweeping generalizations or to up the stakes in an exchange of accusations, nor is it extremism. It is simply to record a fact of which Muslims' children should be informed. Seeing things in that perspective clarifies our perception of events in Bosnia, which is a war of civilizations in the strict sense of the word. Otherwise, how do we account for the savage shelling of civilians in cities, the murder of pregnant women and the killing of fetuses, the refusal of certain European countries to apply the embargo against the Serbians ... the humming and hawing and procrastination by the UN Security Council on enforcement of its own resolutions, and the timorous wait-and-see attitude of Western ministries of foreign affairs which contrasts so sharply with their speedy reaction in the case of the Gulf War?'[36]

The Euro–Islamic dialogue

The Islamic discourse on Europe presents a number of surprises. It is not unusual to read very violent outbursts which reflect a Manichean approach stressing what is seen as the intrinsical incompatibility between the Judaeo–Christian and Muslim traditions. But it is increasingly common to find Islamists dropping their litanies against the latter-day 'Crusaders' and bringing their discourse more into line with strategic and geo-political considerations close to the theory of critical dialogue dear to German and European diplomacy.

The first of the above-mentioned positions, characterized by great hostility and a visceral mistrust of the West, is reflected by the extremely violent declarations of Shaykh Abd al-Salam Yassin:

> At the head of the Islamist caravan advancing with assurance on the road towards power and autarchy, you will find no Westernized fellow-travellers given over to the enemy both intellectually and culturally. You will find no friendships or alliances with the enemy. Neither will you find anyone of neat appearance and 'position of responsibility', who is in fact a dreary spy and whose life is spent in a succession of apparatchniks' conferences and parties where information about the potential of the country is hawked about in exchange for hard currency. You will find no clients of Hilton hotels, dance halls and other dens of vice or habitués of seminars airing views akin to those of free-masons, Zionism, capitalism or intelligence agencies. You will find only soldiers of God mobilized to serve the material and economic cause of the community and considering this as an act of worship rewarded by God ... [37]

The second type of position is more surprising since it is less widespread and more recent in the ideological field of the Islamists. One can read for example in a collection prepared by al-Furqan who is close to the Islah wa al-Tajdid movement: 'Islamists have greatly neglected the counsels of religion on the need for dialogue.' He then cites a verse of the Koran to illustrate his point (*ud'u li-rabbi-ka bi-l-hikmati wa-l- mau'idati al-hassana*) and continues: 'Islamist movements have not practised responsible, direct dialogue with the countries of the North and the West, despite benefiting from the rationality found in Islam and the tolerance and proximity to natural law of the Islamic *shari'a*. We also have the arguments and the answers contained in the philosophy and the logic of the Islamic *kalam*. They are closer to the Western mentality than generally imagined and it is only from Western civilization that we can hope to derive some benefit. At present Islamists are best placed to conduct a dialogue with a secular and hostile North, especially after the collapse of the main explicitly atheistic movements such as communism or existentialism. So why should Islamist movements not enter into this dialogue since until quite recently such philosophies were considered by left-wing Muslim writers as typical products of Western colonialism and its representatives in the region? Although the Gulf War showed such accusations to be unfounded, it did not fully dispel the view that Islamists have concentrated their efforts first and foremost on combating the Left and Communism and done so indiscriminately without differentiating between the various positions. This has made them the privileged interlocutors of the secular, liberal West, with the weighty responsibility of explaining Islam's position and convincing the West of its viewpoints.

Firstly, Islam is not against the West's materialistic civilization. On the contrary, it is actually propagating certain values of the West, even if it seems to be their enemy (these values include liberty, pluralism, fairness, equality and human fraternity), and there are sufficient arguments and evidence of this in the Muslim religion to dispel any doubts or pre-conceived views on the matter among Westerners.

Secondly, we must ask: have Islamists really presented Islam in its universal version, i.e. in a way compatible with the possibility of assimilation by the Western mind? And have they taken advantage of the principles, values, laws and instruments of Western society to present Islamic values in their true light? One can also question how far the strategy based on *preaching* which currently predominates among Islamist activists really meets the requirements for communicating the meaning of Islam in the framework of an institutionalized, popular dialogue.

Thirdly, communism founded its struggle against capitalism on the basis of the principle of complete incompatibility between the two and the need to build communist society on the remains of capitalism (which in communist theory contained the seeds of its own destruction and by an implacable historical logic would disappear and be replaced by socialism). There was no point of convergence or possibility of mutual recognition between the two world views. But in the case of capitalism and Islam this is not so. There are several points of convergence in the economic and social sphere. Islam contains a number of interesting aspects which could help correct certain errors in capitalism. The important point to note is that in Islam there are no precepts calling on believers to combat capitalism and destroy it by force and revolutionary violence so that it can be replaced by an Islamic system. On the contrary, Islam aims to improve on the best aspects of capitalism. And both systems agree on several points, e.g. the need for economic liberalism, private property, etc. If capitalism formally accepts at least the outer expressions of religion and belief in the beyond, there is a major point of convergence and a springboard for initiating a dialogue aimed at building a unitarian structure on the basis of popular dialogue and the institutions of prayer. Islam and Islamists are confident in the ability of Muslim thinkers to conduct such a dialogue with the West on an equal footing and free from complexes.'[38]

Conclusion

The relationship of Islamists in the south of the Mediterranean region with Europe cannot be dissociated from that of young people as a whole, be they militants or not. The relationship is one of both fascination and rejection. As stressed elsewhere, there is no single Islamist vision of Europe but rather a number of visions telescoping within each other, frequently within the same person. The satanization of the West is in the process of becoming outdated insofar as it no longer serves as a rallying cry for mobilization. Even emblems of the West and its cultural influence such as satellite dishes, Western-style suits and even Western life-styles are no longer attacked outright. Islamism is becoming something quite normal, part of our daily landscape, as reflected in the increasingly political, less emotional ways in which it expresses itself. The West still remains, however, the sphere of total difference, where the presence of Muslims must be dealt with at the level of the *da'wa* but where proselytization is relegated to a secondary level. In becoming more political, Islamists have come to appreciate the status of public liberties and the democratic state, even when they are found among the 'impious'.

Notes

1. Adelkhah, Bayart & Roy (1992).
2. Tozy (1989).
3. Gellner (1983).
4. Burgat (1997, 77).
5. Kepel & Richard (1990).
6. Al-Ghannushi (1990) speaks of the 're-invention of the ideological

and cultural frameworks of modernization'.

7. Etienne (1987, 61).

8. We have stressed the importance of Sayyid Qutb and al-Mawdudi in the constitution of the Islamist frame of reference, in Tozy (1984, 223 ff.).

9. Roy (1992, 38).

10. Roy, ibid.

11. Giddens (1995).

12. Ibid., p. 29.

13. Ibid., p. 184.

14. Ibid., p. 144.

15. Ibid., p. 185.

16. The survey carried out by the Conseil National de la Jeunesse et de L'Avenir (CNJA) on 27 February 1991 found that of 100,374 young graduates, 61 per cent were male. The 25–29 years age group represents 58 per cent of the population. See Conseil National de la Jeunesse et de l'Avenir, *Le Chômage des Jeunes Diplômés* (Rabat, 1991), p. 11.

17. Tozy (1990, 71–102).

18. Kepel (1984, 17).

19. Bennani Chraïbi (1994).

20. Labat (1994, 53).

21. Ibid., p. 57.

22. Vergés (1994, 75).

23. Burgat (1997,103).

24. Review *al-Furqan* 14 (1988), p. 2.

25. J. F. Burgat, 'Les mutations d'un Islam pluriel', *Le Monde diplomatique*, June 1993.

26. Weekly *Sahwa* 26 (1993): 15.

27. *Al-Jama'a* 34 (1989).

28. Survey of students' union leaders at Université Hassan II, 1995.

29. *Araya* 32, Nov. 1992.

30. Carré (1984).

31. El-Manjra (1992).

32. *Al-Furqan* 26 (1992): 2.

33. Rashid al-Ghannushi, 'Les mouvements Islamistes et le nouvel ordre international', *al-Furqan*, 25 (1991): 21.

34. Hungtington (1993, 22–49).

35. Association for the support of Muslim Bosnia led by Doctor Khatib, a prominent moderate Muslim leader close to the palace.

36. *Al-Furqan* 27 (1992): 10.

37. Yassin (1996, 20).

38. *Al-Furqan* 26 (April 1992): 35/35.

12

Techniques and Values: Contemporary Muslim Debates on Islam and Democracy

GUDRUN KRÄMER

The relationship between Islam and democracy or, to put it differently, the democratic potential of Islam as a religion, culture and civilization, remain highly controversial issues. In the debate, theory and practice are not always kept apart, and nor are religion and political culture: some think of Islam as doctrine ('real Islam'), i.e., Islam as the Koranic text or the authoritative tradition more generally, others look at what could be called 'Islam in history', that is Islam as understood and lived by Muslims, while yet another group refers to Islamist thought and practice that presents Islam as a political programme able to compete with secular ideologies, and indeed superior to them. History is read and misread to prove one point of view or another: the so-called constitution of Medina, which in all likelihood dates to the period shortly after the Prophet's *hijra* from Mecca to Medina, and which seems to have been in force for a very limited period only, is referred to by those who argue that the exemplary community established by Muhammad was democratic, with consultation *(shura)* being made obligatory even on the Prophet himself, and citizenship being granted to both Muslims and non-Muslims. According to them, Medina provides the model of an Islamic state based on *shura* and equality.[1] Critics point to the absence not only of liberty, democracy and participation in the Islamic past, but of the very notion of autonomy on the individual as well as the collective levels, of freedom, equality and responsibility. Islam in history was marred, as they see it, by a 'cluster of absences': no concept of liberty, no autonomous corporate institutions and assemblies, no self-confident middle class, etc.[2] Having lacked the socio-cultural preconditions for (liberal) democracy in the past, Muslims will not be able to produce them in the future.[3]

Yet references to 'Islam as such', to 'real Islam' and to Islamic history are of limited use and relevance to the present context: what we are dealing with is a debate solidly grounded in the modern age, reflecting modern ideals and mirroring differing views of what it means to be a Muslim and to establish an Islamic order *(nizam islami)* that is at the same time modern and 'authentic' (whatever that may mean for the individual or group concerned). We are, therefore, not speaking about Islam writ large, but about Muslims (most of them urban male literate middle class Muslims), interpreting, in the light of specific social, cultural and political concerns and conditions, the authoritative sources in order to define what a modern Islamic political order should or could be like. What we are dealing with, then, are 'readings' of Islam (and the allusion here is, of course, to Mohammed Arkoun's 'lectures de l'Islam' as opposed to 'Islam as divine word', or 'text'). That most participants in the debate present their own reading as the 'position of Islam' on any given subject should not obscure the fact that there is no position of Islam on the precise form and nature of an Islamic state or, for that matter, almost any other aspect of social, economic and political life. There are only interpretations of the texts, and of past experiences, reflecting different views, ideals, and interests. The latter point will be taken up later.

The following will be based mainly on the writings of twentieth century Sunni Muslims, most of them Arabs writing in Arabic or one of the major European languages. Oral contributions such as sermons, speeches, radio and TV interviews, audio and video cassettes, e-mail and Internet messages will be excluded unless printed: though they do, of course, touch on social and political issues, they do not, as a rule, aim at systematic reflection. Sociologically speaking, the authors are mostly urban middle class, and well educated in Islamic and/or Western thought and history. Most of them are men. Some belong to the Islamic trend or movement in the widest sense, meaning that they are not necessarily affiliated to any particular Islamist group or movement, but that they believe Islam to provide for a distinctive social, economic and political order which they wish to see established. The Arabic *'tayyar islami'* and the French 'mouvance Islamiste', or even more so, 'la nébuleuse Islamique', serve to convey the sense of vaguely defined boundaries that often make it difficult to distinguish the Islamist from the non-Islamist. In particular, since in the late 1970s and the 1980s, a number of former nationalist, leftist and liberal academics, intellectuals and political activists, now collectively known as 'neo-traditionalists' *(al-turathiyyun al-judud)*, adopted an 'Islamic' point of view. Other participants in the debate are not affiliated to this trend, and some are highly critical of Islamism and the Islamist discourse, especially when it comes to democracy, human rights and the status of women and non-Muslim minorities in an 'Islamic' society. Contrary to what is often said, many of the Islamist writers and activists do in fact have some training in Islamic studies, in certain cases even a solid one; some belong to the class of *ulama*, which, however, can hardly be called 'traditional' any longer considering the deep changes in the curricula and organization of higher Islamic learning from the Sunni al-Azhar and the Qarawiyyin mosques to the Shi'i centres in Qum and Najaf. The distinction between modern 'secular' and 'traditional' religious learning should, therefore, not be exaggerated, at least not with regard to the present subject. The writings include book-length studies, articles, draft constitutions, academic theses, printed speeches and sermons, discussing a variety of themes from the Islamic state in general and its specific features to the compatibility of Islam and democracy. Some are comparative, others focus on a specific case study, area or period. Altogether, the bulk of literature is considerable, and selection therefore a difficult task.[4]

The primacy of values or the 'application of the shari'a

One of the most interesting points in the debate on Islam, the state and democracy is the distinction frequently made by Muslim scholars and Islamists alike between 'values' on one hand and 'techniques' on the other: techniques are declared to be neutral from a religious and/ or moral point of view (technically speaking, they are *mubah*). They can be freely adopted and adapted from non-Islamic cultures and societies, provided Islamic values be preserved intact and uncorrupted. The argument is well known from the discussion about culture, development and modern technology. It is especially relevant to the present context because democracy in general, and liberal, pluralist democracy in particular, clearly include both techniques and values.

And it is liberal, pluralist democracy that most Muslims and Islamists have in mind when they speak and write about 'democracy' and its suitability for an Islamic society, no matter whether they welcome it, cautiously or warmly, or openly reject it. The distinction raises serious problems which are not always, in the existing literature, tackled with the required rigour.

Another differentiation, as intriguing as the first and intimately linked to it, needs clarification: the differentiation between the essentials, or the fundamentals, of religion (*al-asl*) and the 'derivations', the positive norms, the non-essentials so to speak *(al-furu)*, or between the 'stable' elements of Islam *(al-thabit)* and the 'flexible' ones *(al-mutaghayyir)*. Whereas the first are considered to have been defined, for all times and localities, by the divine will and word *(al-nass)*, the latter have to be derived by human reason (though not autonomous reason freed from the constraints of the faith) from the authoritative texts. They require a structured interpretation *(ijtihad)* of revelation and the tradition.

The differentiation appears at first sight to be perfectly reasonable, natural even. Yet the distinctions made and the boundaries drawn between the essentials and the non-essentials, and between the stable (fixed, eternal, immutable, untouchable and divine) elements of Islam and its flexible (changeable, human) ones are, to a large extent, arbitrary, and anything but well-defined, let alone universally agreed upon. On this issue like on so many others, a consensus *(ijma')*, so highly valued by conservative Muslim scholars and radical activists alike, has not evolved. It is, at any rate, not God who distinguished between the two domains, but Muslim thinkers, jurists and theologians. To justify their distinctions, they revert to the concepts and categories of Islamic jurisprudence *(fiqh)* and reinterpret them to fit a context, and a purpose, that is essentially political: The juridical category of the 'duties towards God' (the *'ibadat*, encompassing by and large the area of cult and ritual) is said to constitute the stable domain, fixed beyond any questioning by God and his Prophet, whereas the 'social duties' (the *mu'amalat*, covering everything else from financial transactions to political organization, and from marriage to international relations) are part of the flexible elements that have to be adapted to the changing requirements of time and place in order to make Islam, as the well-known formula runs, truly relevant to all times and places. To complicate matters even further, interpretation is not admitted in cases where there is an unequivocal and authoritative text *(nass qati' al-dalala)* of the Koran or the prophetic *Sunna*. Again it need not be stressed that it is Muslim scholars and Islamist activists who determine whether a text is indeed unequivocal and authoritative, and whether it is the precise wording *(lafz)* or the wider meaning, intention, spirit or finality *(maqasid)* of this text that should prevail.[5] The distinction between the 'stable' and the 'flexible' domains comes very close to the one between the 'sacred' and the 'profane', or the 'spiritual' and the 'temporal' known from the Western tradition, though it is hardly ever defined in these terms.

The differentiation is all the more remarkable since most of the Muslim and virtually all of the Islamist authors writing about Islam and democracy, or about the ideal 'Islamic order', subscribe to the view that Islam is religion and state *(al-Islam din wa-dawla)* or religion and world *(din wa-dunya)*. Many do not seem to have any problem with the wider implications of this thesis, but equally many do. Following the Egyptian reformer Muhammad Abduh (1849–1905), whose modernist approach still inspires much contemporary Islamic thought, Muhammad Ammara (widely known as Imara) formulated a compromise: he considered the two spheres of religion (worship, ritual) and of politics to be differentiated, but subject to the same moral and religious code and law, the *shari'a* ('not separate ... but nonetheless distinct', as Abduh had put it).[6] Again, the question of what this notion of differentiation implies for the organization of an Islamic state and society remains. It could be understood to allow for autonomous decisions in the social and political spheres, so long as they continue to be, in the widest sense, inspired by Islamic codes and values. It could also open the way to secularization, though it would be unavowed and indeed unwanted secularization. But it need not do so. All depends on the political will of the interpreters – and their political clout.

Government or governance *(al-hukm)*, most Sunni contemporaries are agreed, is part of the social duties, the *mu'amalat,* and therefore changeable. Its mechanisms and procedures can be adapted from non-Islamic sources provided the results conform to Islamic norms and values and, by the same token, do not neglect, contradict or violate explicit commands of God or his Prophet *(nass),* i.e., the Koran and the (binding) *Sunna.*[7] This assumption has far-reaching implications, for it allows for great flexibility in matters of social and political organization which are basically regarded as mere 'techniques', employed to secure certain fixed ends ('values'). God, it is thought, left the details of political organization to the Muslim community to be determined according to its varying needs and aspirations. Indeed, he did not even grant the Prophet a son, thereby barring hereditary rule, enjoining instead consultation *(shura)*, free choice and, some would say, democracy. According to this view, the caliphate provides one model of political organization, but not the only one and perhaps not even the one best suited to the demands and realities of the late twentieth century. It is at any rate not the decisive element in making a given socio-political order into an Islamic socio-political order.

The hallmark of the Islamic order is the *shari'a*, comprising both law and ethics, in which Islamic values are enshrined. No state can claim to be Islamic, so the Islamists argue, that does not 'apply' the *shari'a*, and apply it exclusively. Basing themselves on a famous passage from the Koran *(sura* 5: 44, 45 and 47), radical and militant Islamists will go so far as to declare as heretic and exclude from the community *(takfir)* all those who do not follow God's judgement *(hukm Allah)* which they identify with the *shari'a*.[8] The *shari'a* incorporates the value system of the Islamic order and gives it its moral and political purpose. Only the *shari'a* can safeguard justice, harmony and stability. Only where the *shari'a* is paramount do legality and legitimacy *(shar'iyya, mashru'iyya)* coincide: *la shar'iyya bi-dun shari'a* – there is no legitimacy without the *shari'a*. The Islamic state or order based on the *shari'a* is the only state in which all men and women are subject to the same (eternal, immutable, divine) law. The compatibility of this notion of the eternal, immutable *shari'a*, fixed for all times and places by God and the Prophet, with the distinction between the stable core and the flexible 'non-essentials' of Islam, and between the 'real', 'divine' *shari'a* on one hand and human interpretation and jurisprudence *(fiqh)* on the other remains, of course, to be explored.[9] Two principles enter into potential conflict: the yearning for a definitive system of norms and values, established by a higher authority and therefore beyond the reach of human manipulation, for certainty, clarity, order and stability, and the recognition of unending change requiring the constant use of human reason, even if it be reason guided by the faith that does not question its truth and demands. If there are ways to harmonize the two, they are not systematically discussed by Islamist authors. The 'myth of the *shari'a*' (E. Sivan)[10] has, to a certain extent, replaced the myth of the 'just ruler'. While some Islamist activists still struggle for the restoration of the caliphate, the majority gives precedence to the 'application of the *shari'a*.' For them it is the abstract system of the law, its ethics, norms and values, that matter and not so much the person of the ruler and his individual qualifications.

Within the framework of what I would call the 'functional theory of government' (or governance), the debate has, then, largely shifted to the nature, adaptability and flexibility of the *shari'a* and the relevance of specific legal provisions, including notably the canonical punishments in criminal matters *(hudud)*, to modern conditions. Does the *shari'a* offer a comprehensive set of norms and prescriptions regulating human life to the smallest detail, or does it merely set down basic rules of piety and moral uprightness aiming at people's well-being on earth and their salvation in the hereafter which still leave ample room for human interpretation of the 'spirit' or the 'finality' *(maqasid)* of the law? Does it require a literalist ('fundamentalist') reading that simply 'discovers' rules and regulations that have been unequivocally set forth in the text, or does it demand a continuous search for the purpose, spirit and finality of God's word – and it need not be emphasized how vague and malleable this notion of finality is, particularly when identified with 'public interest' *(maslaha amma* as the modern, essentially political adaptation of the juridical concept of *maslaha mursala*, i.e., interest that cannot be directly derived from the authoritative texts).[11] 'Enlightened', modernist authors such as al-Awwa, Ammara or al-Ghannushi have, of course, every incentive to magnify the role of reason and to define the scope of human interpretation as widely as possible, an endeavour once dismissed by Malcolm Kerr as the attempt to define the *shari'a* primarily by its 'empty spaces'.[12] Their dilemma is all too obvious, for if the *shari'a* is to provide for order and stability, human interpretation reflecting constantly changing needs, aspirations and interests must have clear limits. Another point has to be made: the heavier the emphasis on the purpose and finality of the law, and the centrality of public interest, the more imminent becomes the question of who is qualified to define them, and according to which rules. It poses the question of authority and of political power. Yet in the internal debate, it is rare to find an author (unless he or she be openly critical of Islamist discourse and practice) who squarely addresses the question of power. Instead, the reasoning usually assumes a moral tone, asking for personal probity rather than institutional checks and balances. A look at model constitutions will serve to illustrate this point.

A model of an Islamic constitution

To resume, most contemporary Muslim scholars and Islamist activists would argue that the precise form of the Islamic state or government is a matter of convenience, to be defined according to the public interest, *al-maslaha al-amma*. They nonetheless share certain assumptions concerning its foundations, purpose and organization. If the ideal type of a modern Islamic state were to be constructed, it would include the following elements: all human beings are born equal, having been installed as God's viceregents *(khalifa, pl. khulafa' or khala'ifa)* on earth. The concept of *istikhlaf* which, particularly when combined with the notion of dignity *(karama)* inherent in all human beings in their capacity as the children of Adam, could serve as the basis of an Islamic concept of human rights but is in need of further clarification.[13] While many authors define *karama* and *istikhlaf* so as to include all human beings, others restrict them to believers, if not Muslims only, making them contingent on the fulfilment of a person's duties towards God that figures so prominently in the general debate about human rights.

Similar problems arise with regard to other values the Islamic state is assumed to be based upon: justice most of all, but also – and here we are moving beyond the classical canon of Islamic social values – equality and freedom as well as responsibility *(mas'uliyya)* on the part of the individual and accountability *(musa'ala)* on the part of the government or ruler. This canon deserves close examination for in it we find incorporated certain notions or values that are, at least in this political context, unmistakably modern. This applies to equality as well as to freedom and responsibility which have been transferred from the legal and religious spheres to the political one. The question remains to what extent these general statements have been harmonized with the notions concerning the status of all those groups and strata which, under classical Islamic law *(fiqh* rather than *shari'a)*, have not enjoyed freedom or equality. In the first place women, non-Muslims and slaves, but also those who are not deemed to be true believers

– the atheist, the sceptic, the agnostic, the artist and the intellectual who do not recognize the boundaries of faith and common decency variously defined. At this point, the subjects of democracy and of human rights become so closely intertwined as to be inseparable. A closer look at individual stands on human rights will reveal that it is on the issues of freedom and equality – full religious, intellectual and political freedom and equality of all men and women before the law as distinguished from their equal worth before the Creator – that the principal limitations on Islamic democracy lie.

Less controversial are the following features: government/the state/ the ruler are needed in order to enforce order and ensure stability by implementing the *shari'a*, i.e., Islamic law and ethics. In the Islamic order, supreme sovereignty *(siyada, hakimiyya)* rests with God alone who has defined the law, the good and the evil *(al-ma'ruf wa-l-munkar)*, the licit and the illicit *(al-halal wa-l-haram)*.[14] However, God does not rule and he is not the head of state. Sovereignty is essentially defined in legal, and moral, terms. The authority *(sulta)* to 'discover' the meaning of revelation and to 'apply' God's law has been trans-ferred to the community as a whole, which is therefore the source of all powers *(asl al-sultat)*. The head of state, no matter whether he be called caliph, imam or simply president (no woman can occupy the highest position of command and authority), is merely the representa-tive of the community *(al-umma)*, the people *(al-sha'b)* or the citizenry *(al-muwatinun)* that elect, supervise and, if necessary, remove him from office.

So far, there is no apparent break with classical notions. The sub-tle changes come out more forcefully once the mechanisms of election, supervision and control are examined. The model is not without con-tradictions, or tensions, to say the least: some of the more obvious ones concern the head of state himself whose importance has been undeniably reduced in favour of the role of the 'umma' or the people, respectively. At the same time, the need for strong leadership, and unity of ranks, is constantly underlined, and considerable space de-voted to the personal qualifications of the 'ruler' *(al-hakim)* down to the question whether, at the end of the twentieth century, descent from the Prophet´s clan, the Quraysh, is still mandatory, or whether that condition served certain functions, including notably the ability to mobilize powerful solidarity groups *(asabiyya)* as Ibn Khaldun had argued, which under the present conditions can be better fulfilled by other means (free consent, elections, democratic legitimization, etc.). The eclectic nature of modern Islamic political theory is clearly reflected in the variety of terms under which the 'ruler' is presented: if it is 'caliph' or 'imam' in one context, it is 'amir al-mu'minin' in another, and 'president' or simply 'head of state' in a third, creating considerable confusion of terminology and, I would argue, thought as well. One point, however, is universally agreed among Sunni authors, distinguishing them from their Shi'i counterparts, especially those influenced by Ayatollah Khomeini's doctrine of the 'Guardianship of the Jurisconsult' *(velayat-e faqih):* the 'ruler' is not sacred and he holds no religious authority. They also reject the historical notion of the caliph as God's 'shadow on earth' who, during Umayyad and Abbasid times, even tried, albeit ultimately without success, to assert religious authority.[15] The interpretation of the tradition is entrusted to the religious scholars, the *ulama* and *fuqaha*, who are 'the heirs of the Prophets', reducing the ruler to his function as guardian and defender of the faith (*'al-din al-usus wa-l-sultan al-haris'*, as Abu Hamid al-Ghazali had formulated it in the eleventh century). But they do not constitute a clergy mediating between God and humanity. According to contemporary Sunni views, the Islamic state is built on the rock of the faith, and founded on sacred law, but it is not a theocracy in the restricted sense of being headed by a divinely appointed monarch or the men of religion. It is a religious, or even an ideological, state with a religious mission, but it has no religious government *(hukuma diniyya)*. For that reason many Sunni authors insist on the term 'civil state' or, to be more precise, 'state of lay persons' *(dawla madaniyya)* to designate the Islamic order. Al-Mawdudi called it a 'theo–democracy' to illustrate the admixture of theocratic and democratic elements peculiar to his concept of the Islamic state; Louis Massignon and Majid Khadduri, to cite two eminent Islamicists, preferred to speak of a 'théocratie laique' or a 'nomocracy', respectively.

Responsibility, participation and control

In spite of some vacillation, there is a definite shift of emphasis away from the person of the ruler and the duty of obedience for the sake of peace and order, even under unjust rule, mirroring the abhorrence of disorder, strife and anarchy *(fitna)* so characteristic of the classical tradition, to the authority of the community and the responsibility of every individual believer. This shift no doubt reflects the impact of modern political ideas as well as the decline and final abolition of the caliphate in 1924. Characteristic of much contemporary writing is its activist bent and the tendency to translate general principles and duties into strictly political ones: the pious believer as active citizen. Three principles are usually invoked in this context: the Koranic command to enjoin good and prohibit evil (*al-amr bi-l-ma'ruf wa-l-nahy 'an al-munkar*);[16] the Prophet's appeal to give counsel *(al-din al-nasiha)*, and the duty to consult *(shura)* which is emphasized in the Koran and the *Sunna*. They are interpreted in such a way as to make political responsibility, commitment and participation the religious duty of every single individual *(fard al-ayn)* which he or she cannot devolve to those in command or better able to understand what is good for the community as a whole (which, according to legal theory, would make it a collective duty, *fard al-kifaya*). Some even individualize the duty of *hisba* (control), which historically was exerted by the state or ruler and delegated to specialized officials, notably the *muhtasib*. Even where the state is retained as the chief agent, *hisba* is largely used as an instrument of moral control, and the enforcement of moral and religious conformity in public, that is to say an instrument of control directed 'downwards', from the ruler towards the people, and not vice versa.[17] As a result of these endeavours, politics is sacralized ('the vote as an act of worship', *shahada)*, and general duties and obligations are systematically politicized, extended and, albeit to varying degrees, institutionalized. Under the impact of modern political thought, the limited involvement of the community in selecting the ruler via consultation *(shura)* and the oath of allegiance *(bay'a)* as it was laid down in classical treatises and intermittently practised in Islamic history, particularly under the four rightly guided caliphs (632–61 AD), is translated into a constitutional system based on a social contract (again *bay'a, mubaya'a*).[18] This obliges the ruler to consult the community and/or their elected representatives on all public matters and makes the ruler not only, like any other believer, subject to the law and responsible before God, like any other believer but also held accountable to the electorate.

The instruments of political control include free and general elections that give the active vote to all (Muslim) men and women (non-Muslims are sometimes excluded from national councils and cabinets, and always from the office of head of state; women are frequently denied the passive vote which would give them access to highest office). Many contemporaries accept the majority vote, especially those coming from countries where Muslims form the overwhelming majority of the population and where a majority vote in favour of Islam, a particular Islamic group or the application of the *shari'a* can be presented as being *ipso facto* democratic.[19] Resistance is stronger where Muslims are in a minority, as is the case in India. Many contemporaries advocate the separation of powers which goes beyond the separation of functions and delegation of authority (*tafwid*) envisaged by, for example, al-Mawardi (d. 1058).[20] Great emphasis is placed on the independence of the judiciary which is responsible for the application of the *shari'a*, and as a consequence usually closed to non-Muslims and women. Several draft constitutions include provisions for the establishment of a Higher Constitutional Court to survey public policy and legislation and ensure its conformity with Islam or the *shari'a*, respectively.[21]

Much thought is given to the forms and procedures of *shura*, participation qua consultation. *Shura* has in fact been given such a wide and sweeping reinterpretation that it is widely regarded as the ('authentic') Islamic equivalent of modern parliamentary democracy.[22] The question is, I think, not so much whether this makes historical sense (it does not, for the community of the Prophet and the state of the rightly guided caliphs was, of course, not a parliamentary democracy), but whether Muslims in general and Islamists in particular wish to give it that meaning. Even after intensive debate, many questions remain controversial: whether the ruler has a duty to consult, and whether he is bound by the decisions of those consulted; whether they are men (women are rarely mentioned in this context) of his own choice, members of the social and political elite the *ulu l-amr* or the *ahl al-hall wa-l-aqd*, the 'men that bind and loosen', to use the traditional terminology), or the elected representatives of the community; individuals only or members of formal organizations such as political parties, trade unions, peasant organizations, etc.; religious specialists *ulama* and *fuqaha* or experts in other fields and community leaders; whether they decide by majority rule, and whether all matters of general import have to be subject to formal consultation. Most authors tend to consider shura to be both required and binding on the ruler *wajiba* and *mulzima*, to include religious as well as other experts and community leaders, and to accept majority decisions as normal and legitimate. Moving far beyond historical precedent, they conceive of *shura* as a formal process and an institution, i.e., a *shura* council made up of elected delegates of the community, an Islamic parliament so to speak.

What has to be emphasized is the ideal of mutual consultation in harmony and equity which sees *shura* as an instrument to safeguard unity, not the forum of debate, contest and competition, reflecting divergent convictions, world views and interests. The latter least of all: interest is to be excluded as much as possible as selfish, divisive and destructive, being largely assimilated to the Koranic concept of *hawan*, blind passion and desire that is the opposite of *Islam*, surrender to God. In the last resort, there is only one legitimate interest, and that is the interest of the community as a whole, or of Islam (and in theory there can be no contradiction between the two, for the community of believers will not err, and hence not stray from the faith). To realize the public good, *al-maslaha al-amma*, has to remain the ultimate aim, and individual, particularistic interests *(masalih)* stand it its way. The ideals of unity *(wahda)*, consensus *(ijma')*, and a harmonious balancing of groups and interests *(tawazun)*, often associated with the theological concept of *tawhid*, the oneness of God, are still paramount. Unity is contrasted with strife, conflict and anarchy, and consensus with the abomination of *fitna*.[23] That puts a limit to legitimate pluralism which comes out quite clearly in the debate about freedom of thought, creed, speech and association, that is in the domain of human rights proper. There is a general recognition that God created people to be different, and that therefore differences of opinion *(ikhtilaf)* are natural, legitimate and even beneficial to humankind and the Muslim community – provided they remain within the limits of the faith and common decency.[24] But most authors are greatly reluctant to permit unlimited freedom of speech or to tolerate religious deviation, whether it is openly voiced scepticism, blasphemy or apostasy.[25] The menace of *fitna* still serves the purpose of stifling open criticism and the spirit of free inquiry.

The discourse of morality

To summarize, the present Muslim/Islamist discourse on Islam and democracy *(shura,* Islamic democracy) has not only adopted, and declared as Islamic or compatible with Islam, certain elements of modern democratic political organization such as elections, representation, parliamentary rule, or the separation of powers. It has also incorporated, on one level at least, key values such as freedom, equality, individual responsibility and accountability, even though a close analysis of Islamist positions on human rights, women, non-Muslims, freethinkers, agnostics and atheists will reveal that the general principles ('no compulsion in religion', 'freedom of thought', 'equality/equal worth', etc.) are in most cases confined to the framework of Islam, the *shari'a*, common decency or what the individual group, thinker or activist may choose to define as such. It is not liberal democracy that they wish to see established but a state of law, justice and order based on stable norms that are beyond the reach of human beings, be they despots or the gullible masses. Certain thinkers and activists excepted (the Sudanese Hasan al-Turabi or the Tunisian Rashid al-Ghannushi may be among them), Islamist writers have in general little respect for those masses, if they do not openly despise them: they are fickle, and they require guidance, not necessarily of the 'traditional' *'ulama*, but of those who have seen the truth. The old distinction between the elite and the masses, *al-'amma* and *al-khassa*, albeit rarely acknowledged, is still very much in evidence.

In this modern utopia of an Islamic order that is based on justice and *shura*, participatory, moral and harmonious, elements of 'traditional' Islamic social and political thought have been reinterpreted in the light of modern ideals, concerns and necessities, sometimes subtly, often less so, but generally with the intent, avowed or unavowed, to give legitimacy to modern concepts by linking them, and be it fictitiously, to the great tradition. It is still primarily a moral discourse rather than an openly political one. That there should be reinterpretation comes, of course, as no surprise given the great richness of the Islamic heritage *(al-turath)* which preserved its very richness because of its capacity to assimilate and integrate diverse ideas, techniques and, yes, values. Yet it is often ignored or at least neglected by analysts of modern Islamic political thought who are struck by the bitter rejection of all things Western and do not look more closely as to how divine sovereignty *(hakimiyya)*, collective authority, individual responsibility and the duty to consult are actually defined, and to what extent modern notions have in fact been 'authenticated' by providing them with an Islamic pedigree. The various attempts to design an Islamic order suited to the modern age are the product of interaction between Muslim and Islamist thinkers, their critics, society at large, and the state who all hold different ideas of what authenticity, modernity and 'the West' imply, or require. They are eclectic, often contradictory, open to further change and modification, and for that reason worthy of attention. In any case, the distinction between values and techniques, so dear to Muslim scholars, Islamist activists, certain ruling powers and some of their sharpest critics alike, that can help to facilitate assimilation and incorporation, deserves closer attention.

Notes

1.   Ammara (1988: 66–9); al-Awwa (1989: 49–61, 120 ff.); al-Ghannushi (1989: 66 ff.); Serjeant (1981), chapters V and VI.

2.   Binder (1988:2); Turner (1974).

3.   Waterbury (1994: 23–47); Sadowski (1993: 14–21 & 40); Kramer, G. (1994: 200–26) & (1995a: 39–67); Esposito & Voll (1996).

4.   The following is based on my *thèse d'état* (1993); Ammara (1988); al-Awwa (1989); Huwaydi (1993) & (1982); Khalid (1981); Khallaf (1993); Uda (1951a) & (1951b); Osman (1985); Jarisha (1985) & (1986) all from the Egyptian Brotherhood; the Syrian Muslim Brother Hawwa (1984); the Tunisian Islamist al-Ghannushi (1993); and the leader of the Sudanese National Islamic Front, al-Turabi (1985). Two studies by prominent Egyptian constitutional lawyers dating from the 1960s are widely quoted in Islamist circles: Muhammad Diya al-Din al-Rayyis (1979) and Abd al-Hamid Mutawalli (1966). Many of their themes had already been presented, in a decidedly modernist vein, by Muhammad Asad (1961), who, in the late 1940s, was involved in elaborating an Islamic constitution for the newly created state of Pakistan.

5.   For representative statements, see Asad (1961: 11–13) or al-Bishri (1989:20–31). For an original view, see Ammara (1989: 98–108).

6.   Ammara (1988: 14ff., 64–82, 208 ff.); for Abduh, see Kerr (1966:3 ff., 151 ff., 189 ff.).

7.   More sophisticated authors who had a training in Islamic law and theology distinguish between the binding and the non-binding *sunna*, i.e., those elements of the *sunna* that refer to Muhammad in his capacity as prophet with full authority to define Islamic norms and obligations as opposed to those that report his saying and doings as a mere political leader, an ordinary human being so to speak. Once again, the distinction is more compelling in theory than in practice for the actual divisions are far from clear and univer-

sally accepted. For details, see al-Awwa (1974: 29–49), or Ammara (1988: 70–80, 195–213); both refer to Mahmud Shaltut, 1958–63 Shaykh al-Azhar, whose *al-Islam aqida wa-shari'a* (1988), is still widely quoted (here pp. 409–505). See now Brown (1996).

8.   For a detail refutation of this interpretation of '*man lam yahkum biman anzala Allah*', see Ammara (1988: 31–82). A good example is Shaykh Omar Ahmed Ali Abdurrahman (1990).

9.   The distinction between the 'pure and uncorrupted' *shari'a* and 'imperfect *fiqh*', its 'frail and fallible filter', has been presented with great clarity by the Indian scholar Kemal Faruki in his *Islamic Jurisprudence* (1988: 12–19), who does not, however, link it to politics.

10.   Sivan (1995: 218–43).

11.   For *maslaha* and the *maqasid* of the *shari'a*, see the Moroccan reformer Allal al-Fasi (s.d.: 133–47, 177–85).

12.   Kerr (1966: 210 ff.).

13.   The principal Koranic references are *suras* 2:30, 17:70, 33:72 and 49:13. For critical overviews, see Steppat (1989: 163–72) and Wielandt (1993: 179–209). The Muslim Brother Abd al-Qadir Uda (1906–54) in his *al-Islam wa awda'una al-siyasa* (1951a: 16–35, 279ff.) developed a concept of the viceregency of man which influenced subsequent Muslim and Islamist thinkers and activist.

14.   The debate about sovereignty in general and *hakimiyya* in particular is inextricably linked to two of the most influential figures of Sunni Islamic political thought, the Indo–Pakistani Mawlana al-Mawdudi (1903–79) and the Egyptian Sayyid Qutb (1906–66). For an in-depth study of the issue, which has raised considerable controversy, see Abd al-Karim (1976).

15.   For the attempt, see Crone and Martin (1986) or Jaadane (1989).

16.   Many contemporary authors base themselves on a treatise by the great Hanbali scholar Taqi al-Din Ahmad b. Taymiya (d. 1328), one of the chief references of contemporary Islamist thought, particularly radical Islamist thought, *Al-amr bi-l-ma'ruf wa-l-nahy 'an al-munkar*, ed. by Muhammad Jamil Ghazi (1987).

17.   Again Ibn Taymiya serves as prime reference; see his *Al-hisba wa-mas'uliyyat al-hukuma al-islamiyya*, ed. by Azzam (s.d.). The duty of *hisba* is claimed by the Saudi religious police, but it was also invoked by the opponents of Nasr Hamid Abu Zayd, a lecturer of literature at Cairo University and outspoken critic of Islamist discourse and practice, who, in 1995, accused him of apostasy and had him forcibly divorced from his wife; see Kermani (1994: 25–49).

18.   For details, see Abd al-Rahman (1988).

19.   Hasan al-Turabi offers a good example of the view that identifies the will of the people (*volonté populaire*) with the demand for the introduction of an Islamic system; see, e.g., his articles (1985: 17) or (1983: 241–9).

20.   Al-Tamawi (1967) and Khallaf (1985).

21.   See, e.g., 'Draft on an Islamic Constitution (1978)', presented by the Islamic Research Academy of al-Azhar, published in *Majallat al-Azhar*, 51 (1979), (April), pp. 4, 151–9 & 81; 'A Model of an Islamic Constitution (1983)' presented at an *International Islamic Conference* held in Islamabad by the Secretary–General of the Islamic Council and published in *The Muslim World League Journal*, 5–6, (*Jumada* I & II 1404), pp. 27–33, chapter X.

22.   Amongst the numerous studies devoted to *shura*, see al-Maliji (s.d.); al-Shawi (1992). Amongst the authors rejecting any identification of *shura* with Western democracy, see the conservative Saudi author Adnan Ali Rida al-Nahwi (1985), or the Jordanian Islamist Mahmud al-Khalidi (1986).

23.   See al-Sayyid (1984) or Djaït (1989).

24.   For details, see my 'Islam and Pluralism' (1995b: 113–28). The conventional view is presented by Yusuf al-Qaradawi (1990); for a critical assessment, see Umlil (1991). Some very interesting statements by Islamist thinkers and activists, amongst them al-Ghannushi and al-Awwa, are included in Tamimi (1993).

25.   Like *fitna*, apostasy (*ridda*) is associated with a historical event firmly rooted in the collective memory, or the *imaginaire social*, in this case the secession of certain Bedouin tribes after the death of the Prophet which was interpreted by Muslim scholars not so much as the political act of treason, but as the religious act of apostasy. The identification of conversion or apostasy with high treason is still commonly made, even where Muslims form the majority of the population and are no longer threatened by individual acts of conversion. For the classical doctrines, see Peters & De Vries (1976/77: 1–25); for a relatively moderate modern view, see El Awa (Mohammed S. al-Awwa) (1982:43–68).

13

Family Restructuring and Affirmation of the Individual in Muslim Countries: The Case of Iran

FARIBA ADELKHAH

We can begin by stating that the problem of the family in Muslim countries is not one of the resilience or resurgence of a single traditional model, as argued by those who subscribe to the thesis of a clash between Muslim civilization and the West, but rather a highly dynamic process involving the re-invention of a social structure in a quite new context. We should first specify what the main components of this process are: firstly, one should note the diversity of Muslim societies themselves and of their cultural and historical heritage. Whatever the force of the Koranic message, there is little in common between family models observed (say) in West Africa or East Africa, the Maghreb, the Balkans, Anatolia, India or Indonesia. This is particularly important because in the view of anthropologists, relations of kinship are not so much a structure as a language through which social actors constantly renegotiate extra-family issues, e.g. of an economic or political nature.[1]

The contemporary economic and political context accentuates this difference between the varying problems of the family in Muslim countries. It is particularly important to note the impact of the economic situation in each. For example, in black Africa Islamic social structures acted to cushion the effects of the serious recession in the 1980s and tend even to take over from a decaying state, just as Christian churches and sects sometimes do. In Central Africa, the advance of Koranic schools is largely due to the succession of 'blank years' in the state-run education system. On the other hand, Islamic social structures may also occur within the context of a 'rentier' type economy (the Gulf states) or in countries with a high economic growth rate, e.g. Indonesia, Malaysia or even Turkey, and resist the ensuing upheaval (migrations, rural exodus, urbanization or re-urbanization). The relationship between religion and the family obviously varies from one type of situation to another.

Likewise, the political conditions in which the question of the family arises are highly diverse. The case of Iran, which is always cited by denigrators of political Islam, is quite original. It is characterized by a genuine political revolution, a popular-based urban movement in the form of vast peaceful demonstrations, which is unparalleled in the Islamic world. Today it has entered a post-revolutionary phase, which can be characterized as 'Thermidorian' and which is giving rise to extensive intellectual and legal debate in a plural press, though under the control of an authoritarian regime drawing its ideology and hegemony from the Islamic principle. In Turkey, on the other hand, the hegemonic and nationalist ideology is secular, although there is no radical rift between it and Muslim concepts.[2] Islamic claims, which are post-Kemalist and neo-positivist are channelled through a parliamentary party, the Refah, or by brotherhoods closely linked to the two major parties of the liberal right. Such claims must take into account a corpus of laws of the West-European type which have irreversibly shaped civil society (for example, the civil code is extensively based on the Swiss model). With its civil war, Algeria tragically illustrates a third political form of the Islamist problem, although this scenario remains exceptional (occurring only in Afghanistan, Tajikistan and possibly in Egypt in the future). It seems to be due less to religion than to an aggravation of factional trends and a specific form of political economy.[3] Between these extreme cases, there is a myriad of other political situations such as charismatic monarchies crossed with parliamentary regimes as in Jordan or Morocco, more or less authoritarian regimes as in Tunisia, Indonesia or even Malaysia, parliamentary democracies with social and religious pluralism as in India or the Ivory Coast, military regimes using Islam for political ends as in Sudan, etc. Each type of situation affects the process of re-inventing the family in its own way.

Family patterns in Muslim countries are not governed exclusively by endogenous laws considered to be particular to an Islamic civilization doomed to clash with the West. They too form part of the globalization trend. But this is not reducible to an effect of uniformization or to a process of reinvention of an Islamic difference. Firstly, the reference models highlighted by the process of globalization vary, especially as regards the family. For example, it has been noted that emigration of North Africans into West-European countries has encouraged the spread of contraception in their home countries and facilitated the demographic transition, while immigration of Egyptians in the Gulf States has had the opposite effect by encouraging a re-traditionalization of the family.[4] In Iran reference to the Western nuclear family with its stress on individualization, which was highly in vogue under the *ancien régime*, is losing ground to the Japanese family model, the attraction of which has been highlighted by the prodigious success of the television series *Oshin*. Secondly, the adoption of foreign perceptions and practices, far from watering down the feeling of being Iranian, has strengthened it. It has two apparently (but not really) contradictory effects: on the one hand, it accentuates the diversity between Muslim societies because it is affected by trends which vary from one situation to another, while on the other it helps disseminate references throughout the *umma*, e.g. in the field of family law or women's dress. From this standpoint globalization acts as a kaleidoscope rather than as establishing a fixed stable relation between Western societies and Muslim societies. Understanding of the question of the family in Muslim countries must be based on the analysis of specific situations, clearly underscoring the historical and contingent nature of these. I am not certain, for example, that the position of women in Islamic society, which remains the main source of misunderstanding between Westerners and Muslims, is doomed to remain captive in the 'scriptural prison' which is how some regard the Koranic message. Inevitably, this message will be renegotiated by real-life women and men believers, as well as by clerics who will alter not its religious meaning from the standpoint of the faith, but rather its social efficaciousness, just as has occurred down the centuries with the Testament of the Christian faith.

The great question today is whether Muslim societies are exploring new types of organization and thought which are bound to have their effects on the family. In this paper we will look at only two possible approaches to the question: the relationship between political mobilization and transformation of the family circle, and the relationship between the family and the individual.

Political mobilization and the problem of the family

For Western public opinion, it is an open and shut case: political Islam's main message is the submission of women and a refusal of their emancipation as has been achieved in the West. Iran's Islamic revolution is a typical example of this type of 'return to the Middle Ages'. It should be noted that certain Islamist militants are not far from sharing this interpretation and ascribe the 'corruption of women' to the West and Westernization. But what is striking in the Iranian Revolution is the very modest rank occupied by the question of the place of women and of the family. The popular movement in the country raised political slogans such as the overthrow of the monarchy, the reconquest of national independence lost to American imperialism and (although only in the first phase of the revolution) the claim for an Islamic government. The problem of the position of women and the organization of the family was only raised in the first months of the Islamic Republic, stemming from the question of the veil, and it opposed the various revolutionary currents although it cannot be reduced to a confrontation between secular and religious elements. Without repeating the results of a previous analysis,[5] we should stress that Iranian women who participated *en masse* in the 1978–79 demonstrations succeeded in maintaining their essential legal rights acquired under the 'Ancien Régime', e.g. divorce, and perhaps even increased their presence in public affairs, under the protection of the *hijab*, through their devotional and charity work or due to the development of unlicensed trading during the economic recession. Due to the pressure of these social developments, the leaders of the Islamic Republic could not keep to a neo-fundamentalist view of women's position and finally recognized the political and revolutionary legitimacy of certain hopes and claims. The Islamic left was understandably more ready to do so than the conservative right which won the general elections in 1992. In any event, the social and political reality of the Islamic Republic cannot be reduced to the submission and segregation of women. On various occasions Imam Khomeini received delegations made up of women and it is in Saudi Arabia, not in Iran, that women are banned from driving. It is also revealing that Iranian society tends to be perceived as modern and open in these matters by public opinion in the United Arab Emirates.

One of the most striking aspects of the recent general elections

(March, 1996) was the election in the first round of Faezeh Hashemi for the party of the 'Servants of Reconstruction'. The significance of this success, which received extensive media coverage, is twofold. It is remarkable firstly in that it is a political success: the 'Servants of Reconstruction' aim to support Rafsanjani and, if possible, help achieve his re-election in 1997, even at the cost of a constitutional revision. Faezeh Hashemi played a key role by putting up a good fight against the president of the Iranian parliament and leader of the outgoing conservative majority, Nategh Nouri, who only won by a slim majority. But this victory by the president's daughter also meant success for a certain class of women, for not only is Faezeh Hashemi the President of the Women's Sporting Federation and a competent horserider, but she also represents the epitome of the 'executive (and Islamic) woman', judging by the way I saw her drive when covering her election campaign. It would be premature to draw conclusions from an election which still has to go to a second round (late April 1996), even though it is likely that the number of women elected to parliament will be considerably greater. But it is already clear that this election has marked a peak for the affirmation and re-structuring of the family in Iranian political society. On this count, the Islamic Republic is proving itself politically capable of institutionalizing the social debate rather than stifling it.[6]

In the very different context (as we have seen) of Turkish parliamentary democracy, the Refah is also bearing witness to the fact that Islam does not necessarily bar women from social participation. The study by Nilüfer Göle[7] paints a picture of women political activists quite comparable to that of the Iranian Islamist women I have studied. The Turkish women likewise are university graduates who see no contradiction whatsoever between their religious and political claims and their aspiration to modernity and who are using the symbol of the veil to renegotiate their place in society. The increased electoral support for the Refah owes much to this type of militancy, especially in Istanbul. It is important to recall that this is occurring in a political society open to the excesses and perversities of permissiveness and consumerism. For many years the popular dailies have regularly published photographs of scantily clad women and they are given to scandal mongering. Against this backdrop, Filiz Ergun, a lady dentist and a Refah town councillor, was involved in a case of adultery with a fellow party official. In a defiant outburst on Iranian TV, the official exclaimed: 'Sure, I slept with her, what the heck is it to you?' (*Libération*, 24 November 1993). One could also cite the case of the imam who demanded a divorce since his wife stubbornly insisted on wearing the chador and would not dress 'like a civilized woman'. In court the cleric justified his stance, saying 'I want a partner in keeping with modern-day society' (*Libération*, 6 May 1993).

However, we should not portray the Refah and Turkish Islam as in any way resembling a red-light district! In the main, militancy amongst Islamic women is channelled through the strategy of doing charity work which is a key point in this type of populist movement in Turkey as in Algeria, Lebanon and India. By helping the impoverished slum-dwellers in the '*gecekondu*' (shanty towns), showing solidarity and sharing with them life's joys and trials (bereavement, marriage, birth, etc.), the women supporters of the Refah are accounting for a high proportion of their party's vote. But Mr Erbakan's party is very heterogeneous sociologically speaking, with support coming from both the large cities in western Turkey and the eastern provinces. In addition, its internal organization is poorly known, so that it is difficult to pinpoint the factor which prompted the decision not to present women candidates at the 24 December 1995 elections. According to certain leaders, the Statutes of the Parliament ban veiled women from taking their seats, but this argument is unfounded and seems like an attempt to hold the republican institutions responsible for a choice made by the Refah leaders themselves. Other Refah leaders actually went so far as to allege that a women's place is in the home and that they are incapable of carrying out the same tasks as men. The party's female committees, purged of their most feminist elements and now controlled by Mr Erbakan's wife, did not feel the need, however, to react publicly. In any event, this decision seems to have harmed the Refah. It won a lower absolute number of votes in Istanbul than in the March 1994 municipal elections (down 1.7 per cent, i.e. 80,000 votes, despite an overall increase in the number of voters enrolled), especially in districts where the mayor was a Refah member. It has still not succeeded in making a breakthrough in the prosperous regions along the Aegean and Mediterranean coasts, although it has strengthened its position in its traditional strongholds in the centre and east of Anatolia. The other parties have not achieved much better results in parliament in promoting women's rights, and the Ciller 'tree' should not hide the 'forest' of machismo in Turkish politics, because women made up less than 5 per cent of the candidates running and even fewer in potentially 'safe seats'.

This all too brief analysis of the case of Iran and Turkey shows that politics is a key medium for the transformation of women's status. Far from being typical of the situation throughout Muslim countries, the present drama in Algeria is a specific case. The Algerian crisis is due to the failure of that transformation medium to function because of the severity of the French colonialist regime, the harshness of the war of liberation, the policy of the post-colonial military regime and finally the implosion of this latter due to the combined effect of repression and terrorism. Nonetheless, the Algerian civil war cannot be reduced to a struggle between secularism (or a progressive attitude) and Islam (or obscurantism), a conflict in which women are the only victims.[8] In its bloody way, the war also reveals developments in the field of the family because joining the Islamic Salvation Front or taking to the 'maquis' enables young people to gain independence from their families, to become consumers and develop their individual personality.[9] More widely, the sharp focus on the question of women in the eyes of Westerners should not lead us to reduce the problem of the Muslim family to that of women.

Restructuring the family and individualization

If we reconsider the situation in Iran, we can see how family restructuring, expressed in the language of Islam, seems to be accompanied by a parallel problem of individualization. Women are clearly concerned by these trends, but so are the remaining members of the family unit who also see the boundaries of their role in the family redefined. In my view, the process of individualization is not occurring against the family or outside the family, rather it is a key part of it and is contributing to the process of bringing the family into line with the new context of the contemporary world. Conversely, the vigour of the family order is not revealed by the permanence of community structures outside or against the state but rather by the marking out of its sphere or its roles and the independence of its members, partly because of interference from the state sphere, e.g. in the legal field. This is an example of the strong relationship observed by de Tocqueville between the omnipotence of the state and the autonomy of the individual. Even if in the early 1980s the totalitarian tendencies of the Islamic Revolution encountered resistance from the private sector, nonetheless the Republic plays a role of centralization and bureaucratic rationalization in Iranian society.[10]

As a starting point we can take the television series *Patriarch* (*Pedar salar*) which has enjoyed a blockbuster success in 1995 and 1996 and which, like *Oshin*, has led to heated debates in the workplace and in families between parents and children and husbands and wives. The TV screen has in fact crystallized the question of these types of relationships. In this 'soap opera' a father plans, with no prior consultation, to house his three married sons under his own roof. The youngest daughter-in-law, whose marriage is being followed by the viewers with bated breath, refuses to accept this arrangement, one thing leads to another and the family shows major signs of strain. The infuriated father chases his children from the home, refuses any contact with them and withdraws his emotional and economic support. The mother, who is the main go-between, and allows us to see the effects of the conflict between father and sons, desperately employs all her diplomatic wiles to reconcile the household. However, only illness opens the eyes of the patriarch and persuades him to accede to his wife's pleas and, in the vivid Persian expression, 'get off Satan's donkey'. He understands that the world has changed. His children are moved and delighted to let bygones be bygones. They return home to the time-honoured tradition of joining their father around the dinner table. The tablecloth symbolizes a pole of family stability and solidarity, an incomparable haven of peace in society. However, still around the symbolic tablecloth, it is the father who takes the initiative and decides to turn a new page, handing a bunch of keys to each of his sons who henceforth, on his suggestion, will live as neighbours in adjoining apartments in a housing block and not share a single house as in olden days.

The message of the plot is clear: there is no salvation outside the family but there can be no family without respect for the autonomy of individuals and couples. Once again, we should not underestimate the emotional force of this type of message which compares today with that of the Koran in a Muslim society. It is well known that the astounding success of this type of melodrama in Asia is a key outlet for the women's self-assertion and the transformation of family roles.[11] Since 1979 there has been an ongoing process of nuclearization of the Iranian family which began in the 1960s and 1970s due to oil wealth and urbanization. This development is inseparable from the innovations of modern life such as accommodation in apartments, the spread of Western-style furniture, the popularity of travel by car and by air, social values and role models influenced by the media (including American cinema which remains very popular). These and other factors interact to shape the role of the individual and the family. One should not think, however, that the family runs counter to the purposes of the regime or the expectations of Islam.

For one thing, by and large state policy backs this trend, e.g. by encouraging birth control, facilitating contraception to protect the health of mothers and provide better education for children or by targeting the bulk of its school support programmes to the nuclear family. School is, *par excellence*, the focal point where state intervention and the role of the family converge and interact, as parents and teachers cooperate in the education of children. But it is also one of the social institutions of the Islamic Republic where one can best appreciate the tremendous thrust for change and innovation, whatever the lingering authoritarianism in the relationship between young people and adults and the material difficulties of an education system in a country facing a severe economic recession and a high birth rate. One advertisement for a private centre in Teheran clearly illustrates this aspiration for a type of school open to the needs, and indeed wishes, of individual children. Under the caption 'Here, your child decides', one group of children are seen working round a table while others have chosen to practice their writing lying traditional-style on a carpet on the floor. In daily life, the remodelling of the family is reflected precisely in this alternative 'between armchair and carpet', although it is inseparable from the public action of the state.

The religious sphere is also involved in this reinvention of the family model. Both in the press and on radio and television, clerics constantly debate and question the social role of women, which ultimately is the background reference to the unending debate about the *hijab*. The debate, it should be stressed, usually occurs on non-religious programmes. The clerics voice their views as religious specialists but also in a good-natured, informal way as family advisers (*moshaver-e khanevadeh*), full of sound advice, rather like Mennie Grégoire in France. A pointer to the importance of this social phenomenon is the fact that the TV-preacher Hujat al-Islam Moussavi-Hosseini, the presenter of the programme *Khanevadeh* ('Family', now off the air), achieved an outstanding success in the first round of the general elections and will certainly be re-elected on April 20. This is amazing given the suspicion with which the Iranian clergy viewed television prior to 1979. Even today, Hojjati-Kermani can be heard debating the advisability of banning satellite dishes. Although the media today are a key instrument for socialization, and hence for the transformation of the family sphere, Islam remains overwhelmingly present, and not only as a system of ideological domination as often thought. Rather, it provides the vocabulary and the grammar by which people are shaping their modernity, including the modern family, (although this latter cannot be reduced to religious language).

Islam too, and the practice thereof, is subject to this ongoing change, and the forms of the various ceremonies, acts of worship, rituals and prayers can themselves contribute to the process of individualization of family members and the rationalization of their behaviour.

Let us consider the difference between Iran in the 1970s and today. In 1970, the population was 33.7 millions, approximately 47 per cent living in towns of over 100,000 inhabitants. In 1996, the population has risen to 60 millions, 58 per cent living in towns. Over the same period the percentage of children in school has risen from 30 per cent to 80 per cent (20 per cent to 70 per cent among girls). Teheran which had 4.5 million inhabitants in 1976 is today a megalopolis of more than ten million inhabitants. These figures underscore the extent of the change due both to overall modernization as well as to specific events (the Revolution, the war with Iraq, an exceptionally high birth rate, the fluctuating economics of oil, etc.). The world of religion was bound to be affected in its turn by this change, as shown by examples from daily life. Thirty years ago a middle-class family living in the capital and practising religion in the common, accepted way in Iran, would exercise great caution in referring to the Koran and Koranic verses out of respect for their sacredness. The Book had an aura, its presence was keenly felt. It was kept in a high place in the room in a cloth cover to avoid contact with dust or impure hands and to keep It out of the reach of children. People would move around the room in relation to the Book, never turning their back on It, avoiding any unseemly, let alone immoral, posture, never for example stretching out their legs towards It, even to sleep. It was deemed improper to rise to one's feet while the Koran remained open for reading. Reference was made to It at every important event in life. For example, a verse of the Koran would be pinned to the clothing of new-born babies, It would be read out at a particular stage of the wedding ritual and brides would be photographed holding the Book. Before setting out on a journey, the traveller would pass three times under the Koran and a glass of water. Consultation of the Koran via a religious authority would be made before taking any far-reaching decision, It would be used to ward off ill fate, e.g. during illness, and, obviously, It would be recited over the dead. Daily life itself was placed under Its protection: house façades would frequently bear ceramic or wrought iron decorations comprising a verse of the Koran. The sacredness of the Koran was so strongly felt that it gave rise to so many constraints that people avoided having too many copies in their possession. For example, a civil servant in the Pahlavi administration would often prefer to get rid of a particularly precious copy of the Koran with intricate calligraphy on gazelle hide by 'giving It to the water' (which had to be pure and running). This was the normal process for destroying religious writings, in particular, damaged or incomplete fragments of the Koran. A religious person might well even systematically cut out Koranic verses appearing in newspapers to protect them from irreverent treatment and eliminate them according to the prescribed rules, even if this meant travelling right across town to find a well or stream guaranteeing the required degree of purity.

Many of these customs are still in use today. Some of them have even developed and acceded to the status of 'invented traditions'. For example, the *va en yakad* pinned to a baby's clothing today is a personalized gold brooch. The bride's Koran heads the dowry list and today is at the heart of the wedding ceremony. Its binding must be of good quality and the wife-to-be will pore over the Book more solemnly than ever, as the moment approaches for her to be immortalized on a video tape shot by a professional (women only) crew. This has given rise to a new profession for women in Iran as camera operators. Trained on the job, they are meeting a new need of modern-minded families, while complying with the Islamic norms which the Republic holds dear. During the long photo session the bride poses repeatedly, holding the Word of God (*kalam ol-lah*) in her cupped hands, gazing ecstatically heavenward. In many ways the new family sociability in Iran and the craving for consumer goods and modern technology are reifying and ritualizing ancient practices, including religious ones.

However, the most obvious innovations relate to the actual dissemination of the Koran. Nowadays, the Holy Book is published in large editions and there are more and more different editions available. Previously all editions shared a similar calligraphy, binding, format and translation into Persian. Now there is great diversity. Drawing on extensive new exegesis, many new, less literal, translations have appeared. The believer has the choice of different presentations for different purposes, ranging from the pocket version in a leather or plastic case with a zip fastener to the quality edition designed to grace a room and impress visitors. The Islamic Republic boasts it is completing the world's largest edition of the Koran. It is also possible to purchase keyrings with miniature Korans printed in characters so small as to be illegible and sheathed in a protective case. It may be exaggerating to talk of a process of 'merchandizing' of the Book. People never say, for example, they are going to 'purchase' a Koran or inquire directly about the price. The ritual consists of asking 'how much is the gift of Koran?' (*hedieh-ye qoran chandeh?*) and bookshop labels read 'gift of the Koran: 5,000 Rials'. However, the widespread presence of the Word of God has perceptibly altered the relationship people have with It. Its contents appear in the daily press, certain newspapers have chosen a Koranic verse for their motto, others punctuate political and social news items with holy quotations, and most of them devote articles to theological debates, studded with *suras*. It has become impossible to take as many precautions as previously in one's day-to-day dealings with the Holy Scripture, even though some believers and clerics voice indignation at this phenomenon, especially since newspapers (newsprint often being state-subsidized) frequently serve as cheap wrapping paper for butchers or greengrocers and eventually end up in rubbish bins. Furthermore, the everyday, commonplace presence of the Koran has divorced It from its previous close connection with the sense of bereavement, so much so that the *bismallah* mania of the leaders of the regime, who never begin a speech without invoking the name of God Almighty and Merciful, is now the butt of frequent jokes. For example, a reporter asks a peasant what he puts on his fruit trees, to which the peasant replies: 'In the name of God Almighty and Merciful, dung … !.' Obviously, these jokes are not to everyone's taste and certain practices and views prevalent thirty years ago still hold today. However, the combined effects of the changes inherent in a 'mass society' in the field of consumption and communications on the one hand, and the Republic's wish for Islamization have irreversibly altered people's concept of the sacred and their relationship with it. Besides the fact that the Book is now the subject of ideological debate in the daily press and reviews (not only legal, theological or philosophical disputes, known as *erfan*, limited to clerical circles), It is now giving rise to new activities for the believer–consumer. For example, it is possible to hear the *sura* of one's choice chanted by simply dialling 114 (corresponding to the 114 *suras*) and this service is soon to be available on Minitel although the number of subscribers in Iran is still low. However, sales of Minitels seem to be rising precisely at the same rate as that of the demand for the '114 Koran' service.

Along the same lines, Iranian television is recommending that the music played while holding the telephone line should be replaced by a recorded Koranic verse. It should be noted that these new forms of Islamic socialization do not really reflect an upsurge in revolutionary militancy. They are manifestations of the 'Thermidorian' period of the Republic and coincide with new kinds of consumer behaviour appreciated by *homo iranicus* or *homo Islamicus*. For example, believers wishing to improve their knowledge of the Book can acquire at least three computer diskettes of what can only be described as 'Koranic games' (*Touba, Rezvan, and Taha*) allowing them to become familiar in Persian, English or French and interactive mode with Koranic verses, religious science and the life of the Saints. There is no reason to suppose that these 'Koranic games' will oust computer games which are all the rage with the younger generation. But they do point to the fact that Islam has entered the era of the mass media and its new communications systems.

Insofar as they are one dimension of the process of rationalization (Max Weber), bureaucratization, technologizing and even merchandizing of the religious sphere, are accompanied by a process of individualization. Religious socialization combines these different aspects. Girls, as is known, are initiated to prayers at the age of nine (whereas boys must carry out their religious duties from the age of 15). The ceremonies marking the attendant rites have been transmitted on television since the early 1990s, something quite unprecedented in Iranian society. Wearing a white veil, young girls recite for the first time, collectively and in public, the prayer which they have learned during the school year. They are fêted and receive floral crowns, gifts and a copy of the Koran. Several remarks may be made about this rite: it recalls the solemn communion in the Catholic faith, it translates the social recognition and esteem for the child celebrated as an individual in his or her own right, and it formally ratifies the child's autonomy vis-à-vis the family who provided his or her education. This new form of religious socialization thus shows that the bureaucratization of Islam both limits the field of action of the family, generates a certain homogeneity of the practices celebrated and disseminated by television, and fosters individualization within this framework at the earliest age.

Islam today is as much a matter of reason as of belonging. This point was already clear in Ayatollah Motahhari's writings. Since the Revolution the dissemination of the regime's ideological discourse, especially during Friday prayers, and the conquest of the media by religion have accentuated this rationalization of the Islamic message. More and more, believers themselves are justifying their practices with logical arguments claiming to have a scientific foundation. Thus polygamy is judged harmful in light of the teachings of Western psychology: the woman who is victim of polygamy is likely to be a poor mother and unable to assume her social role. If only because times are hard and money short, the Foundation of Martyrs backs this argument and only recognizes the first wife's entitlement to social benefits.

This rationalization of religion and its relationship with the process of individualization of believers is furthered greatly by the development of this widespread media cover. For example, when religious meetings are convened announcements are made by computer-generated posters, flags placed in public thoroughfares, advertisements and inserts in the daily press. Radio also publicizes the meetings. The names of religious speakers at the meeting are clearly mentioned and notice is given if there are to be questions and answers (*porsesh-o pasokh*). In other words, religious meetings now constitute an individualized, interactive sphere, whereas previously people came to listen only. Believers choose between these religious meetings, preferring one speaker or one type of sociability to another. It must be added that these changes are also affecting women: their *jalesseh* are subjected to the same rules of publicity and competition. Without repeating our previous analyses, it may be recalled that the religious sphere has provided women with numerous possibilities of access to the public urban sphere, with full social, and even political, legitimacy. At present, many women are in charge of Islamic institutions or associations, particularly in the charity field, participating fully in the structural differentiation of the religious sphere. This is not to say that the emancipation of women necessarily involves Islam in Iran. Some prefer to open body-building centres (this, it should be added, is perfectly in keeping with Islamic morals as recommended by the regime and is legitimized by gender segregation). But in any given traditional society, religion may be a key factor for individualization. On this count it may be interesting to compare Iran with Victorian England. It has been said that women's charity work paved the way for the militant feminism of the Suffragettes in a context of urbanization, industrialization and development of a popular press.

This brief overview of trends in family restructuring in Iran shows up a landscape which is much more complex than supposed by the thesis of the 'clash of civilizations'. Islam, while clearly not to be underestimated, is only one of many factors involved and will have to come to terms with them. For example, the economic recession and the war with Iraq have played a key role in the move towards independence for women, either by obliging them to work in unlicensed trading to supplement family incomes or to take over as head of the household due to the absence or death of their husband, as in the case of the heroine in *Bachu, the little stranger* (Bayza'i, 1989), or indeed Fa'ezeh Hashemi whose husband died shortly after the Revolution and who is raising her two children single-handed. Likewise, the portrait of the dead on tombstones and in death notices, even when the deceased is a woman, owes more to the worship of the young martyrs killed in the war than to any Muslim conviction (the status of anthropomorphic reproduction has traditionally posed problems in Islam).

By taking due note of this complexity, we will understand better that the religion of the Prophet does not, in itself, constitute an insurmountable obstacle to changes in the family occurring and that it probably brings about different effects in different situations. I do not have the time nor have I researched the matter fully enough to deal with other Muslim societies here. However, my impression is that the way in which (say) Turkish women reproduce the family framework in the context of their paid work in the textile sector while some of them probably vote for the Refah[12] or the way in which Egyptian women legitimize their presence in factories by wearing the *hijab*[13] are individual examples of social situations which exist throughout the Muslim world. By taking into account the differences within that world, one can correctly pose the question of the relationship between Europe and Islam in the field of family behaviour and customs. All too often, Islamic civilization is identified with the Arab countries in closest geographical proximity, especially the Maghreb, or more exactly with what we think we know about those countries. However, this overlooks one obvious fact: the immense majority of Muslims are not Arabs and do not speak Arabic. It may well be that the search for an 'Islamic specificity' in years to come will receive its main impetus from the Muslim countries of Asia. Already, Pakistani networks are assuming growing leadership in the neo-fundamentalist movement and their influence in British Islam in general, and the Rushdie affair in particular, is well known. Likewise, Malaysian and Indonesian Islam are exploring a model of Islamic modernity which is exerting considerable influence in the Gulf.

Conclusion

How then should we perceive the process of affirmation of an Islamic specificity in relation to Europe in the family sphere today since we seem to be dealing with a highly differentiated movement which is inseparable from its surrounding environment?

Firstly, Islamic strategies consistently emerge in relation to the Western world from which they adopt a number of elements, albeit in terms of conflict. However, the way in which these strategies are viewed in the West, i.e. with hostility, in its turn alters and shapes them. For the moment, the inevitable interaction between the two civilizations is gravitating towards tension as two opposing identities face each other. But this tension should not conceal the vast grey area of compromises and arrangements, particularly in technology in the 'worldly time' sphere.[14] In the context of West European industrial societies with their own values and practices, but also with their economic difficulties, Muslims will develop family models of their own which may borrow their main emblems from Islam but will not be determined only by the religious dimension.

One of the factors involved in this process of re-inventing the family relates to the boundary between private and public, and this is neither clear nor stable. As Charles Taylor has pointed out, it is constantly being negotiated. It is unfortunate that people do not fully understand that wearing the veil is precisely one manifestation of the wish for re-definition and may even be a claim by young women for independence from their family by gaining access to school and, in a host society which ignores them, to a personality in their own right. In particular, not enough emphasis is placed on the fact that this aspect of dress coincides with a stage in the search for identity by the individual or her family, rather than a testimony of the inalterable difference of Muslim identity. We repeatedly hear dogmatic stereotyped views on the decision to wear the veil while less attention is paid, for example, to any decisions to give up wearing it. Paradoxically, the most emotive cause of strife and friction between the two cultures may actually be a practice offering most hope for compromise and osmosis.

Notes

1. Geschiere (1995).
2. Tapper, Richard & Nancy (1991, 56–83).
3. Martínez (1995).
4. Courbage, Benhaïm & Leveau (1994).
5. Adelkhah (1991).
6. Adelkhah (1996).
7. Göle (1993).
8. Leveau (1995).
9. Labat (1995).
10. Adelkhah, Bayart & Roy (1993).
11. Dissanayake (1993).
12. White (1994).
13. Elowe MacLeod (1991).
14. Laïdi (1996).

Part Four

Islam in Europe, the Islam of Europe

14

The Re-Islamization of Muslim Immigration in Europe

JOCELYNE CESARI

The pattern of countries emerging from authoritarian regimes which spread during the 1980s from Latin America to the former Soviet Union, passing through Sub-Saharan Africa, marked a sharp contrast with what was, or was claimed to be, the 'exceptions' of Arab and Islamic countries. In their attempts to explain why and how Arab countries failed to benefit from this wind of freedom which was favouring the move to political liberalization in other latitudes, certain analysts were again tempted to base their explanations on the supposedly irreducible nature of the Islamic frame of reference. Their analyses failed to consider the importance of the context and the need for a historicist approach, frequently placing excessive emphasis on textual analysis and falling prey to a very essentialist vision of religion and an extremely linear conception of progress.

On the Northern shores of the Mediterranean, Muslims have been settled in European societies for some considerable time. With the increasing 'visibility' of signs of Islamic identity over the last decade and its accompanying forms of collective commitment, this question has again been raised with the same conceptual shortcomings. Here too, the 'totalization' effect has come into play: Muslims are as it were the victims of an 'assignation to be', as if the fact of professing the Islamic faith must necessarily be accompanied by unwavering compliance with the precepts and the ritual codes. The use of the term 'Islam' exercises a kind of 'totalizing' effect, rendering it inconceivable that Muslims can exercise the liberties and compromises vis-à-vis their revealed Law that believers of other faiths enjoy.

In the North as in the South, this 'totalizing' attitude generates at least three types of distortion. Firstly it conceals the remarkably modern form of relationship which more recent generations of immigrants maintain with Islam. In considering Islam as a cultural or ethical frame of reference which is fairly detached from the constraints of practising the religion, the vast majority of these young Muslims today exemplify a secularized use of religion and their behaviour as believers-cum-consumers is quite comparable to that of young Catholics of the same age.

The second price to pay for this 'essentialist' vision of religion overlooks the influence of cultural differences in people's relationship to Islam. It is necessary to stress, yet again, that Muslim history in its entirety demonstrates how 'ways of being a Muslim' vary greatly according to different cultural and historical contexts in which the Koranic message has taken root.

And the third cost of regarding Islamic countries as 'exceptional' or a case apart and the opaqueness this generates is that, more widely, it thwarts intellectual efforts to move beyond the well known dichotomy which continues to be repeated today [1] between those forging ahead actively with the task of political and social modernization on the one hand and Islam on the other.

In analysing forms of commitment to Islam manifested by a population of young people of Muslim background, my aim is to avoid explanations in terms of a 'return of religion' and rather to consider these forms as modalities of reconstruction of collective identities in contexts where the points of reference have become shifting and blurred since the collapse of East–West polarity. By focusing attention exclusively on the problem of the supposed 'return of the religious', one is assuming a differentiation between politics and religion, i.e. a distinction peculiar to the modern Western world which is in fact being questioned today even in countries where it arose and which, above all, blinds us to the full scope and variety of such manifestations. What we are witnessing is *not* a disappearance of the political sphere under the force of hammer blows from religion, but the utilization of religion, or merely the *vocabulary* of religion, to express new forms of politics which can no longer be expressed in the traditional words and concepts. On this count, to suggest that politico–religious movements are primarily religious movements using politics in order to resacralize public affairs or, conversely, primarily political movements using religion to gain political power, leads nowhere. Should we not rather consider them as movements seeking both political power and a resacralization of public affairs and whose distinguishing feature is that they can only conceive of power in the context of, and by reference to, the religious and vice versa? As Patrick Michel writes, 'These movements have been built on the double failure of nationalism and communism. Both take Western modernity as a reference: its liberal version is simultaneously fantasized, desired and rejected. They are above all indicators of the recirculation of ideas which, by permitting the expression and (to a certain extent) the overcoming of a feeling of frustration, translate the opposite of what they claim to voice. Far from attesting to a 'return of the religious', they point to its effacement by revealing a deficit in politics at the present time, a vast, cruel void where even the political vocabulary is lacking to express it. Hence the recourse to religion as a register of discourse, as a language.'[2]

In this situation of almost complete disenchantment with the world, or precisely because of this disenchantment, the affirmation of particular characteristics has acquired stronger force than ever. Recognition, authenticity, respect, etc. have become part and parcel of political claims and bear witness to people's greatest fear at the end of this century, that of fading into uniformity. This anguish about a loss of identity is explained by the shattering of individual and collective points of reference, obliging us to re-address the question of our relationship with the universal. The development of societies and nations is caught in the choice between two apparently irreconcilable options: the search for the universal and the assertion of difference. In this new – and still faltering – redistribution of meaning, religions are particularly sought after as vectors to explain and understand the changes under way.

The religious even so

In the light of these new factors, it is essential more than ever to develop a 'conceptual framework allowing us to control the consequences of both the modern processes of institutional differentiation and the equally modern process of dissemination of collective meanings.'[3] To this end, it is important to bear in mind that there are social and symbolical mechanisms common to both the religious sphere and the political sphere, and stress the fluidity of belief in modern societies.[4] The religious nonetheless remains a particular type of belief insofar as it calls on the legitimizing authority of a tradition.[5] Two risks emerge here: the tendency to enclose oneself within dogma and the imposition of a thought police enforcing conformity of behaviour and belief. This is a demand inherent to any system founded on the authority of a tradition but intolerable and incomprehensible for any honest-minded person today, accustomed to the easing of this type of imperative in secular societies.

However, this tendency is re-emerging and is developing its ambitions in two different, irreconcilably opposed, directions: 'It is deploying *ad extra* in the search in different ways for a 'religious organization' of the world and *ad intra* as a withdrawal from the world of those involved in the lineage of believers.'[6]

The connection between the internal dimension and the external dimension is formed by one of several possible models which produce different types of religious association. The problem is to establish how a religious group is affected by the tension between *ad extra* fundamentalism based on conformity to the tradition in *extension* and an *ad intra* fundamentalism based on conformity to the tradition in *intensity*. In my opinion, the difference between investments in Islam according to whether they occur in the Arab world or in Europe reflects this dual orientation: in the Arab world Islamism refers more to an identity mechanism based on extending references to Islam to the social, cultural, economic and political spheres from which it had been removed at least since the independences, whereas Islamization in Europe seems to be a means of intensifying religious practice and people's relationship to Islam in a context of religious and cultural pluralism. The other essential difference relates to the process of Muslims learning their minority role in the democratic countries of the North, i.e. a completely new situation in the history of the Muslim peoples.[7] The process of cultural adaptation of the young generations of Muslims attending school in Europe has led to considerable changes in the way they identify with the Islamic frame of reference, opening up a gap with methods of appropriation prevalent in the Muslim countries of the South.

Visibility is not a 'return to the religious'

Visibility should not be mistaken for a return of religion: this is the first pitfall to avoid in discussing the renewal of religious forms. Certain behaviour is interpreted as evidence of a return to religion simply because in a certain context it is more conspicuous. When for example in the early 1980s, immigrants built prayer centres in suburban tower blocks, many enlightened people, even in the world of science, did not hesitate to talk of a 'return of Islam'. But the Muslims in question had not become more practising. They had simply changed their attitude to French society and decided henceforth to claim their right to places of worship. We need to analyse the nature of the visibility of certain religious acts because it is sometimes more revealing about the group considering the act as visible rather than the act itself. The 'head scarves question' in France is symptomatic of this extreme partiality and relativity of the nature of visibility. In other words, the Islamic head scarf is visible in France but much less so in Germany or the United Kingdom.

In the context of European societies, certain ways of relating to Islam can reveal a change in the way people present themselves and define themselves collectively in civil society and can thus disturb the prevailing consensus about the boundary between the public and the private but without this type of behavioural pattern vis-à-vis others necessarily constituting a return to religious practise.[8]

Here Islam functions as a vector for professing a collective identity. Statements about belonging to Islam coming from young people born and/or socialized in France have to be replaced in the context of a highly fragmented society where the ideas of progress and the future have been called into question. Reference groups are no longer constructed solely on the basis of social status and in particular economic status. Categories such as 'working class', 'worker', and even 'immigrant', 'suburban youth', etc. no longer provide easy identification. This is why people are having recourse to a religion for that purpose. They are seeking to reconstruct an identity on the basis of the Islamic frame of reference which offers them meaning both individually and collectively, facilitates understanding of the world in which they live and functions as a kind of 'map' or reference grid marking out the directions to follow in both individual behaviour and social intercourse.

Islam can also provide a vector for protest against people's social conditions, offering alternative methods of social or political action. Certain young people decide to invest in Islam after trying out political or cultural activism such as the fight against racism, the struggle for civil liberties, etc. These channels often seem to them artificial or doomed to failure, especially when they have failed to counter the mechanism of exclusion. Difficulties of finding employment, the feeling of social relegation and discrimination, perception of the highly negative image of Islam in public opinion, the vivid memory of the humiliations of the French colonial past passed on by their family (as if part of their history was not included in the French national identity), and the bankruptcy of a whole series of ideologies such as Marxism or the Third World movement which fired the ideals of their elder brothers and sisters: all of these reasons merge to ensure that belonging to Islam occupies a central position. Reference groups with universal aspirations, i.e. the usual channels of collective action, be they trade unions or political parties, fail to mobilize these young people. This was already clear in the 1980s when the 'beur' associative movement appeared as a means of entering the political arena and replacing institutionalized forms of commitment. But it has become even clearer since that movement proved incapable of developing a genuine reference group rooted in a social movement. For the past five years, French suburbs have witnessed the emergence of associations of young people openly declaring themselves to be Muslims and developing their social militancy through a wide range of activities, ranging from help with school work to sports. They are competing with teachers and social workers on their own terrain and doing so in the name of Islam whose values they claim are better suited to facing the challenge posed by marginalization.

One should not, however, conclude too hastily that the relationship is only between Islam and the suburbs. These forms of identification in fact reflect the search for identity of all young people in France who live in a society where the authorities and organizations which in the past helped foster social bonds and cohesion have lost a great deal of their influence. Our modernity has incorporated the legacy of its religious matrix in the strict sense via the idea of accomplishment. But today we are experiencing a situation where the Utopian structures of modernity are collapsing, dramatically raising the question of the foundations of the social bond. The perception of citizenship reflected by the various forms of commitment in the name of Islam is rooted in the civil sphere to the detriment of the civic sphere. The civic dimension of citizenship refers to our allegiance to centralized, universal political institutions and to the public authorities. It expresses itself, for example, through institutional channels such as exercising our right to vote or by militancy in political parties or trade unions. On the other hand, civil citizenship involves a proximity type of participation in areas and issues which are not usually political, e.g. children dropping out of school, the environment, racism etc. Civility is built on the basis of relationships between individuals and implies the recognition of groups who are different within the social fabric. In other words, it is based on awareness of the diversity of civil society seen as an assembly of different groups with, however, a common bond linking them to the social order. In this context, people act politically not simply by voting in elections but especially by their involvement and participation in daily activities in various sectors. They want, for example, to mediate between certain categories of the population and politicians, especially at a local level. And for such actors, the distinction between one's commitment as a citizen and one's religious commitment is irrelevant, whereas usually it is considered to be one aspect of being a citizen and is the basis of the contract between individuals and the political community.

The challenges of pluralism

In this way new poles of identification are emerging in civil society, expressing themselves by the defence of the specific interests of religious, ethnic or cultural groups and restoring individuals' sense of belonging to a community. Does this imply that an ethnicization of politics is occurring along Anglo–Saxon lines? It is far from certain. There is a clear trend towards more and more claims being made in terms of specificity's and the feeling of belonging to a national community is weakening. But this does not mean that participation in the political life of the nation is being radically altered by those groups identified as ethnic entering the political arena. It seems rather that through this emergence of the civil bond a shift is occurring in the focus of political participation which is increasingly centred on urban areas and on local action. This may lead to a fragmentation of citizenship into a series of groups each with its more direct, almost physical sense of belonging, to the detriment of the overall political community. At the same time, this situation strengthens these groups' allegiance to the state insofar as it is the only body empowered to arbitrate and allocate resources among them. The question of their loyalty to the political community and how far they share even a minimal common concept of that community remains open. Thus building a common future and especially a shared memory are again raising difficulties which modern democracies had, at least partly, put behind them.

In this respect, the process of Islamization, which in the case under consideration involves rooting Islam in a country not initially Muslim, leads to changes and innovations not only in people's 'way of being Muslim' but also in the status accorded to all religions in the public sphere. The appearance of Islam in secularized societies has re-opened debates about religious freedom, tolerance, the limits of public, collective expressions of faith, etc. In the case of France, the appearance of Islam in the religious and cultural arena has shown up the historicity of a law on secularism which claimed to be universal. In proclaiming the principle of secularism, the aim was not so much to ensure parity and balance between existing religions as to keep all religious activities out of the public sphere, even if, paradoxically, to achieve this end the law recognizes the principle of the equality of all religious expressions.[9] Stemming from a conflict between the French Republic and the Catholic Church, the law on secularism was the result of a compromise which though not actually contested today, is nonetheless a focus of debate.

The situation has changed considerably since the law on the separation of the Church and the State was passed almost a century ago. The Catholic Church has come to terms with the principle of secularism, establishing an extensive network of private schools to further its educational aims and obtaining state recognition for them. Thus the terms of the relationship imposed by the secular revolution have not been radically altered: religion was confined to the private sphere and remains there. Spatio–temporal events in the life of society are largely free from religious references of any kind. The social context has contributed to this: the gradual loss of interest in religious practices explains why believers have accepted more and more readily a separation which in its day was highly controversial but which today enjoys a near-consensus.

Contestation has of course continued to exist, largely thanks to believers less 'exotic' than the adepts of Muhammad and focused in schools, which remain a sensitive issue for secularism. Issues are the inclusion in curricula of courses on 'religious science' or 'history of religions', which day of the week should be a holiday to allow children the possibility of religious instruction outside school, the fact that the school year is structured in accordance with Catholic holidays and fails to allow for other minority religions, etc. But this is like an in-family debate. In the case of the 'head scarf', however, it is Islam – still perceived as the religion of the alien – which enters the arena, raising doubts and questions.

The outcry is primarily due to the difficulty people have in accepting that henceforth a certain number of French citizens are Muslims and wish to be seen as such. One reason for people's doubts is that in French collective consciousness Islam occupies a particular – and frequently negative – place as a result of a colonial past with which many have not yet come to terms.[10] Furthermore, Islam today crystallizes a range of negative, off-putting images regarding the status of women. The position of women in Islam seems diametrically opposed to the principle of non-discrimination governing relations between individuals in French society. In some cases this negative perception goes so far as to equate the head scarf with other signs or symbols, including the swastika. This kind of association of ideas reflects misunderstanding and a refusal to accept the other's beliefs. It must be stressed that in its famous edict of 27 November 1989, the Conseil d'Etat does not refer to the head scarf as such but to the wearing of signs of religious conviction in general. In another controversial ruling in 1992, the members of the Conseil d'Etat rightly recall that the head scarf in itself expresses nothing. As such it cannot be equated with other outer signs such as the swastika which constitute a direct incitement to hatred. The head scarf can be perceived as an aggression against women's dignity only by a process of reconstruction of what we know or think we know about the Islamic religion and civilization. Such an interpretation of a religious symbol, regardless of who is wearing it, is in itself a violation of freedom of conscience.[11]

Furthermore, the visibility of signs of belonging to Islam blurs the border between the public and private spheres and questions the prevalent view that religion is a private matter of confession, because Islam (like Judaism) is primarily a way of living. This implies that a practising Muslim cannot reduce his faith to acts of worship within the mosque because certain of his religious precepts relate to daily relationships between individuals, eating habits, or relations between men and women.

If Islam is a life-style and can be lived as such by certain believers, this sharply focuses attention on the question of the social dimension of religions. Do religions not enshrine a certain number of values which could have a bearing on public and social life? This position is defended increasingly vocally by a number of religious authorities[12] and the visibility of Islam can be seen as highlighting their stance.

Summarizing, one can say that the entry of Islam in the French religious sphere has shaken the apparently stable balance between the three main principles underpinning the principle of secularism, viz. republican unity, respect for religious pluralism and freedom of conscience. If pluralism is part and parcel of democracy, this latter no longer refers to the integration of embattled minorities, the abstract concept of the citizen or a re-balancing of the elites in power. Today, it concerns rather the combination of multi-culturalism and communitarism. The new pluralism is no longer really that of voluntary associations based on free, part-time participation of individuals, but rather the combination of the pluralism of 'plural societies'. This brings to the forefront the concept of moral pluralism, according to which there is no single project or single common good, but rather multiple concepts of the common good between which a rational choice has to be made.[13]

What then is the public importance of our identity?[14] The liberal view is that neutrality in the public sphere is the price to be paid for equality and that public institutions should only take general needs into account regardless of cultural specificities. Those who favour policies of cultural difference take the opposite view and stress the recognition of identities: 'With the policy of equal dignity, what is established is supposed to be universally the same, an identical body of rights and privileges. With the policy of difference, we are called on to recognize the unique identity of this individual or this group, what distinguishes them from others.'[15] In the case of the policy of difference, there too the foundation is a universal potential: the freedom to shape and define one's identity as an individual and as a culture. But this involves the further demand of equal recognition for all cultures, which goes beyond the recognition of the equal value of all human potentialities and generates a considerable number of difficulties in governing political communities. There are thus two differing conceptions of respect. One involves 'turning a blind eye' to differences and respect is for what is common to all of us. In the other view, difference must be favoured or at least recognized, and hegemony and discrimination in the name of a dominant culture must be denounced. This antithesis is now at the heart of the political debate in Western societies. Islam is just one element, though not the least important because it frequently is the factor revealing a latent crisis in the case of secularism in France.

The challenge of the transnational

The question of pluralism in democracies cannot be addressed exclusively from the viewpoint of the relations of one and the same national community. It must be faced also because of the pluralism of allegiances which today characterizes certain categories of citizens, e.g. Muslims in France or in Europe. In this context, one must allow for the fact that the main centres of Islam where the Muslim '*doxa*' is developed are outside Europe, in the Middle East, Asia and possibly in the Maghreb. This raises the question of the training of the Muslim religious authorities whose role includes passing the religious message on to future generations. This explains why the socialization of Islamic educators has become so crucial in the major European countries. The polarization of Islamic minorities towards events abroad coincides with ongoing turmoil in the Muslim world, exemplified by events such as the Rushdie affair, the Gulf War, the rise of political Islam, etc., which could lead to the radicalization of certain sectors of the Muslim population living in Europe. There is little point in expecting European Islam to cut itself off from such outside influences. The real question is how it will achieve autonomy and build its specificity as a minority without breaking with its roots.

This identification with an Islamic sphere cutting across national borders is conducive to the multiplication of networks, especially on both banks of the Mediterranean. Initially, the religious demands of first-generation immigrants were made independently of any influence from their countries of origin. But subsequently these countries have proved quite incapable of meeting new demands, in particular, the demand for Koranic schools. Frequently, places of worship established by immigrants in their host countries are taken over by 'imams' from the countries of origin. By running these religious centres, the 'imams', who have an education but no prospects for social promotion in North African countries, can settle in France and build up networks providing relative safety in the political sphere and financial resources to fund political resistance to the regimes in power back in their North African home countries. It is however important to keep one's perspective about the extent of involvement of immigrant populations in these networks because they sometimes operate independently of the immigrants even when adopting the centres and circuits used by them. To many immigrants, the proselytization methods of certain neo-orthodox currents seem much more effective than the more intellectual, modernist methods of radical Islamists. There are of course militant Islamists in France, but the extent of the indoctrination of immigrant youth is much less than that suggested by certain sensationalist media who are quick to classify pietists and Islamists under the blanket heading of 'fundamentalists'. These militants, who have left their countries of origin because of the repression against them by the regime in power, often use their country of exile as a safe haven to take stock and train before returning to fight for an Islamic state. However, some of these Islamist leaders may show interest in the Muslims living in France, in which case they often feel the need to re-orient their preaching towards criticism of Westernization and assimilation, dropping more overtly political connotations. In any event, this kind of solidarity shows the transnational bonds countering the nationalist state logic prevalent in Europe and the Arab world and does not always fit neatly in the well-orchestrated ballet of Euro–Mediterranean diplomacy.

Notes

1.   Cf. e.g. M. Kramer (1994), ' … Democracy, diversity, accommodation, the fundamentalists have repudiated them all. (…) (Their) principles bear no resemblance to the ideal of Europe's democracy movements; if anything, they evoke more readily the atavism of Europe's burgeoning nationalist right'.
2.   Michael (1994, 107–8)

3   Hervieu-Léger (1995, 13–25).

4.   *Idem* p. 17

5.   Hervieu-Léger (1986, 121).

6.   Hervieu-Léger (1995, 24).

7.   Cesari (1994). Cf. also 'L'Islam, ultime recours?', *Confluences* 16 (1995–1996) (Winter), pp. 55–63

8.   Certain intense forms of religious practices are possible without requiring visibility. Wearing certain garments with an 'Islamic connotation' or carrying out religious practices in public reflect the wish to be known and recognized as religious practising. These signals are intended for fellow Muslims also and can be used as leverage in struggles for power and influence.

9.   On this point it should not be overlooked that this aspect of the Bill finally adopted gave rise to wide debate in the secular camp and that the first draft submitted in 1904 proposed that religions separated from the state should be subject to close surveillance by the state. See Baubérot (1994, 57–68).

10.   See Cesari (1994).

11.   See Kessler (1993, 98–9).

12.   In an interview with *Le Monde*, 15 October 1988, Monsignor Lustiger said that the ideologization of the ephemeral, the 'levelling off' of values, were leading to a major crisis in which younger generations were losing the key to Western culture. The Church has a social role to play here: that of a guardian of memory.

13.   See Leca (1994).

14.   See Taylor (1994).

15.   Taylor (1994, 57).

15

Muslims and European Education Systems

JØRGEN S. NIELSEN

It has long been clear that education is the field which has most continuously been at the centre of the encounter between Muslims and their European environment. When wives and children started joining their menfolk in the process of family reunion following the immigration stops in the early 1970s (ten years earlier in Britain), education quickly became crucial. This was where the immigrants hopes for the future lay, while suddenly large numbers of native Europeans, teachers, educational administrators, and children and their parents, were brought into direct contact with communities and traditions of which they had hardly heard before. The immigration had changed from a temporary migration to becoming a settlement.

I do not intend to revisit the process of immigration or to analyse the educational backgrounds of the countries of origin of the Muslim communities in Europe. Rather, I propose to outline the presuppositions of the European systems of education and then discuss their responses to the new Muslim presence, in both cases paying particular attention to the nature and role of religious education (RE). I would stress that this is being written from the point of view of someone who is not an expert in European education, rather as someone who has spent some time in getting to know the experience and perspectives of the Muslim communities.

The development of mass education in Europe during the nineteenth and early twentieth centuries did not take place in a vacuum. It took place on the background of existing traditions of education and in the context of specific, if mixed, objectives. The experience, on which the new systems drew, was obviously that of the medieval church, whether in schools directly under church control or independent foundations, usually with a Christian purpose and run by clergy or people trained by the clergy. The tradition, in other words, was one heavily imbued with Christian ideas and intents of various kinds. The development of mass education built on this experience, and the churches continued for a long time to play a central role in the expansion and progress of these new systems. It is when one begins to look at the political and other circumstances behind this radical expansion of education that a general European pattern begins to break down.

At one level mass education was part of the overall project of the development of the modern bureaucratic and centralized state. This alone required a minimally literate population, a factor which was common across all European states including the Ottoman Empire, even if the timings differed from one country to the next. The process of industrialization and the associated urbanization also raised the requirements for a better educated population, especially in the technological and administrative professions. A basic mass system was required to provide the recruitment base for more advanced educational and training sectors.

It was, however, at the fundamental level of the rationale or, if one prefers, the ideology of the project that we find the elements which form the specific character and agenda of the educational systems which we have inherited today - what the British often call the hidden curriculum which often is not, in fact, all that hidden.

At this level we are dealing with mass education as one of the main mechanisms for the creation of the modern European nation state. It is, therefore, also here that the systems of different countries part company, especially as regards the place of religion.

Following the end of the wars of religion, arising especially out of the Reformation and symbolized by the 1648 Westphalian principle of *cuius regio eius religio*, Europe had settled down to a system of monarchical states in which the old decentralized feudal power had been weakened in favour of a stronger central monarchy. This was to become the period of the divine rights of kings and royal absolutism, enlightened or otherwise. The post-Reformation ecclesiastical systems were closely tied into the new statist order. The theological justifications presented by the churches differed as between Lutheran and Calvinist traditions with the former especially tending to become closely identified with if not totally assimilated to the state. On the Catholic side kings had to reach some form of mutually agreeable accommodations to the Church, protecting its privileges in exchange for its support while living with the constant threat of the appeal to an external authority.

It is in the post-1648 settlements that the ground was laid for very different experiences with relations between church and education, even though starting from essentially the same point of church control. As Protestant churches, especially Lutheran ones, became more integrated into the state so the state obtained a foothold in the process of education ultimately leading to its absorption, in turn, into the state. It was thus a comparatively simple matter for later absolutist monarchs of the Enlightenment to decree the establishment of mass obligatory primary education, as was done in Denmark already in 1815. Here the foundations were laid for a state-owned and financed school system.

In the Catholic world, on the other hand, the Church tended to retain a dominant role, if not a monopoly, in education, often as the price for supporting the monarchy. As Europe moved into the era of popular revolutions and demands for popular participation in government, the Church ran the risk of being seen as an obstacle to progress. In France a century of tense and often conflictual relations between the republics and the Church developed out of the French Revolution, with relations swinging between concordat and confrontation. In an increasingly anti-clerical atmosphere, relations with the Church were settled in the 1905 legislation at the centre of the *republique laicque*. Similar patterns pertained in parts of Switzerland, while in Bismarck's Germany the Catholic Church was put in its place through a *Kulturkampf* which left its mark on German society for decades. Elsewhere, kings and republics succeeded in negotiating more favourable arrangements through concordats with a church weakened by the unification of Italy and the disappearance of the Papal State in all but name and by the general process of social and cultural secularization.

In Eastern Europe it took the disasters of the first world war and the communist revolution to finally break the influence of the Orthodox churches over both state and education.

It is these various developments of the nineteenth and early twentieth centuries which usually explain the place and nature of religious education in the school systems of Europe today, especially in the West.

In a recent survey of the situation of religious minorities in member countries of the Council of Europe, one of the questions included was the status of religious education in schools.[1] This confirmed information otherwise available that, in general terms, it is possible to consider the approach to religious education (RE) in state schools in three categories.

The fully laicist approach in which the state school makes no provision at all. The best example of this is France, with the exception of the Alsace-Moselle region, but it is also common in most Swiss cantons. In the French situation, the Catholic Church retains a large number of private schools in which Catholic RE is provided. The Spanish policy seems to have been recently to move in this direction.

The most common approach is to be found in most countries with a Protestant tradition and in those countries which have inherited a Vatican concordat tradition. Here the pattern in general is for the state to have arrangements with the church or the main churches by which they provide denominational religious education within the framework of the state school curriculum. It is usual in these circumstances for children who do not belong to the 'recognized' denominations to have the right to be withdrawn from such classes.

In some countries like Greece and Portugal it is respectively Orthodox and Catholic Christianity alone which are taught. In the state church countries of Scandinavia it used to be determined by law that Christian education should be provided in school according to the teachings of the 'Evangelical Lutheran Church'. In others, such as the Netherlands, Germany, Belgium, Austria and the Alsace-Moselle region of France, there are several such 'recognized' communities (in Austria and Belgium including the Muslim) each of which has its particular arrangements with the state education system. This usually involves teachers, sometimes but not always clergy, recognized and trained by the religious community as well as by the state teaching to a syllabus and using text books which have been developed by the religious community but with state approval. The funding usually comes from the state.

Within this general category, England stands out as being somewhat unique. The provisions of the 1944 Education Act required that RE be given according to a syllabus agreed by a process involving the local education authority, teachers and representatives of the main religious communities - at a time when this could only mean various

Christian denominations.

The third approach is a comparatively recent development, one which has come about specifically in response to the settlement of new religious communities. Secondarily, this has also been response to the secularization of society and the consequent declining role of the traditional churches. We are here talking about some form of multi-religious RE. It has appeared primarily in countries where the state has directly offered RE according to the denomination of the state church.

England was the pioneer in this approach although its introduction was not systematic in a subject which was governed by the wishes of 104 different local education authorities. It was the West Riding of Yorkshire which started the process in 1966 with a careful attempt to make space for the main world religions in a syllabus which was still overwhelmingly Christian, although non-denominational as the 1944 Act required. The radical breakthrough came with the introduction of Birmingham's new RE syllabus in 1975. Here all the major religions were given equal status and space, with a recommendation that schools concentrate on Christianity and two others. The syllabus was a minimalist document leaving the very extensive teacher's handbook and its subsequent supplements and revisions to give detailed guidance. Representatives of all the religious groups concerned were involved both in the syllabus consultation and in vetting the handbooks. This pattern was followed with local variations by most authorities over the following ten years and was supported by an extensive restructuring of RE teachers' training.[2]

The English model was closely studied by the Netherlands and Scandinavian countries, which had changed their RE syllabuses in the same direction by the mid-1980s. Under the impact of the growing number of children from the new religious minorities, religious educationalists in other countries were also seeking to include a broader dimension in what otherwise remained denominational RE. This was the case in some German states as also in some of the more progressive Catholic dioceses across the continent.

However, as the English model was beginning to receive more enthusiastic support in some parts of mainland Europe, it was beginning to show signs of some of its weaknesses. Some of these were clearly due to political and financial factors. RE was not a popular subject among most teachers or children, and it is generally recognized that in primary schools less than half of RE lessons were being given by teachers not qualified in the subject. As a debate developed during the 1980s over the relationships between schools and ethnic minorities, it soon became politicized.

On the one hand was a complex of institutional issues. The English system had in 1944 incorporated the large number of church schools into the publicly-financed system while leaving a degree of control in the hands of the churches, mostly the Church of England and the Roman Catholic Church. The legislation was formulated so that new so-called voluntary schools could be established - and many were as new suburbs developed in the post-1945 economic reconstruction. A small number of Jewish schools also existed in this system, and occasionally new Jewish schools were also established under the general legislation.

However, by the early 1980s Muslim organizations had reached a stage when they were beginning to be increasingly active on the local scene - they were in effect successfully integrating into local politics. And they began to demand access to the same facility. The first coordinated demands came from Bradford. The Islamic school in the London Borough of Brent put in a series of requests for recognition, and several other schools have joined the queue. But all requests, even when supported by local education authorities and civil servants, have so far been turned down, in contrast with requests from churches and the occasional Jewish school, often made at the same time and in the same district. This has caused a growing resentment based on the belief that the government is deliberately opposed to the formation of publicly-funded Muslim schools, a belief which anecdotal evidence would seem to support.[3]

A further set of issues which was also related to politics, although this time a more general educational political debate at the national level, was the general discussion around the role of multicultural education. Through the 1970s and into the early 1980s multicultural education had come to be perceived as the right way to develop the education system. Enormous effort, if not always systematic effort, had been devoted to developing multicultural education and a whole generation of teachers had been trained with at least a rudimentary expectation of multicultural education. Inevitably there was a wide spectrum of practical implementation ranging from nothing, through notional attempts to serious sustained programmes. Linked to this was a more recent concept of anti-racist education. Here one immediately got caught in a growing ideological debate where common sense, and ultimately the children in school, often became the victims.

At the time that the high point of official approval for multicultural education was reached in the 1985 publication of the government document *Education for All*, the so-called Swann Report,[4] a backlash had already started. Parents in some areas refused to have their children placed in schools with large numbers of children of south Asian background. The Bradford Council of Mosques ran a successful campaign for the dismissal of a head teacher who had expressed sceptical and anti-Muslim views in a right-wing journal, and Muslim organizations were increasingly expressing their dissatisfaction with a school system which they saw as encouraging the devaluation of religious belief in favour of a process of secularization. The outbreak of public protests against Salman Rushdie's *The Satanic Verses* in early 1989 was in great part the coming together of frustrations around these matters on the part of the Muslim community.[5]

Most recently we have seen how Muslim dissatisfaction even with the multifaith RE experience has found open expression. This latest series of events can be traced back to careless and often populist political manoeuvres at the time of the parliamentary debate on the 1988 Education Reform Act. This legislation was intended to deal with very different issues, namely the national curriculum and the contest between a Conservative central government and local authorities, especially the urban Labour ones, over control of schools. It was originally intended that the religious settlement of the 1944 act was to remain unchanged, until some right-wing members of the House of Lords demanded that Christianity be restored to the centre of RE and school worship. A compromise was found through a negotiation coordinated by the Anglican Bishop of London. The compromise explicitly recognized the centrality of Christianity, as being the main religion of England, while also guaranteeing a space for the world religions represented in the country. At the same time provision was made for special arrangements to be granted where the population of a particular school warranted this.

The emphasis in the political debate on the reassertion of the centrality of Christianity in the school system communicated to the minorities, and especially the Muslims, a sense of being marginal: they were exceptions. In practice the law also gave them a guarantee of a place in the system which had not previously been available. But it was the noise, not the fact, which set the public tone which then coloured the subsequent processes of implementing the forms of school government and the development of the national curriculum. The fact that much of the older Muslim leadership was distracted by the Rushdie affair and then the second Gulf War during 1989–91 meant that it excluded itself from active participation in these implementation phases.

Finally, the change of generation played an increasingly significant part in developments. It was the frustrations of young Muslims born and brought up in Britain which lay behind much of the anger during the Rushdie affair. These Muslims were now marrying and sending their children to school. Such young parents knew how to function within the English system like any other native, and how to use it to gain the maximum advantage for their own children, something the English middle classes have always done. The new forms of school government, especially the provision for elected parent governors, gave these young Muslim parents a role in determining the atmosphere and educational provision their schools were offering their children. The various education acts since 1988 had provided them with the tools to negotiate exceptions and special provision to take account of the particular character of the individual school.

It might be pertinent also to turn ones attention at this point back to the way multifaith RE had developed. The choice of the term 'religious education' was not a careless one: this was not to be religious instruction, but education into an understanding of the nature of religion as a human phenomenon. The research and theories of people like Piaget and Goldman were important: RE was to be child-centred and use the child's own sense of curiosity, wonder and spiritual development as its foundation. This meant almost by definition that RE had to be multifaith because only in this way was it possible to show the variety of human responses to the ultimate spiritual questions of purpose and the transcendent. The newly multireligious nature of society provided a convenient political argument for the introduction of such new approaches to RE.

From the point of view of those committed to these various religions, this approach was not without its problems. It seemed, at least by implication, to be saying that while the questions being put were deeply spiritual - and therefore this was not a secular or materialist approach to the subject - the human responses as developed in the religions were just that: human. This was particularly dangerous to the Abrahamic religions with their core belief in divine revelation, in other words that the religion was from God. Among more conservative Christian trends, the new forms of RE were never given more than a reserved welcome, if that. As Muslim leaderships became more integrated into the political processes, they also began to question seriously the underlying assumptions. Quite critical documents were published by Muslim organizations in response to the Swann report's comments on RE, and a proposed new RE syllabus produced by the now defunct Inner London Education Authority (ILEA) towards the mid-1980s attracted the first systematic Muslim opposition.[6] The cause of the new RE was not helped by its proponents or the educational establishment. To meet its objectives the teacher of RE actually needed an unusual combination of skills, some of which could be acquired by training but much not. Again the lack of political and funding support meant that the subject remained under funded and under resourced. In practice, therefore, much multifaith RE was, frankly, badly taught, leading to the common caricature of the 'Cooke's tour' image of the subject: the teacher would pick a theme as suggested by the syllabuses and the handbooks, for example light, and deal with the role played by light in the various religions. This could, of course, be done at various levels of understanding according to the maturity of the children, but it remained a superficial tour. Only the secondary school student who selected to do religious studies after the age of fourteen would be likely to get a systematic understanding of the overall nature of, say, Islamic belief and practice.

The reluctance of many schools and educational authorities to deal with their local religious communities as partners - Muslim communities in particular were often regarded with distrust - meant also that the schools understood themselves as the only place where education, in any proper sense, was being carried out. One result of this was that local mosques continued to practice their traditional forms of Islamic instruction led by unqualified teachers whose only conception of how to deliver the material was as they themselves had received it in the village of origin. Both sides, school and mosque, were divided by a gulf of mistrust and misunderstanding which prevented them from exploring where they might cooperate.

A conference organized by the Islamic Academy in Cambridge in the late 1980s sought explicitly to legitimize to the Muslim community the multifaith education of the state system - young Muslims needed to be informed about the beliefs of their neighbours in a multifaith society - and to the RE establishment the Islamic instruction of the mosque - Muslim youth needed to be founded firmly in their own faith.[7] The two sectors ought to be able not only to recognize each other's specific reasons for existing but also for finding ways of cooperating.

But many, if not most, of the Muslim centres for religious instruction remained in the hands of the older generation, most of whom did not or would not understand, while the pressures of continuing educational changes meant that most schools did not have the time or energy to engage also in such a further new demand, if they were able to see its necessity.

Most recently this whole complex set of misunderstandings has hit the headlines with the decision of a primary school in Birmingham to make provision for Muslim religious instruction for the majority of its pupils whose parents wanted them to opt out of the city's multifaith RE syllabus. While it was quite clear that the move was within the law, some media reaction has talked of isolation and Islamic fundamentalism. To the credit of the press, there has been an equal recognition that the failure of the government to grant voluntary status to applicant Muslim schools in the past has contributed to the perceived crisis.

The movers behind this development are precisely that generation of Muslim young parents which has also created over thirty private, mostly small, Muslim schools. Among these are the ones which have so far unsuccessfully applied for voluntary status and, with that, public funding.

To my mind it is absolutely clear that European countries, among them Britain, are in danger of losing a significant opportunity and thereby generating problems for themselves for the future. In some cases it may already be too late. I would argued that the European-educated generation of Muslims is probably the most valuable resource shared by both the Muslim community and the wider society in the task of integration of the two into a future multicultural society. They are difficult to deal with because they upset the preconceptions of both their own elders and of the established institutions of Europe. But it is precisely such preconceptions which need to be upset.

The schools and other educational efforts being established formally and informally across the continent by this generation at the
present need to be cultivated and nurtured. It has, in the end, been
the Netherlands which has possibly achieved most so far. The decision a dozen or so years ago to support the establishment of publicly
funded Muslim schools - not as exceptional privilege but on a par
with existing Christian schools - was viewed by many as a great risk.
Most of the Muslim organizations founding the schools were widely
regarded as 'conservative' not to say' fundamentalist'. Today it appears
to be the case that, whatever the religious 'colouring' of the founders
(actual or perceived), the result has been schools which have successfully integrated (not assimilated): they are Dutch and they remain
Muslim.

The Danish experience has been more ambivalent, as far as I can
judge. The legal and political tradition has made it probably the most
favourable European country for the establishment of publicly-funded,
parent-led, 'free' schools. However, the absence of some form of central government supportive and understanding policy seems to have
mitigated against developing the kind of positive and constructive
experience there appears to have been in the Netherlands, even though
the latter started later.

My own conclusion is that Britain is in danger of losing an opportunity the foundations for which it, in its own rather muddled way,
had laid possibly a decade before anyone else. The government should
at least ten years ago have taken a policy decision to encourage the
recognition of, say, six Muslim voluntary schools spread around the
main centres of Muslim residence and spread around the main Muslim organizations. (The spread would have helped to insulate the
programme from internal Muslim community politics.) It should have
told its inspectors to advise and support the efforts of those schools
(there were many inspectors positively ready to do so) while at the
same time encouraging the training of suitable teaching staff, not limited to Muslims, for such schools while also encouraging the
recruitment and training of Muslims as teachers for the main stream
state sector. It did the latter finally five years ago when it approved
the establishment of a BEd teacher training programme with Islam
as the main subject; but this was not as part of any overall policy. It
should have encouraged closer links between schools and local religious centres (which some education officials in Bradford, Birmingham

and elsewhere have long been trying to do) and the development of forms of training for the teachers of such centres (which some Muslim leaders of the older generation first asked for fifteen years ago).

The Netherlands have not solved their problems, but at least they have tried to identify them and to adapt policy and practice towards solving them. Britain and Denmark have each in their own way also moved. So have other countries which attract less headline attention: Austria, Sweden, Norway, for example.

But my greatest fears arise from France and Germany, each in their own way. France's almost 'fundamentalist' attachment to its *laicism* blinds its officials and politicians to the enormous riches the country has in terms of well-educated, francophone (and often also anglophone) young Arab and Turkish educated Muslims. They want to become French Muslims and to build an 'Islam of France'. But the anticlerical republican tradition, reinforced by almost paranoid fears of Algerian Islamic extremism, regularly forces these people into the margins. They are undermined and delegitimized in their own communities in France, just as French-led accusations against Rashid al-Ghannushi (exiled in Britain) has undermined his innovative and constructive leadership of the Islamic opposition in Tunisia. The almost pathological French focus on a square meter of cloth covering women's heads has deprived France and the rest of Europe of the experience and expertise of the largest group of educated Muslim young people anywhere in Europe.

Germany is a cause for concern for a different reason. Here also there is a rising generation of young educated Muslims who are European and (not but) Muslim. The stubborn policy of the Federal Republic of Germany to deny that it is a country of immigration provides the justification for refusing Muslim applications for recognition as a public law body, such as is granted to the churches. Muslims cannot be recognized because they are not permanently settled. But who says they are not permanently settled? The same legal and political system which refuses them permanent settlement!

A couple of years ago German federal officials were reported as saying that - *al-hamdu li'llah* - they had stuck to their policy: look at the trouble the British were getting themselves into with schools and education crises, Rushdie affairs, and urban riots. This may be a short-sighted view.

To use a geological simile, we are here dealing with a phenomenon similar to the interaction of tectonic plates: where they meet the build-up of tension can be dissipated either by regular small earth tremors or by much rarer, and therefore much larger, earthquakes. The constant process of manoeuvre and negotiation so characteristic of Britain and not unfamiliar to the Netherlands and Scandinavian countries has made us used to looking for constructive solutions to conflicts and tensions. The apparent stability of the French and German systems is, I suggest, more likely to produce serious earthquakes which heighten tensions in the long run rather than solve them.

Notes

1.   *Study drawn up by the Group of Consultants on Religious and Cultural Aspects of Equality of Opportunities for Immigrants*, Council of Europe doc. MG-S-REL (95) 3, 25, January 1996.

2.   See Howarth (1983).

3.   For sources regularly referring to these and following developments, see *News of Muslims in Europe* (bi-monthly, 1980 and 1988), and *British Muslims Monthly Survey* (from 1993), both published by CSIC, Selly Oak Colleges, Birmingham B29 6lQ, UK.

4.   Department for Education and Science, *Education for All*, Cmnd. 9453, London: HMSO, 1983.

5.   Lewis, P. (1994) deals with this subject in some detail. See also my concluding chapter of Nielsen (1995) and its bibliography.

6.   ILEA press release 84/93, 11 June 1984, and press release of the National Education Council, quoted in *News of Muslims in Europe* 27 (1984), 27 July.

7.   Islamic Academy (1984).

16

Isolation or Integration: The Development Towards Multicultural Societies

FRANÇOIS ZABBAL

The concept of 'multi-culturalism' is amenable to as many definitions as that of 'integration'. The apparent consensus in recognizing cultural diversity, which has existed for some two decades in Europe, in fact hides widely diverging views, even within the same country. This is particularly so in a country like France, which is a latecomer to the idea of the multi-cultural society and gives the impression of having had to move with the times in going against the basic principles of its national ideology.

It is necessary, therefore, to analyse each European country individually to see how the policy of integration of foreign populations is being constructed and what future developments are likely. To grasp overall trends which will affect Europe in the future, however, more will be required than the mere comparison of different systems as is becoming the norm in an increasing number of publications and seminars.

The parallels drawn do of course provide useful data on countries whose influence will be decisive on other European societies because of their economic and political 'clout' or their relatively high number of immigrants, e.g. Germany, the United Kingdom or France. But analyses available to date have simply compared institutional policies and the forms of organization set up by immigrants, or defined categories, without shedding light on these policies or the mechanisms which will operate in favour of one model or another. Furthermore, they very often adopt a (more or less open) apologetic stance which prevents strictly ideological obstacles being taken into account.

Throughout the entire stormy debate about 'integration French-style', for example, no one questioned the basic tenets of secularism which are still held to be a universal model by elites of all types, including Catholic elites.

Research also seems lacking when it comes to providing a new content for multi-culturalism. This is because it is a new problem for European societies, hence the tendency to use the American example as a model to follow or a case to avoid. But it is also due to the focus given to research by universities, political organizations and the media, as can be seen in the studies on immigration carried out in France over the last twenty years.

The problem is compounded by the difficulty of defining the concept of 'culture' whose content varies with use. As a result, the clearly political slogan 'recognition of cultural diversity' often appears a superficial concession, if not a mere electoral gambit. However, the idea of culture in its widest sense (as understood by the Anglo–Saxon or anthropological tradition) frequently crops up during discussion of widely varying issues, such as teaching immigrants the language and culture of their country of origin, regulating cultural practices or conflicts between different legal codes. But as soon as an attempt is made to isolate and define the notion of 'culture', one gets into the abstract debate about the relationship between Islam and the West or the question of the dialogue between revealed religions. Historians may try to show that previous waves of immigration into France, e.g. from Poland, Italy or other populations (Catholic, Jewish, etc.) also raised problems of cultural integration, but some reference is always made to the exceptional nature of the new immigration, ascribing it to Islam.

It seems necessary, therefore, to describe developments in European societies facing immigration of an unprecedented type in their recent history from three viewpoints: that of anthropological determinism, that of trends and patterns due to the intervention of various social actors, that of the cultural characteristics specific to immigrant populations and the effects of their relations with their societies of origin.

The anthropological perspective

Not surprisingly, anthropological analysis provides the most solid basis for comparisons in a field where many of the data are approximations. It rests on the objective reality of family behaviour patterns and the model it constructs provides the most stimulating hypothesis to account for ongoing trends. Probably the most highly developed theoretical schema to describe the relation between family structures and political and national ideologies is provided by Emmanuel Todd (1994).

The anthropological criterion seems particularly relevant to the analysis of developments in the system of kinship in immigrant groups. It shows up the disintegration or the durability of a given system as a function of the reception facilities, although it fails to convince when the author attempts to provide a general system of interpretation applicable to all societies. This is clear if one considers certain key aspects of social and family development either in immigrants' countries of origin or their host country.

Firstly, developments in the system of kinship in the countries of origin are not really taken into account. It is the majority system which is considered, whereas a number of indicators show conclusively that rapid change is occurring in the endogamous system (cf. the work of demographers such as Philippe Fargues and Youssef Courbage). In addition, modern legal codes and institutions have had their effects on these systems, as have population movements. When, for example, Emmanuel Todd stresses the 'break with the Arab–Muslim model' which the appearance of single-parent families in proportionally significant numbers among Algerian immigrants in France represents, he fails to note that the phenomenon is very widespread in Algeria itself.

This development is overlooked using a methodological subterfuge: for reasons of statistical convenience, the exogamy of immigrants is viewed from the standpoint of the community, which is important and symptomatic of a considerable break with the family model. But talk of such a break presupposes a fixed endogomous system in the countries of origin, whereas there has in fact been remarkable progress towards family exogamy, even in rural environments. For Algeria or for Turkey, it is essential to analyse developments in the family system and their accelerating pace between the 1960s and 1980s. This is particularly important because successive waves of immigration have given rise to populations with distinct cultural and sociological characteristics. The groups who came directly from a rural environment in the 1960s are not identical to those who come from a rural background but have experienced the phenomenon of urbanization after their move to the city or the extension of state and urban structures to the countryside.

Secondly, newcomers bring a different culture with them because in their country of origin there has been a dissemination of national culture (state culture or otherwise) by various institutions such as the education system, television, state-owned firms, the social security system, etc., as well as a development of that national culture.

It is thus possible to show quite clearly that the system of kinship alone cannot account for the development of immigrant populations. The point is shown *a contrario* by the explanation offered for the cohesion and group identity of Turks and Algerians. Discussing the situation of the Turks in France, Emmanuel Todd finds no other explanation for their cohesion than the dissemination of a model acquired in Germany and transferred to France via Alsace. This overlooks the important force of Turkish nationalism. Born out of Pan-Turanism at the beginning of this century, it played a key role in the formation of a Turkish nation tightly-knit around its language and forged on the basis of negating other populations, e.g. the Armenians in the 1910s and then the Kurds.

The same applies to Muslim universalism. Here too nuancing is required because the situation cannot be deduced, as it were 'automatically', from the system of kinship which provides for equality of brothers. Whether he is discussing Turkish secularism or the development of modernity in other countries, Emmanuel Todd implicitly assumes societies to be closed systems developing on their own. Especially since the mid-nineteenth century, however, there have been transfers of universalistic European ideologies and institutions and, as a result, a process of grafting leading to a specific set of connections between the state, the nation and the individual, as well as an Islamization of the state.

This accounts for the simplistic analysis of the Islamization of the Turks in Germany as a reaction to a hostile environment. It is the only explanation possible for Emmanuel Todd once he accepts literally the secularism of the Turks, failing to realize that secularism did not deeply affect all aspects of Turkish society.

The social actors

Another failing of Emmanuel Todd's analysis is its excessive anthropological determinism in the classification of universalist and differentialist ideologies. Admittedly, the author does take into account the distortions that occur between objective anthropological structures and their expression in the political and ideological field. But overall he attaches too little importance to factors which have a decisive effect on the development of integration, namely: the intrinsic force of ideology and consequently its capacity to resist the phenomenon of cultural assimilation, even though the structures undergo profound changes; the accumulated effects of the attitudes and decisions adopted by the social actors, i.e. the various bodies and authorities responsible in one way or another for dealing with the immigrant population, or individuals from that population who provide guidance and leadership or develop adaptation or withdrawal responses. In other words those who participate in their various ways in the process of adapting to the host country culture.

To clarify the first factor, a classic example from anthropology suffices. As is well known, endogamy in Arab societies is expressed by the preference given to marriage between patrilinear cousins. Arabic reflects this in its vocabulary relating to kinship: 'husband' and 'wife' are rendered as '*ibn al-amm*' and '*bint al-amm*' respectively (i.e. son and daughter of the paternal uncle), even when their forebears share no common bond of kinship. Generally the Arabic language and the implicit ideology it conveys preserve this endogamous assumption even in countries where exogamous marriage has become the rule.

The same can be said of polygamy, although with one difference, namely that it is not linked exclusively to family structures but refers to Islamic legal principles and as such sheds light on the way that ideology can rest on dogma and deny the objective reality of social structures. Institutional, i.e. legally recognized, polygamy has not only become less prevalent in Arab countries but in many social strata it is actually looked down on and considered a sign of backwardness. Nonetheless, apart from Tunisia, no family code has actually gone so far as to ban it.

On the other hand, the same symbolic and powerful bond between religious dogma and family practices makes the recognition of

Muslim polygamy impossible in Europe although it is in fact accepted in a certain manner by custom and even by the legal system. In theory there is nothing to prevent legal recognition of Muslim polygamy, given that a number of European countries have moved from recognition of successive polygamy to recognition of simultaneous polygamy and in certain precisely defined conditions, actually codified the rights of both the wife and the partner ('la compagne'). This point is openly acknowledged by jurists like Ibrahim Fadlallah who point out that the principles considered non-negotiable by European countries (even those willing to reach an accommodation as regards certain customs of immigrant populations) relate less to polygamy than to the matter of women's rights. I will come back to this question later.

Nonetheless, polygamy remains unacceptable because of its symbolic dimension both for the host country and for Islamic activists whether in Muslim countries or in Europe. For European societies, it is an emblem of difference at its most extreme. It symbolizes the inferior status of women in Islam and allows Westerners to point their finger at a social group considered alien, even when its members do not actually practice polygamy. Although polygamy is mainly practised by black African immigrants in France, it is often ascribed by public opinion to the North African population where in fact its prevalence is minimal.

This takes us on to the question of law. Its role has, unfortunately, been neglected both by anthropologists and political scientists although it is in fact extremely important and is a central issue both in Arab countries and in Europe. If proof is required, one only needs to recall the bitter controversy that has raged over the last two decades in Egypt, Algeria and elsewhere about the reform of the 'family code'. And in Europe, this has been the approach taken in the attempt to ensure adoption of certain principles of the Islamic *shari'a*.

Developments in European jurisprudence will affect key questions relating to family structures and the symbolism that surrounds them. The danger is that a fully-fledged Muslim law – tolerated if not recognized – could develop which would be a pure product of the interaction of the various actors involved in the process of integration of Muslim populations in Europe. Such a system of law would be neither classical Islamic law nor the present-day law in force in Arab countries and whose development depends on the internal balance of power specific to each.

The legal conflicts which are fought out in European courts reveal the unstable, shifting border between the sphere of application of the official legal system and aspects of the personal status code of the immigrant's country of origin to which recourse is possible in specific situations, e.g. in the case of marriage in the country of origin. Bilateral agreements between European countries and a number of Arab and Muslim countries, e.g. the conventions between France on the one hand and Morocco, Tunisia and Algeria on the other, have attempted to create some order out of the inextricable conflicts which have arisen among subjects with dual nationality. But in fact they have perpetuated the unfair treatment which North African women received compared to their French counterparts, whose interests *were* preserved. Furthermore, many spheres are not covered by existing codes and conventions and the actual legal proceedings, which take the form of legal councils, take place under the control of the mosques or associations. Unfortunately, the extent and the effects of this situation are not known with any degree of precision because of the lack of any systematic surveys.

Another problem is that the magistrates, judges and so on who have to deal with these complex day-to-day problems of culture and education (juvenile delinquency, forced marriages of under-age girls, custody of children, etc.) are often ill-equipped to do so. They are not trained to understand the anthropological context and thus cause inevitable stress and strain in changing family structures where parental authority is being shaken. Moreover, rulings by supreme courts and other legal bodies have not yet established the intangible basic principles without which daily compromises amount to a rolling back of the principle of the universality of the law. Before addressing the question of which practices can be recognized in order to defend a given interest, e.g. the rights of minors in the case of polygamy, or to foster gradual integration, the essential underlying principles of the legal and social order must first be defined.

Cultural diversity

Anthropology and the law enable us to base our analysis of the processes of integration on the most common social institution which immigrants have imported into their host country with them. Whether the family is disintegrating as in the case of the North Africans in France or enduring as with the Turks, surveys offer ample evidence that the institution is proving incapable of providing the new generation with attitudes, patterns of behaviour and a code of morality, in short the family culture which is the ultimate factor unifying the group.

However, the solidarity which remains reinforces and perpetuates perceptions of the enduring relationship with the country of origin. Associations of all kinds and courses in the language and culture of origin were intended to maintain what was considered an essential link with the 'home country'. Such programmes were set up at a time when it was confidently expected that immigrants would return home one day. Subsequently, they have been replaced by a host of initiatives throughout Europe. As far as cultural initiatives are concerned, the aim generally is to re-establish links with a tradition and (implicitly or explicitly) to enhance the prestige of the immigrant vis-à-vis Western modernity which parades its absolute superiority and asserts the immigrant's backwardness. This relates to the trend towards recognition of cultural diversity which has gathered momentum in certain European countries since the 1970s and has spread as anti-immigrant movements have burgeoned. But the case of France has stood out with its so-called 'beur' culture which has been hailed as a sort of cultural symbiosis.

One is however bound to raise questions about the elements making up this culture and those considered to be its sources of inspiration and standard bearers. One of the most curious cultural phenomena to emerge over the last two decades has been the proliferation of self-styled specialists in inter-cultural dialogue. Individuals or institutions, whose proclaimed mission is to bring different peoples closer together, bridging the historical gap between estranged societies and fostering symbiosis of the respective cultures. Inter-culturalism is supposed to be an intermediate area where exchanges occur and a blend is achieved between two cultures.

Clearly the scope of the phenomenon and its particular features are due basically to the massive foreign immigrant population in Europe today. As far back as one cares to scan history, there have always been individuals or groups playing the role of mediators between the various regions of the Old World and encouraging the flow of people, ideas and merchandise. But while in the past, contacts and mutual awareness occurred on the fringes of society, today they are taking place both between and at the heart of European societies. And contrary to the past, it is no longer a case of Europeans forging close ties with Arab or Muslim societies abroad as part of the colonial venture. European expansion, whether peaceful or violent, was accompanied by a vast programme of research, discovery, surveys and accumulation of knowledge, giving rise to one of the emblems of contemporary science, Orientalism. Conversely, new local elites, dubbing themselves 'modernist', borrowed *pêle-mêle* from Europe ideas, institutional models, scientific knowledge, etc. thereby resuming contact with their own history. The paradox today is that immigrants are having what is thought to be their own culture meted out to them, that is, an Arab–Muslim tradition which has been re-interpreted by modernity in general and Western science in particular. Then by a curious mirror effect, Westerners imagine that they are in dialogue with that cultural tradition.

But for immigrants from a rural background who arrived in Europe before national institutions had extended to cover all of their home country, the city culture of the elites, who in their manner had appropriated the ancient cultural heritage, was foreign to them. As for more recent waves of immigrants who learned to read and write and were educated in the new national institutions, their assimilation to the host country culture is such that the probability of their contributing to a cross-fertilization of cultures seems highly remote.

At the same time, Europe's middle and upper classes, who have very little contact with immigrants, discover the dead culture of the Arab–Muslim past in their museums and read about the living culture of today's Arab and Muslim countries in translated literature.

Bibliography

Abd al-Karim, Fathi (1976) *Al-dawla wa-l-siyasa fi l-fiqh al-islami. Dirasa muqarana*, Cairo.

Abd al-Rahman, Ahmad Siddiq (1988) *Al-bay'a fi l-nizam al-siyasi al-islami wa-tatbiqatu-ha fi l-hayat al-siyasiyya al-mu'asira*, Cairo.

Adelkhah, Fariba (1996) 'Les élections législatives en Iran. La somme des parti(e)s n'est pas égale au tout', *Les Études du Ceri*, 18, (July). Paris.

——(1991) *La révolution sous le voile. Femmes islamiques d'Iran*, Paris: Khartala.

——(1993) & Bayart, Jean-François & Roy, Olivier *Thermidor en Iran*, Brussels: Complexe.

Abdurrahman, Omar Ahmed Ali (1990) *The Present Rulers and Islam. Are They Muslims or Not?*, London.

Abed al-Jabri, Mohammed (1995) 'Ibn Ruchd et le dialogue des cultures' in Thierry Fabre (ed.) *L'Héritage Andalou*, Paris: L'Aube, pp. 39–47.

——(1990a) 'Al-Islam laysa kay nafsila-hu 'an al-dawla' in Hassan Hanafi & Abed al-Jabri (eds) *Hiwar al-Mashriq wa-l-Maghrib*, Cairo: Madbuli.

——(1990b) *Al-aql al-siyasi al-arabi: muhadidatu-hu wa tajaliyatu-hu*, Casablanca.

Abedin, Syed Z. (1990) 'Muslim Minority Communities in the World Today', *Islamochristiana* (PISAI), 16, pp. 1–14. Rome.

Alvarez-Pereyre, Frank ed. (1995) *Le politique et le religieux*, Jerusalem: Peeters.

Amin, Ahmad (1952) *Yawm al-Islam*, Cairo.

——(1945–1952) *Dhohr al-Islam*, Cairo. 4 vols.

——(1933–1936) *Doha al-Islam*, Cairo. 3 vols.

——(1929) *Fajr al-Islam*, Cairo.

Amin, Husayn Ahmad, 'Mulahazat hawl al-da'wa ila tatbiq al-shari'a', *al-Musawwar*.

Ammara, Muhammad (1989) 'Hal yajuz al-ijtihad … ma'a wujud al-nass?', *al-Hiwar*, 13, pp. 98–108.

——(1988) *Al-dawla al-islamiyya wa-l-sulta al-diniyya*, Cairo/Beirut.

Anderson, Lisa (1995) 'Democracy in the Arab World: A Critique of the Political Culture Approach' in Brynen, Korany & Noble (eds) *Political Liberalization*, pp. 77–92.

Al-Aqqad, Abbas Mahmud (1952) *Al-dimuqratiyya fi l-Islam*, Cairo.

Arkoun, Muhammad (1996) 'Transgresser, déplacer, dépasser', *Arabica*, 'L'Ouvre de Claude Cahen, no.1, pp. 28–70.

——(1993a) 'Les Fondements Arabo-Islamiques d'une culture maghrébine' in M. Arkoun, *Penser l'Islam aujord'hui*, Algeria.

——(1993b) 'Algérie 1993: Réflexions sur un destin historique', *REMMM*, 65 , pp.197–207.

——(1989) *Ouvertures sur l'Islam*, Paris: Jacques Grancher.

——(1988) 'Une autre histoire de la pensée en Méditerranée', *L'Evènement méditerannéen*, 2.

——(1984) 'Modes de présence de la pensée arabe en Occident musulman' in Muhammad Arkoun *Pour une critique de la raison islamisque*, Paris: Maisonneuve & Larose, pp. 299–326.

——(1981) 'Al-Islam wa-l-ilmaniyya', *al-Waqi*, 1, pp. 14–22.

Asad, Muhammad (1980) *The Principles of State and Government in Islam*, Gibraltar. New ed.

Al-Ashmawi, Muhammad Sa'id (1987) *Al-Islam al-siyasi*, Cairo: Sina li-l-nashr. Partly translated into French as *L'Islamisme contre l'Islam*, Paris: La Découverte, 1989.

Al-Awwa, Muhammad Salim (1989) *Fi l-nizam al-siyasi li-l-dawla al-islamiyya*, Cairo/Beirut. 6th ed.

——(1982) (Mohamed S. El-Awa) *Punishment in Islamic Law: A Comparative Study*, Indianapolis.

——(1974) 'al-Sunna al-tashri'iyya wa-ghayr al-tashri'iyya', *al-Muslim al-Mu'asir*, (November), pp. 29–49.

Ayubi, Nazih (1991) *Political Islam: Religion and Politics in the Arab World*, London: Routledge.

——(1995) *Over-stating the Arab State*, London: I.B. Tauris.

Al-Azmeh, Aziz (1992) *Al-Ilmaniyya min mandhur akhar*, Beirut: Markaz dirasat al-wahda al-arabiyya.

Barakat, Halim (1984) *Al-Mujtama' al-arabi al mu'asir. Ba'z istitla ijtima'*, Beirut: Markaz dirasat al-wahda al-arabiyya.

Baubérot, Jean (1994) 'La France, République laïque' in Jean Baubérot (dir) *Religions et laïcité dans L'Europe des douze*, Paris: Syros, pp. 57–68.

Belhassen, S. (1979) 'Femmes tunisiennes islamistes', *Annuaire de l'Afrique du Nord*, pp. 77–94.

Ben Achour, Yadh (1992) 'Islam et laïcité: propos sur la récomposition d'un système de normativité', *Pouvoirs*, 62, pp. 15–31.

Bennani Chraïbi, M. (1994) *Soumis et rebelles, les jeunes au Maroc*, Paris: CNRS.

Al-Bishri, Tariq (1989) 'Shumuliyyat al-shari'a al-islamiyya: anasir al-thabat wa-l-taghyir', *al-Hiwar*, 13, pp. 98–108.

Bill, James & Sprinborg, Robert (1984) *Politics in the Middle East*, New York: Glenview, IL: Scott Foresman/Little Brown.

Binder, Leonard (1988) *Islamic Liberalism. A Critique of Development Ideologies*, Chicago/London: Chicago University Press.

El-Bizri, Dalal (1995) *L'Ombre et son double. Femmes islamistes, libanaises et modernes*, Beirut: CERMOC.

Bonhoeffer, Dietrich (1967) *Letters and Papers from Prision*. New York: Macmillan. Rev. ed.

Boutaleb, Abdelhadi (1995) *Le monde islamique et le projet du nouvel ordre mondial*, Paris: PUF.

Brik el-Hannachi, Salah (1994) 'Interdépendance et partenariat transméditerranéens', Rome Symposium held on 17–19 January 1994, published in Lisbon: North-South Centre of the Council of Europe.

Brown, Daniel (1996) *Rethinking Tradition in Modern Islamic Thought*, Cambridge.

Brynen, R., Korany, B. & Noble, P. eds (1995) *Political Liberalization and Democratization in the Arab World. Theoretical Perspectives* (vol. 1), London/Boulder, CO: Lynne Rienner Publishers.

Bucaille, Laetitia (1994) 'L'engagement Islamiste des femmes en Algérie', *Maghreb-Machrek*, 144, pp. 105–18.

Burgat, François (1995) *L'Islamisme en face*, Paris: La Découverte.

Buzan, Barry (1991) 'New Patterns of Global Security in the Twenty-First Century', *International Affairs*, 67, no 3, pp. 431–51.

Carré, O. (1984) *Mystique et politique: lecture révolutionnaire du Coran par S. Qotb, frère musulman radical*, Paris: Le Cerf & Presse de la FNSP.

Cesari, Jocelyne (1994) *Être musulman en France*, Paris: Khartala.

Charfi, Abdelmajid (1982) 'La sécularisation dans les sociétés arabo-musulamanes modernes, *Islamochristiana* (PISAI), 8. Rome.

Corm, George (1989) *L'Europe et l'Orient. De la balkanisation à la libanisation: histoire d'une modernité inaccomplie*, Paris: La Découverte.

Courbage, Youssef, Benhaïm, Raymond & Leveau, Rémy (1994) 'Le Maghreb an suspens', *Les Cahiers du Ceri*, 8, Paris.

Cox, Harvey (1984) *Religion in the Secular City: Toward a Postmodern Theology*, New York: Simon & Schuster.

——(1965) *The Secular City — Urbanization and Secularization in Theological Perspective*, New York: Macmillan.

Crone, Patricia & Hinds, Martin (1986) *God's Caliph. Religious Authority in the First Centuries of Islam*, Cambridge: Cambridge University Press.

Dissanayake, Wimal ed. (1993) *Melodrama and Asian Cinema*, Cambridge: Cambridge University Press.

Djaït, Hichem (1990) *Europa y el Islam*, Madrid: Libertarias.

——(1989) *La grande discorde. Religion et politique dans l'Islam des origines*, Paris: Editions Gallimard.

—— (1974) *La personnalité et le devenir arabo-islamique*, Paris: Seuil.

Domenach, Jean-Marie (1990) *Europe, le défi culturel*, Paris: La Découverte.

Eickelman, Dale F., & Piscatori, James (1996) *Muslim Politics*. Princeton: Princeton University Press.

Elowe MacLeod, Arlene (1991) *Accommodation Protest: Working Women; The New Veiling and Change in Cairo*, New York: Columbia University Press.

Esposito, John L. (1996) & Voll, John *Islam and Democracy*, New York/Oxford: Oxford University Press.

——(1995) *The Islamic Threat: Myth or Reality?*, New York: Oxford University

Press. 2nd ed.

——(1991) & Piscatori, James P. 'Democratization and Islam', *The Middle East Journal*, 45, no.3, pp. 427–40.

——(1991) *Islam and Politics*, Syracuse, NY: Syracuse University Press. 3rd. ed.

——ed. (1987) *Islam in Asia: Religion, Politics and Society*, New York: Oxford University Press.

——ed. (1983) *Voices of Resurgent Islam*, New York/Oxford: Oxford University Press.

Etienne, Brunno (1987) *L' Islamisme radical*, Paris: Hachette.

Fandy, Mamoun (1994) 'Tribe versus Islam', *Middle East Policy*, 2, pp. 40–51.

Faruki, Kemal (1988) *Islamic Jurisprudence*, New Delhi.

Al-Fasi, Allal (s.d.) *Maqasid al-shari'a al-islamiyya wa-makarimu-ha*, Casablanca.

Ferchiou, Sophie (1989) 'Pouvoir, contre-pouvoir et société en mutation', *Peuples Méditerranéens*, 48–9.

Foulquié, P. (1986) *Dictionnaire de la langue philosophique*, Paris: PUF.

Fuller, Graham (1995) 'The Next Ideology', *Foreign Policy*, 98, (Spring), pp. 145–58.

——& Lesser, Ian O. (1995) *A Sense of Siege: the Geopolitics of Islam and the West*, Boulder: Westview Press.

Gellner, Ernest (1983) *Nations et nationalisme*, translated into French by B. Pineau, Paris: Payot.

——(1981) 'Flux and Reflux in the Faith of Men' in E. Gellner, *Muslim Society*, Cambridge: Cambridge University Press.

Geschiere, Peter (1995) *Sorcellerie et politique en Afrique*, Paris: Khartala.

Ghalioun, Burhan (1991) *Naqd al-siyasa: al-dawla wa-l-din*, Beirut: al-Mu'assasa al-arabiyya li-l-dirasat wa-l-nashr.

Al-Ghannushi, Rashid (1993) *Al-hurriyat al-amma fi l-dawla al-islamiyya*, Beirut.

——(1989) 'Fi l-mabadi al-asasiyya li-l-dimuqratiyya wa-usul al-hukm al-Islami' in R. al-Ghannushi, *Mawahir islamiyya*, Cairo, 1989.

——(1990) *Al-haraka al-islamiyya wa-l-hadatha*, Beirut: Dar al-jil.

Giddens, Anthony (1995) *Les conséquences de la modernité*, Paris: La Découverte.

Göle, Nilüfer (1993) *Musulmanes et modernes. Voile et civilisation en Turquie*, Paris: La Découverte.

Guazzone, Laura ed. (1996) *The Islamist Dilemma. The Political Role of Islamist Movements in the Arab World*,Berkshire (UK): Ithaca Press.

Haddad, Yvonne Y., Voll, John O., & Esposito, John L. (1991) *The Contemporary Islamic Revival: A Critical Survey and Bibliography*, New York: Greenwood Press.

Hakiki-Talahite, F. (1991) 'Sous le voile … les femmes', *Cahiers de l'Orient*, 23, pp. 123–42.

Halpren, Manfred (1963) *The Politics of Social Change in the Middle East and North Africa*, Princeton: Princeton University Press.

Hamdi, Mohamed Elhachmi (1996) 'The Limits of the Western Model', *Journal of Democracy*, 2 (April), pp. 81–5.

Hamilton, William & Altizer, Thomas (1966) *Radical Theology and the Death of God*, Indianapolis: Bobbs Merrill.

Hawwa, Sa'id (1984) *Al-madkhal ila da'wat al-ikhwan al-muslimin*, Cairo. 3rd ed.

Hervieu-Léger, Danièle (1995) 'Quelques perspectives théoriques pour une sociologie religieuse du politique' in Frank Alvarez-Pereyre (ed.) *Le politique et le Religieux*, pp. 13–25.

——(1986) *La religion pour mémoire*, Paris: Le Cerf.

Hippler, Jochen & Lueg, Andrea eds (1995) *The Next Threat: Western Perceptions of Islam*, London: Pluto Press.

Hodgson, Marshall G. S. (1993) *Rethinking World History: Essays on Europe, Islam and World History*, Cambridge: Cambridge University Press.

Hourani, Albert (1992) *Arabic Thought in the Liberal Age, 1798–1939*, Oxford: Oxford University Press.

Howarth, R. (1983) *Agreed Syllabuses of Religious Education 1975–1982*, Unpublished Med thesis, University of Birmingham, 1983.

Huntington, Samuel (1993) 'Clash of Civilizations', *Foreign Affairs*, 72, no.3, pp. 22–49.

——(1984) 'Will more countries become democratic?', *Political Science Quarterly*, 99, no 2.

Husayn, Taha (1938) *Mustaqbal al-thaqafa fi Misr*. Translated into English by S. Glazer as *The Future of Culture in Egypt*, Washington, D.C.: American Council of Learned Societies, 1954.

Al-Husri, Sati (1944) *Ara wa-ahadith fi l-wataniyya wa-l-qawmiyya*, Bagdad: Dar al-ilm li-l-malayin.

Al-Huwaydi, Fahmi (1993) *Al-Islam wa-l-dimuqratiyya*, Cairo.

——(1981) *al-Qur'an wa-l-sultan: humum islamiyya mu'asira*, Cairo.

Ibn Taymiya (1987) *Al-amr bi-l-ma'ruf wa-l-nahy an al-munkar*, Cairo. 2nd ed.

——(s.d.) *Al-hisba wa-mas'uliyya al-hukuma al-islamiyya*, ed. by Salah Azzam, Cairo.

Ibrahim, Anwar (1995) 'The Need for Civilizational Dialogue', Washington, D.C: Center for Muslim–Christian Understanding, Georgetown University.

Islamic Academy (1984) 'Religion and Education in a Multicultural Society: An Agreed Statement', *Muslim Education Quarterly*, 2, no 1 (Autumn), pp. 68–71.

Ismail, Salwa (1995) 'Democracy in Contemporary Arab Intellectual Discourse' in Brynen, Korany & Noble (eds) *Political Liberalization*, pp. 93–112.

Jaadane, Fahmi (1989) *Al-mihna. Bahth fi jadaliyyat al-din wa-l-siyasa fi l-Islam*. Amman.

——(1981) *Usus al-taqadum inda mufakiri al-Islam fi al-alam al-arabi al-hadith*, Amman.

Jarisha, Ali (1986) *Al-mashu'iyya al-islamiyya al-ulya*, al-Mansura. 2nd ed.

——(1985) *I'lan dusturi islami*, al-Mansura.

Kebabdjian, G. (1994) 'Les pays du Maghreb ont-ils intérêt à une zone de libre-échange avec l'U.E.?', *Cahiers du GEMDEV*, (October).

Kepel, Gilles (1984) *Le prophète et pharaon*, Paris: Seuil.

——& Richards, Yann, eds (1990) *Intellectuels et militants de l'Islam contemporain*, Paris: Seuil.

——(1994a) *A l'Ouest d'Allah*, Paris: Seuil

——ed. (1994b) *Exils et royaumes. Les appartenances au monde arabo-musulman aujourd'hui*, Paris: Presse de la Fondation Nationale des Sciences Politiques.

Kermani, Navid (1994) 'Die Affäre Abu Zayd. Eine Kritik am religiösen Diskurs und ihre Folgen', *Orient*, no. 1, pp. 25–49.

Kerr, Malcolm H. (1966) *Islamic Reform. The Political and Legal Theories of Muhammad 'Abduh and Rashid Rida*, Berkeley/Los Angeles.

Kessler, David (1993) 'Du combat au droit', *Le Débat*, 77, (November–December), pp. 98–9. Paris.

Khader, Bichara (1994) *L'Europe et la Méditerranée de la proximité*, Paris: L'Harmattan, Academia.

——(1990) 'La Méditerranée entre les tentations solitaires et les projets solidaires', *Cahiers du Cermac*, pp. 75–6.

Khalid, Muhammad Khalid (1981) *Al-dawla fi l-Islam*, Cairo.

Al-Khalidi, Mahmud (1986) *Nizam al-shura fi l-Islam*, Amman.

Khallaf, Abd al-Wahhab (1993) *Al-siyasa al-shar'iyya aw nizam al-dawla al-islamiyya*, Beirut. 5th ed.

——(1985) *Al-sultat al-thalath fi l-Islam*. Kuwait. 2nd ed.

Khoury, Rami G. (1995) 'Democracy East and West: Culture and Universal Values', *American-Arab Relations. A New Beginning?* The Foundation of Democratization and Political Change in the Middle East, (Summer), pp. 68–76.

Kodmani-Darwish, B. & Chartouni-Dubarry, M. eds (1997), *Les Etats arabes face à la contestation islamiste*, Paris: Armand Colin/IFRI.

Köhler, Martin (1994) *Pour un cadre de négotiation politique globale de l'Union Européene en Méditerranée.* This study was conducted for the General Directorate for Studies of the European Parliament, Doc. FR/DV266/266628, 18 November 1994.

Krämer, Gudrun (1995a) 'Cross-Links and Double Talk? Islamist Movements in the Political Process' in Laura Guazzone (ed.) *The Islamist Dilemma*, pp. 39–67.

——(1995b) 'Islam and Pluralism' in Brynnen, Korany & Noble (eds) *Political Liberalization*, pp. 113–28.

——(1994) 'The Integration of the Integrists: A Comparative Study of Egypt, Jordan and Tunisia' in Ghassan Salamé (ed.) *Democracy Without Democrats*, pp. 200–26.

——(1993) *Islam, sura und Demokratie. Studien zu Theorie und Praxis zeitgenössischer sunnitischer Muslime*, Hamburg.

Kramer, Martin (1994) 'Islam versus Democracy', *Current Issues*, Moshe Dayan Centre, Tel Aviv University.

Labat, Séverine (1995) 'Le FIS à l'épreuve de la lutte armée' in Rémy Leveau (ed.) *L'Algérie dans la guerre*, Brussels: Complexe.

——(1994) 'Islamismes et Islamistes en Algérie. Un nouveau militantisme' in Gilles Kepel (ed.) *Exils et royaumes*, pp. 41–67.

Laïdi, Zaki (1996) 'Les temps mondial. Enchaînements, disjonctions et médiations', *Les Cahiers du Ceri*, 14. Paris.

Lerner, Daniel (1958) *The Passing of Traditional Society: Modernizing the Middle East*, New York: The Free Press.

Leveau, Rémy (1995) *L'Algérie dans la guerre*, Brussels: Complex.

Lewis, Bernard (1996) 'Islam and Liberal Democracy. A Historical Overview', *Journal of Democracy*, 2, (April), pp. 52–63.

——(1988) *Le langage politique de l'Islam*. Paris: Gallimard, Coll. Bibliothèque des Sciences Humaines.

Lewis, P. (1984) *Islamic Britain: Religion, Politics and Identity among British Muslims*, London: I.B.Tauris.

Lueg, Andrea (1995) 'The Perception of Islam in the Western Debate' in Jochen Hipler & A. Lueg (eds), *The Next Threat: Western Perceptions of Islam*.

Al-Maliji, Ahmad Muhammad (s.d.) *Mabda al-shura fi l-Islam ma'a muqarana bi mabadi al-dimuqratiyya al-gharbiyya*, Alexandria.

El-Manjra, Mahdi (1992) *La troisième guerre des civilisations*, Paris.

Martín Muñoz, Gema (1995) 'L'Egypte dans l'échiquier arabe face au mouvement Islamiste', *Hérodote*, (October), pp. 142–74.

——(1992) *Política y Elecciones en el Egipto contemporáneo, 1922–1990*, Madrid: ICMA.

——(1994) et. al. *Democracia y Derechos Humanos en el Mundo Árabe*, Madrid: ICMA.

——(1997) 'Le régime algérien face aux Islamistes' in Basma Kodmani-Darwish & May Chartouni-Dubarry, *Les Etats arabes face à la contestation islamiste*, pp. 41–70.

—— 'The Image of Islam and the Arabs in the West. The prevalance of culturalist visions' in J. S. Nielson & S. A. Khasawnih (eds) *Arabs and the West: Mutual images*, Amman: Jordan University Press, pp. 59–72.

Martínez, Luis (1995) 'Les groupes islamistes entre guerrilla et négoce. Vers une consolidation du régime algérien?', *Les Études du Ceri*, 8. Paris.

——(1998) *La guerre civile en Algérie*, Paris: Karthala.

Mayer, Ann Elizabeth (1995) 'Reform of Personal Status Laws in North Africa: A Problem of Islamic or Mediterranean Laws?', *Middle East Journal*, 49.

——(1991) *Islam and Human Rights: Tradition and Politics*, Boulder, CO: Westview Press.

Mehden, Fred R. von (1988) *Religion and Modernization in Southeast Asia*, Syracuse, NY: Syracuse University Press.

Michel, Patrick (1994) *Politique et Religion, la grande mutation*, Paris: Albin Michel.

Monshipouri, Mahmoud & Kukla, Christopher G. (1994) 'Islam, Democracy and Human Rights', *Middle East Policy*, 3, pp. 22–39.

Munif, Abdelrahman (1989) *Cities of Salt*, New York: Vintage Books.

Mutawalli, Abd al-Hamid (1966) *Mabadi nizam al-hukm fi l-Islam*, Cairo. 7th ed.

Al-Nahwi, Adnan Ali Rida (1985) *Al-shura al-dimuqratiyya*, Cairo. 2nd ed.

Nielsen, Jørgen S. (1995) *Muslims in Western Europe*, Edinburgh: Edinburgh University Press.

——& S. A Khasawnih (eds) (1998) *Arabs and the West: Mutual Images*, Amman:

Jordan University Press.

Nora, Pierre ed. (1984–1992) *Les lieux de mémoire*, Paris: Gallimard, 7 vols.

Norton, Augustus Richard ed. (1994) *Civil Society in the Middle East*, Leiden: E.J. Brill, 2 vols.

Peters, Rudolph & De Vries, J. J. (1976/77) 'Apostasy in Islam', *Die Welt des Islam*, N.S., 17, pp. 1–25.

Pipes, Daniel (1983) *In the Path of God: Islam and Political Power*, New York: Basic Books.

Piscatori, James P. ed. (1983) *Islam in the Political Process*, Cambridge: Cambridge University Press.

Poulat, Emile (1987) *Liberté, laïcité, la Guerre des deux France et le principe de la modernité*, Paris: Cerf.

Pryce-Jones, David (1974) *Weber and Islam*, London: Routledge.

Al-Qadarawi, Yusuf (1990) *Al-sahwa al-islamiyya bayna al-ikhtilaf al-mashru wa-l-tafarruq al-madhmum. Fiqh al-ikhtilaf fi daw al-nusus wa-l-maqasid al-shar'iyya*, Cairo.

Al-Rayyis, Muhammad Diya al-Din (1979) *Al-nazariyyat al-siyasiyya al-islamiyya*, Cairo. 7th ed.

Revel, Jacques (1995) 'Passé Recomposés', *Autrement*, pp. 150–1.

Roy, Olivier (1992) *L'échec de l'Islam politique*, Paris: Seuil.

Rushdie, Salman (1988) *Satanic Verses*, London: Viking.

Saaf, Abdallah (1995) 'L'Europe insaisissable et l'Europe intériorisée', *Le Maroc et l'Europe*, Nantes: Ouest Editions.

Sadowski, Yahya (1993) 'The New Orientalism and Democracy Debate', *Middle East Report*, 183, (July–August), pp. 14–21. Reprinted in Joel Beinin & Joe Stork (eds) *Political Islam. Essays from Middle East Report*, Berkeley/Los Angeles: University of California Press, 1996, pp. 33–50.

Said, Edward W. (1981) *Covering Islam*, New York: Pantheon Books.

——(1979) *Orientalism*, New York Vintage Books.

Salamé, Ghassan ed. (1994) *Democracy Without Democrats? The Renewal of Politics in the Muslim World*, London/New York: I.B. Tauris.

Al-Sayyid, Ridwan (1984) *Al-umma wa-l-jama'a wa-l-sulta. Dirasat fi l-fikr al-siyasi al-arabi al-islami*, Beirut.

Serjeant, R. B. (1981) *Studies in Arabian History and Civilisation*, London. Reprint.

Shaltut, Mahmud (1988) *Al-Islam aqida wa-shari'a*, Cairo/Beirut. 15th ed.

Sharabi, Hisham (1988) *Neopatriarchy: A Theory of Distorted Change in Arab Society*, Oxford: Oxford University Press.

Al-Shawi, Tawfiq (1992) *Al-shura wa-l-istishara*, al-Mansura.

Sid Ahmad, Abdelkader (1995) *Un projet pour l'Algérie: élements pour un réel partenariat euro-méditerranéen*, Paris: Publisud.

Sivan, Emmanuel (1995) *Mythes politiques arabes*, Paris.

Smith, Wilfred Cantwell (1962) *The Meaning and the End of Religion*, New York: Harper & Row.

——(1957) *Islam in Modern History*, Princeton: Princeton University Press.

Steppat, Fritz (1989) 'God's Deputy: Materials on Islam's Image of Man', *Arabica*,

36, pp. 163–72.

Taarji, Hinde (1991) *Les Voilées de l'Islam*, Casablanca: Eddif.

Talbi, Muhammed (1992) *Iyal Allah, afkar jadida fi alaqat al-Muslim bi-nafsi-hi wa-l-akharin*, Tunis, Dar Siras li-l-nashr.

Talha, Larbi (1995) 'Une zone de libre-échange entre le Maghreb et l'Europe, un projet par défaut', *Études Internationales*, 55, no.2, pp. 39–57.

Al-Tamawi, Sulayman Muhammad (1967) *Al-sultat al-thalath fi l-dasatir al-'arabiyya al-mu'asira wa fi l-fikr al-siyasi al-islami. Dirasa muqarana*, Cairo.

Tamimi, Azzam ed. (1993) *Power-Sharing Islam?*, London: Liberty for Muslim World Editions.

Tapper, Richard & Nancy (1991) 'Religion, Education and Continuity in Provincial Town' in Richard Tapper (ed.) *Islam in Modern Turkey, Religion, Politics and Literature in a Secular State*, London: I.B.Tauris, pp. 56–83.

Taylor, Charles (1994) *Multiculturalism, différence et démocratie*, Paris: Aubier.

Todd, Emmanuel (1994) *Le Destin des immigrés. Assimilation et ségrégation dans les démocraties occidentales*, Paris: Seuil.

Tozy, Mohammed (1990) 'Le prince, le clerc et l'état' in G. Kepel & Y. Richard, *Intellectuels et militants de l'Islam contemporain*, pp. 71–102.

——(1989) 'Islam et Etat au Maghreb', *Maghreb-Machrek*, 126 (December).

——(1984) *Champ et contre champ politico-religieux au Maroc*. Thèse d'Etat, Aix Marseille III.

Al-Turabi, Hasan (1985) 'Al-shura wa-l-dimuqratiyya: ishkalat al-mustalah wa-l-mafhum', *al-Mustaqbal al-arabi*, 75, (May), pp. 4–22.

——(1983) 'The Islamic State' in John Esposito (ed.) *Voices of Resurgent Islam*, pp. 241–9.

Turner, Bryan (1974) *Weber and Islam: A Critical Study*, London: Routledge & Kegan Paul.

Uda, Abd al-Qadir (1951a) *Al-Islam wa-awda'u-na l-qanuniyya*, Cairo. Partly translated in 'Débats autour de l'application de la Shari'a', *Études Arabes-Dossiers* (PISAI), pp. 70–1 (1986), Rome.

——(1951b) *Al-Islam wa-awda' una al-siyasiyya*, Cairo.

Umlil, Ali (1991) *Fi shar'iyyat al-ikhtilaf*, Rabat.

Uthman, Muhammad Fathi (1985) *Dawlat al-fikra*, Jidda, 4th ed.

Vatin, Jean-Claude (1992) 'Les partis (pris) démocratiques. Perceptions occidentales de la démocratie dans le monde arabe', *Démocratie et démocratisations dans le monde arabe*, Cairo: CEDEJ.

Vergés, Myriam (1994) 'Le casbah d'Alger. Chronique du survie dans un quartier en sursis' in G. Kepel (ed.) *Exils et royaumes*, pp. 69–88.

Voll, John O. (1994) *Continuity and Change in the Muslim World*, Syracuse, NY: Syracuse University Press.

——(1994b) & Esposito, John L., 'Islam's Democratic Essence', *Middle East Quarterly*, (September), pp. 3–11, with ripostes, pp. 12–19 and Voll & Esposito reply in *Middle East Quarterly*, (1994), (December), pp. 71–2.

Waterbury, John (1994) 'Democracy Without Democrats?: The Potential for Political Liberalization in the Middle East' in Ghassan Salamé (ed.) *Democracy Without Democrats?*, pp. 23–47.

White, Jenny B. (1994) *Money Makes us Relatives. Women's Labor in Urban Turkey*, Austin, Texas: University of Texas Press.

Wielandt, Rotraut (1993) 'Menschenwürde und Kreiheit in der Reflexion zeitgenössischer Muslimischer Denker' in Johannes Schwartländer (ed.) *Freiheit der Religion. Christentum und Islam unter dem Anspruch der Menschenrechte*, Mainz.

Wright, Robin (1992) 'Islam, Democracy and the West', *Foreign Affairs*, (Summer), pp. 131–45.

Yassin, Abd al-Salam (1996) *Sur l'économie, préalables dogmatiques et régles charïques*, Rabat: Imprimerie Horizons.

Zakariyya, Fu'ad (1986) *Al-haqiqa wa-l-wahm fi l-haraka al-islamiyya al-mu'asira*, Cairo: Dar al-Fikr. French translation by Richard Jacquemond, *Laïcité ou Islamisme. Les arabes à l'heure du choix*, Paris: Le Découverte, 1991.

Zartman, I. W. & Habeeb, W. M. eds (1993) *Polity and Society in Contemporary North Africa*, Boulder: Westview Press.

Zubaida, Sami, (1993) *Islam, the People and the State*, London: I.B. Tauris.

Index